Private

Voices from the Front

Peter Whittle

THE
SOCIAL
AFFAIRS
UNIT

British Library Cataloguing in Publication Data
A catalogue record of this book is available from the British Library

Designed by Hands On Design, Riverhead, Kent
Printed and bound in the United Kingdom

ISBN - 978-1-904863-43-4

Social Affairs Unit
314-322 Regent Street
London W1B 5SA
www.socialaffairsunit.org.uk
www.newcultureforum.org.uk

Cover photography credits:

Michael Burleigh - Jillian Edelstein
Daniel Johnson - Pavla Yeats
Cosmo Landesman - Francesco Guidicini/Sunday Times
James MacMillan - Eric Richmond/ArenaPAL
Dame Vivienne Westwood - Christian Shambanait

Illustration photography credits:

Sons of York - Marilyn Kingwell
England People Very Nice - Johan Persson
The English Game - Keith Pattison

Private Views:

Voices from the Front Line of British Culture

CONTENTS

Acknowledgements

Sincere thanks are due, first, to the 17 interviewees in this book. All of them were generous with their time, and none received payment. I would also like to thank Michael Mosbacher, director of the Social Affairs Unit, for offering to make this project a co-publication with the NCF, and Clive Liddiard who, as editor, was as usual a pleasure to work with. I'm grateful, too, to Hannah Stone, who listened to and transcribed hours of material, and Frances Weaver, who helped out towards the end. Thanks are also due to Adrienne Connors, Tizer Bailey, Sarah Bettsworth and Samir Ceric.

Finally, and most importantly, I would like to express my gratitude to Alan Bekhor and Donald Kahn, whose support for the NCF has made this book possible.

LIST OF ILLUSTRATIONS

Scene from *The English Game* by **Richard Bean**, as performed at the Yvonne Arnaud Theatre, Guildford, 2008

Scene from *England People Very Nice* by **Richard Bean**, National Theatre, London, 2009

Adam Smith statue by **Alexander Stoddart**, unveiled Edinburgh, 2008

Scene from *Sons of York* by **James Graham**, as performed at the Finborough Theatre, London, 2008

Bush. Collage by **Jonathan Yeo**, 2007

Tony Blair. Oil on canvas by **Jonathan Yeo**, 2008

The New Black by **Sarah Maple**, as shown at the SaLon Gallery, London, 2008

Haram by **Sarah Maple**, as shown at the SaLon Gallery, London, 2008

ABOUT THE AUTHOR

Peter Whittle is founder and director of the New Culture Forum.

He has written features, social commentary and cultural criticism for the *Sunday Times, Spectator, Sunday Telegraph, Daily Mail, Los Angeles Times* and *The Times*, among many others. He is film critic and a feature writer for *Standpoint* magazine.

Peter has appeared on the BBC's *Newsnight Review, Daily Politics* and *The One Show*, ITV's *Tonight Extra*, Sky News and Channel Five News. He is film critic for Claudia Winkleman's Radio 2 show, and has also been a guest on BBC Radio's *Moral Maze, Front Row* and Jeremy Vine's show. He was host of the Carlton Cinema Channel, and was producer and host of *Culture Clash*, the weekly cultural review show on 18 Doughty Street, the UK's first internet TV channel.

He has produced and directed numerous factual programmes for UK and US television.

His first book, *Look at Me: Celebrating the Self in Modern Britain*, was published by the Social Affairs Unit in 2008.

INTRODUCTION

A gathering global financial storm, a historic presidential campaign in the US – and some unpleasantness on Radio 2. These were just a few of the events which unfolded in the background while the interviews for this book – the first to be produced by the New Culture Forum – were under way. With the sole exception of the conversation with Vivienne Westwood, which took place in March 2008 at London's Institute of Contemporary Arts (in front of an audience of 200 or so), all of them were conducted, one to one, over the summer, autumn and winter of 2008.

The aim of these conversations was to produce a picture of the issues, trends and preoccupations that currently shape our culture – from the effects of multiculturalism in arts policy to the cult of celebrity; from the existence of a cultural and political class to the question of bias at the BBC; and from the difficulties of talking about immigration to the prospects for freedom of expression itself in the face of radical Islam. The one thing that unites the interviewees, from sculptor and novelist to critic and broadcaster, is that all of them are creators or practitioners in their particular field. And all of them, in their different ways, offer valuable insights into the cultural state we're in.

I chose the interview format, firstly, because asking busy people to write individual essays would have set them an onerous task, and, secondly, because there was simply a greater chance of covering more ground within a conversation. The tone and emphasis of each one varies. Sometimes they are general: Sir Richard Eyre's concerns about what he calls a growing 'cultural apartheid' in Britain, for example, do not necessarily or wholly spring from his work as a director; and Lionel Shriver's thoughts on anti-Americanism do not rely solely on her work as a writer. Sometimes they are specific, such as the composer James MacMillan's observations on what he (happily) calls the 'chaos' current in our musical life, or the comedian Reginald D Hunter's thoughts on the audiences that come to see him perform. Similarly, the young artist Sarah Maple draws mostly on her personal experience, whereas the perspective offered by Daniel Johnson, as the editor of a newly launched cultural and political magazine, is necessarily wide-ranging.

Despite the increasing view that the terms 'Left' and 'Right' are unhelpful in contemporary political and cultural discussion, the New

Culture Forum (NCF) is viewed (by those who like things wrapped up nicely) as being on the Centre-Right. Certainly, the issues that I see as being of greatest importance to us right now influenced the questions I put to each interviewee.

However, many of those who have followed and supported our work and attended our meetings would find it irritating to be so classified. They simply share an exasperation and frustration with the orthodox set of views and approaches that continues to dominate our culture and that has narrowed and deadened debate. Certainly, one of the main incentives in founding the NCF was to challenge and then change this.

A few years ago, Nicholas Hytner, the director of the National Theatre, said in a radio interview that one thing he would like to see would be a 'good, mischievous right-wing play'. The implication of his words was, of course, that such a thing would be an unusual occurrence, a guilty pleasure, a naughty gesture to the mainstream by those who are not seriously seeking to challenge it. But still, the subsequent discussion of his comments provided evidence of a dissatisfaction among many with the status quo. Even those who considered themselves to be of the liberal Left thought that things did indeed need to be, as one prominent figure on the cultural landscape put it to me (perhaps somewhat complacently), 'shaken up a bit'.

That there is something 'in the air' can be confirmed by a few events that occurred just before I started putting this book together. A panel discussion held at London's Southbank Centre considered the question 'Is all modern art left wing?' It drew a packed audience, and although the guest speakers – who included Jonathan Yeo and Munira Mirza – came to no hard and fast conclusions, the fact that the question was being asked in the first place was significant. Around the same time, James MacMillan wrote an important article in the *Spectator*, in which he described his frustration at the assumption that he was a 'liberal left-winger'.

But it was a piece written by the American playwright David Mamet which was, for the cultural world, the biggest news. In an article in New York's *Village Voice* entitled 'Why I Am No Longer a "Brain-Dead Liberal"', Mamet, a self-described child of the Sixties, wrote: 'I took the liberal view for many decades, but I believe I have changed my mind.' Coming from somebody of Mamet's artistic stature, this was something of a bombshell, at least in US arts circles.

It is against this background that I embarked on these interviews. But politically no assumptions should be made about the 17 interviewees here. Lord Smith was, after all, a Labour minister, and Sir Richard Eyre a long-time Labour supporter. The playwright Richard Bean has described himself as a 'liberal hawk', but by no stretch of the imagination a Conservative. On the other hand, the broadcaster Jon Gaunt would make no bones about being a man of the Right. Munira Mirza might be London Mayor Boris Johnson's cultural advisor, but I would find it hard to classify her politically (much to her satisfaction, I am sure!). Much of Jonathan Yeo's work would be characterised by some commentators as being in traditional genres, James Graham has written three plays centring round the Tory party, and Reginald D Hunter is known for upsetting the liberal sensibilities of some on the comedy circuit. But none of this can be taken as some sort of reflection of their general political outlook or how they might vote at elections, both of which were unknown to me when I initially approached them, and more or less remain so.

Finally, as some might point out, there are no actors or singers in our line-up. However, we are treated to the views of pop stars and movie actors on quite a regular basis; and, in their predictability, one can pretty much set the clock by them. I'm sure many people feel they know intimately Bono's views on climate change, or how Annie Lennox would solve the Middle Eastern crisis. When an actress who is about to depict Margaret Thatcher in a television drama talks of her abiding hatred for the former prime minister, no eyebrow could really be raised in surprise. It is fair to say that there would have been little new to hear from these quarters.

Peter Whittle
April 2009

The Playwright – Richard Bean

*The politics of the theatre, self-censorship,
and outmoded political labels*

Richard Bean's latest play, *England People Very Nice*, opened at the National Theatre in February 2009. Formally an occupational psychologist and a stand-up comedian, Bean's prolific output includes *The Mentalist* (2002), *The God Botherers* (2003), *Harvest* (2005), *Up on Roof* (2006), and *In the Club* (2007).

His most recent play before *England People Very Nice* was *The English Game*, a comedy centring on the members of an amateur cricket team. When it opened in 2008, it was praised by the *Daily Telegraph*'s critic, Charles Spencer, as marking 'a defining moment on the English stage when the conventional liberal pieties that largely obtain in our theatre are finally put under fierce scrutiny, and Jihadist Islam is at last denounced as a malign evil'.

Peter Whittle (PW): Charles Spencer of the *Daily Telegraph* called one particular exchange in *The English Game* a 'defining moment' – what did you make of that?

Richard Bean (RB): Yes, it's a fantastic phrase, isn't it – 'A defining moment on the English stage'. Well they didn't think that at West Yorkshire Playhouse when nobody turned up, so... Yeah, what did I think of that? I think I know what he's saying: it's basically that we haven't really had a play that says that jihadists are actually murderers. Because, for some reason, people are able to conflate jihadist murderers and ordinary, good, hard-working British Muslims, which makes no sense at all. For some reason I don't understand, you can't criticise one without claims that you've besmirched the other.

PW: What has the reaction generally been to *The English Game*?

RB: In many ways, I thought Michael Billington's review in the *Guardian* was really sharp, because he saw it as a picture. I think this is something that kind of appeals to you, Peter, because I've heard you talk two or three times, and you often use the word 'community' in a way where you're talking about a picture of 'community' that's been fractured, don't you? I've heard you say that two or three times. And I think Michael Billington saw it as a portrait of Britain as a fractured community, where the fault lines are very clear. There are other cricket plays, and they tend to be bucolic kind of village-green stuff, or middle-class suburbia where the

1

men are having affairs, the wife is unhappy, that kind of thing. But this one was more overtly political, I suppose. In the sense that there were two representatives of immigrant communities in the team: an Indian – a gay Indian – a 100 per cent integrated, in the sense that, if you look in the stage directions, it says 'wearing rave culture accessories' – because I wanted to make him more English than the English, if you like. And there's a black British guy – he works for the British Council, so he's selling the product abroad: Britishness. You never see any immigrants in that cricket match who are not integrated. You hear them talked about. And, of course, there's Reg, who's kind of on the edge of the BNP – I suppose you'd have to call him a racist, wouldn't you? I don't suppose Reg would vote BNP: he'd be one of those guys who's quietly chuffed when they get a council seat, but who never votes for them.

PW: I thought that perhaps the whole point of the play was that they were trying to play this game while everything seems to be crashing down around them – that they're trying to keep something together.

RB: There's a lot of that, yes. Of course, there are all the trappings of modern society around them: the dog dirt, the chav who burgles their kit, takes all their stuff, the burnt-down community hall... It's funny, I played cricket about two weeks after we opened, and we were on the boundary – our team was batting, at a park near Battersea – and these two really thuggish-looking blokes – extraordinarily thuggish-looking blokes, the type who spend all their lives in the gym, you know what I mean?.. Just wearing singlets and stuff, on tiny little Chopper push bikes, and being pulled by those attack dogs... What are those dogs called? – Pit bull terriers. Huge. So they were being pulled along by them, like sleighs, and they went right across the cricket pitch, just as we were playing. It was like: 'Fuck you!' If I could have put that in the play, I would have. But of course you can't, it's difficult to do that kind of thing in the theatre.

PW: What was your reaction to that incident?

RB: Well, one of the guys in our team is from Ulster, and he shouted out: 'Get off the pitch!' And I said: 'Just shut up!' Because seriously, Peter – I know what you're thinking! You're thinking: 'Well that's really terrible! Somebody should have gone up to them and said something.' But they would have *eaten* us, know what I mean? They would have *barbecued* us on the spot, and I'm really not exaggerating. I'm a big bloke, look at me – but they were just a couple of the nastiest-looking blokes I've ever seen. And it was so ostentatious – right across the middle of the pitch. They knew what they were doing.

There's a part of me, in my worst moments, which wants to have a rule that nobody can comment on our modern society unless they've been violently mugged. It's kind of – why would you listen to a virgin talking about sex? I've been violently mugged once. And on a separate occasion, in Bethnal Green, I would have been killed or hospitalised by a gang. I'm pretty sure of that. I saw them mug an old woman, and they ran off with about three quid of hers, and she was left bleeding on the road. I was the first one on the scene, so I rang the police, and I rang an ambulance. They'd all dispersed. Then I noticed one of them. I couldn't tell whether he was one of the muggers who actually hit the woman, but he came back and he was on his phone. I didn't think much of it at the time. There was an AA [Automobile Association] man about a hundred yards down the road. This other guy went off a bit, and I went down to see the AA man, because he'd also seen the mugging. So I tapped on his window and said: 'Can you please not drive off, because the police will be here any minute, and I saw the back of the men, I didn't see the front of them.' And then bam!! About fifteen 16-year-olds with iron bars, sticks, everything, came...

> There's a part of me, in my worst moments, which wants to have a rule that nobody can comment on our modern society unless they've been violently mugged.

PW: Where was this in London?

RB: Russia Lane, Bethnal Green, where I was living. They arrived and went rattling the railings with these iron bars, around the whole area where it had happened. But I hid in the AA van. They'd come to get me, because I'd stood there and rung the police. And I also told two schoolgirls, who were about 8 years old or whatever, not to go home, because they'd seen it as well. I said: 'The police will be here in a minute, just stay there.' I spent that night in Stoke Newington. I was living in Bethnal Green at the time, but I thought: I'm not going back to Bethnal Green tonight, because I lived about a hundred yards away.

PW: This kind of everyday violence and anti-social behaviour seems absent from the theatre, film and TV – even though it's on everyone's mind.

RB: Well, I don't think it is, actually. But I think it started in a different kind of way. There are quite a lot of films like *Kidulthood* or *Bullet Boy*, that kind of thing, about the breakdown in community. In theatre, you would have things like *Gone Too Far!*, which has just finished at the Royal Court. It's basically about this young Nigerian lad, comes and joins his brother, who lives on a South London estate. The young Nigerian lad is a nice lad, you know: good values, be nice to everybody, treat everyone with respect, help old ladies across the road – values, you know? And his brother has been sucked into the South London values of 'Don't diss me; if you diss me, I'll kill you!' All those kinds of values. And that's what the play is about.

It's interesting: I haven't read it, but as a writer you can imagine what it looks like on the page. On the page, I imagine it looks like it's the young Nigerian who is the hero, and he would have all the solid values of the playwright, one would suspect; but on stage, the way it was staged, it looked like he was the buffoon, and the cool street values of the others kind of dominated. So I think there's a danger of doing plays like that. And *Bullet Boy*, or especially *Kidulthood* – it was the first in a series of two; the other one's called *Adulthood*, which is *Kidulthood 2*, essentially. But it's grotesque; you would run off to France and cry for a week if you saw *Kidulthood*, if there was any truth in that portrait of British society. You know, you could be quite jolly after *The English Game*, but seeing *Kidulthood*, you think that's it, we're finished. And the danger, I think, with those things is that sometimes they look like a celebration.

Take, for instance, *Gone Too Far!* It looks like a celebration of that culture, the hoodie, South London – why do we keep saying South London? It's all of London, isn't it? The actors do this kind of choreographed dance: they've all got their hoods up, looking mean and dangerous, doing all those kind of adolescent, jerky moves that Fred Astaire never invented, know what I mean? And the audience is going 'Yeah, yeah!' at all that celebration of aggression and violence. I'm really not criticising the playwright, because it can sometimes be the production; but every bit of dialogue is just conflict, conflict, conflict. There's no kind of...discussion.

PW: Doesn't that come from an inflated admiration for street-smartness?

RB: I know what you're saying, but I think good gangster movies, good mafia movies – they really do that as well, don't they? They celebrate the family, they celebrate the mafia, and the art of it is actually the critique of their evil. And I suppose it's the same thing. I left wanting to go and live in Wiltshire, you know. It's interesting, I walked past a group of lads who'd been at the play, been in the theatre. And I overheard a bit of conversation. One of them was saying something like: 'How do I get her to come to me, man?' I don't know what it was about, but the other one said: 'You beat her.' When have you left the Royal Court and heard a group of theatre-goers saying that you should 'beat your girlfriend'? I mean, the Royal Court will be celebrating getting younger people into the theatre and everything; but if that means... It's scary.

PW: You didn't become a full-time playwright until you were about 40, did you?

RB: Yes, 42. I was doing stand-up before that, and a little bit of writing. I was an occupational psychologist by training, but I worked for Amnesty International for 10 years, as a freelance – I was never on the payroll – as a freelance occupational psychologist. It sounds a bit clever, that, but it was basically management recruitment. It's very complex with Amnesty, because you advertise all around the world, of course, and you would get somebody flown in from Sierra Leone, say. They arrive jetlagged, and you can't give them a battery of psychometric tests, because they're culturally specific. So I had to design a series of culture-free exercises to see whether they could manage a department. That's what it was, mainly. I got very interested. I've always been interested in politics, but I got particularly interested in it, in the way that Amnesty works, and in their universalist take on human rights. It was a good grounding in some of these ideological issues.

PW: *The English Game* isn't the first time that you've referenced Islam in your writing. There was an instance connected to one of your plays, *Up on Roof*, where you had to rewrite a character. Could you tell me about that?

RB: It was the timing of it, really, that was the main thing. Because it was right in the middle of the Danish cartoon scandal, and the whole management at [Hull] Truck [Theatre] got a bit silly and paranoid, actually. It was a prison play, where one of the prisoners decided to become a Muslim, because in the Seventies – the play is set in the Seventies – you could keep long hair in prison if you could claim some religious reason. So this guy converted to Islam, without any knowledge of Islam. He basically just said 'I'm a Muslim', when in fact he was a member of the Angry Brigade. And it's based on truth. There was an Angry Brigade guy in Hull prison during the riot. Part of the play was that Jesus Christ was also in the prison – you can do that as a playwright! And so, in the original draft, Jesus Christ would occasionally challenge the Muslim guy, as you might expect, on why he was a Muslim. Actually, that's all, really. That's pretty much all.

PW: And that had to be changed?

RB: Yes, there was a bit of a stand-off between me and the theatre, and in the end I gave in. I capitulated in the end. It's no big deal: it's just that Hull's my home town, and I've got a great relationship with the theatre and I wanted to keep that. It's a little bit of expedience, but I mean… The main problem that came out of that for me was that I went to the Royal Court and I said: 'Look, this theatre's asking me to keep the word, the name Mohammed, out of the play, and we can't have that, can we?' There was a whole group of writers that came along, and writers are usually very homogeneous in their views when it comes to censorship, but…

PW: This was a meeting, was it?

RB: It was a meeting that I called, and I said: 'I don't really know what to

5

do; it's getting very difficult, and I want to be strong, and I need support.' Caryl Churchill stood up and said: 'Well, in my opinion, Muslims are persecuted throughout the world and you should be writing plays about that.' She turned around and walked out. And I thought: 'Oh yes, right, now I know what *you* think of free speech...'

But there was a lot of support from – it's weird, but younger male writers, although I'm sure there's not really a gender thing going on. Quite a few of them said: 'If you want some support, Richard, that's fine; we're sticking with you.'

> **She turned around and walked out. And I thought: 'Oh yes, right, now I know what *you* think of free speech...'**

We had a little plan at one time to write a play called the 'Life of Iqbal', which would be like the *Life of Brian*, you know: you would choose some guy who gets mistaken for Mohammed. You know, just doing the Monty Python thing. There were four or five of us at the Royal Court wanted to do this; but of course, those things never work, you know. It never happened. It's interesting, because [former Dutch MP and critic of Islam] Ayaan Hirsi Ali suggested that what the West needs at the moment is a Muslim *Life of Brian*. I came across that after we'd had that idea, actually.

PW: Did the theatre say: 'Under no circumstances can we do it'?

RB: Well, it wasn't like that, because it was just getting the other writers to commit to it and do it. It's interesting, all this fuss about Random House not publishing the Sherry Jones novel on the life of Aisha, *The Jewel of Medina*: that kind of action is not isolated. It just stops everybody writing. Because they think, well there's an interesting critique to be had about Mohammed as a role model, but no one's going to publish it. So you don't bother, do you? It doesn't get done.

PW: You mentioned that younger writers were more supportive. So the older ones weren't?

RB: Well, Caryl Churchill was the only older one there, to be honest. But I think you wouldn't get any support from Harold Pinter or David Hare, for example. Actually, me and David Edgar had a good thing going via email about this – he had a play recently, *Testing the Echo*, at the Tricycle, about British citizen 'contracts'. He had a scene in it where someone quotes from the Koran, and it's that famous quote: 'He who kills one man kills the whole of humanity.' I saw the play, and I picked this out – I don't know if you know the next two sentences? In the Koran, the next bit in that quote is something like: 'Unless he's causing disruption throughout the land, then you can kill.' So it's like: 'Don't kill anyone, because you kill the whole of humanity – unless he's causing disruption throughout the land!'

PW: It actually leaves it wide open who you can kill.

RB: Of course it does.

PW: So he quotes this in the play?

RB: Yes, so I emailed him – I know him, so it's kind of first-name terms. I said: 'David, what's going on here? I've just had a look in my Koran, and you've missed out two sentences there; you've put a full stop where there is no full stop.' Now he takes the mickey out of me – Richard Bean, the only playwright who's memorised the Koran...

PW: Do you know what your reputation is in the theatre world?

RB: I think there are one or two critics who think of me as non-PC, although I think most people think of me as the guy who writes those blokey work plays.

PW: For example, in *In the Club*, which was a kind of old-fashioned farce about the EU, most people in Hampstead might have been shocked to hear some of the lines. Did you get a reaction?

RB: The first thing that needs to be said about *In the Club* is that some of the critics really didn't like it. And people who like my work considered it to be slightly perverse, and not really the kind of thing that I would usually write. OK, it's a sex farce, on one level, and that's not really me anyway: it might be my life, but it isn't my work! So Michael Billington didn't like it, and not many of the quality newspapers liked it. They might have laughed a bit, but they didn't take it seriously. I think that's another problem that we've got with theatre: apart from Billington, there are not many really serious political animals among the critics. It's a problem, because you wouldn't trust some of them with anything seriously political to review – you know, [Nicholas] de Jongh at the *Evening Standard* and whatever. They just wouldn't understand it.

PW: Would you say there's a general approach in the theatre that is liberal left?

RB: I'm unsure what liberal left is nowadays, but I think generally it's the case. I've only seen one pro-war – pro-Iraq War – play.

PW: What was that?

RB: That was at the Tricycle: it was called *The War Next Door*, by Tamsin Oglesby. Very simple premise. It's a metaphor: English bloke living next door to some guy who beats his wife up regularly – what do you do? Do we go in and stop him, or do we let him carry on? The obvious analogy is with Saddam Hussein. Over 20 years, how many Shia Muslims did he kill? A million, is it, over 20 years? What do we do? Let him carry on, or go in and do something? The play was a metaphor, and, of course, Nicholas de Jongh didn't even get it – even though it's called *The War Next Door*! If you read his review, he thinks it's a play about domestic violence!

PW: You would not consider yourself right wing, would you?

RB: Not at all, no.

PW: So what do you make of it when someone like Nicholas Hytner, the director of the National Theatre, says, as he did a couple of years ago, that he would like to see a 'good, mischievous, right-wing play'?

RB: Right wing for me always means anti-immigration and racist. That's not me, can never be me. I'm what I would call a 'liberal hawk': that means that I'm prepared to defend the liberal values of this country against cultural imports. What I'm talking about is defending the hard-won rights of women, ethnic groups, homosexuals – defend their rights to equality, defend English liberal democracy essentially. No ghettos, no cantons, nowhere in England where a woman is not equal to a man, or where a homosexual gets vilified.

> **What I'm talking about is defending the hard-won rights of women, ethnic groups, homosexuals – defend their rights to equality, defend English liberal democracy essentially.**

PW: So Hytner might more usefully have said anything other than...

RB: Anything other than left wing, yes – that really ought to be the expression. 'Can we have some plays that are anything other than liberal left?' Which is more interesting, of course. I think that tends to be what I do now.

PW: So anything other than what we've come to expect – which comes from the assumption that to be educated and enlightened means being liberal left.

RB: I think that's essentially true. And people are very suspicious of you at dinner parties if you say anything else. I remember at a dinner party recently someone was banging on about Guantanamo Bay, and I just said: 'OK, who would you like to be taken prisoner by – the Taliban, or the Americans?' Do you know what I mean? You'd get beheaded by one lot, for sure; the others, they'll put you in an orange jumpsuit and lock you up. Which one do you want? And you can't say these things without people presuming that – 'Oh, that Richard Bean: he's a bit funny!'

PW: You've talked before about there being a lot of self-censorship now going on in the theatre...

RB: An enormous amount of self-censorship.

PW: Since you started working in the theatre, have you noticed any change at all, politically? Or is it still roughly the same? Maybe the theatre is becoming less brave and less relevant. I recently saw *The Female of the Species*, Joanna Murray-Smith's comedy, which rips into Germaine Greer's generation of feminists. And it struck me how rare it is to see something which is not giving you the same basic line.

RB: That's where the fun is to be had. That's where the fun is. I'll give you an example, actually. One of my students – that's the wrong word, because I don't teach; but when you become an established playwright, you get a few people that you end up mentoring. Anyway, she wrote this play, set in the world of advertising – lots of personal stories and stuff, but essentially it was a satire on advertising. And I read it and I said: 'Why have you picked on advertising? Everybody hates advertising. It's been done, you know. Why don't you pick a sacred cow? That's exciting. Pick charity workers.' Charity is something that hasn't been dissected properly in culture, you know. So the point I'm trying to make is: if you get oppositional, then you can have exciting theatre, I think.

The problem you've got is that some people who think they're cool and rebellious and oppositional – all they're doing is writing plays against America, which is the most tedious and boring and brainless thing that you can do, in my opinion. But if you write a play about an AIDS charity in Zimbabwe, and pull it to pieces, I'd go and see that play. I'd find that interesting. And I think a lot of the audience, a lot of people would think: 'Oh, this play really ought to be about what a wonderful charity this AIDS charity in Zimbabwe is, and how it's saving lives, not how it's falsifying its books, and making up statistics...'

> 'Why don't you pick a sacred cow? That's exciting. Pick charity workers.' Charity is something that hasn't been dissected properly in culture, you know.

PW: Would a play such as this stand more chance of being produced now than, say, 10 years ago?

RB: I think quite a lot of artistic directors are really bright people, and – let's take her play – they would really step back from a satire on advertising, and they'd say: 'Well, that's been done. But oh! A satire about charity workers where they're all lining their pockets, all expenses paid in Africa? This is a play!' And they wouldn't necessarily politically agree with whatever's in the play; but they could see that they've found the vein of drama. I think there's always got to be that vein of drama, in other words.

There's an example I use with students, which is: if you're going to write a play about domestic violence – a man beating up his wife – you have to make the man attractive; you have to make him witty and charming, and every time he's on stage he's got to light up the theatre; and you want him to come back on stage, because he's the entertaining one. Then you've got a drama, because he also beats his wife. If you write a play about a guy who always beats his wife and he's a horrible bugger, you've got no drama at all.

PW: Could you imagine a play that was about immigration, but that saw it from an indigenous perspective? Or that was really critical of multiculturalism?

RB: Well, I've written a play about immigration, and Nick Hytner is doing that play in February 2009, on the main stage of the Olivier. It's about immigration into Bethnal Green. It's called *England People Very Nice*, as in pidgin English – *England People Very Nice*. And, very briefly, it's four acts, and it covers French Huguenot immigration into Bethnal Green; then Irish immigration; then Jewish – these are all different acts; then Bangladeshi, with a little bit of Somali thrown in, as it were. And the idea of the play is that... There's a kind of racist pub – well, it's a bit unfair to call it racist, but it's just a typical East End pub – where people stand around saying: 'Fucking frogs, they come over here...' So every wave of immigration gets the racist chorus – this East End pub which slags them off, of course. So I think you've got your play there. Essentially, it's a behavioural scientist's analysis of what happens when there are waves of immigration. It's normal to have conflict over jobs, housing and culture.

> The problem you've got is that some people who think they're cool and rebellious and oppositional – all they're doing is writing plays against America, which is the most tedious and boring and brainless thing that you can do, in my opinion.

My technique of writing is that I have to have comedy. I'm not a poet: you give me any subject and it's going to end up being a bit funny. And there will undoubtedly be people who say that a serious subject like racism shouldn't be given a light treatment; but what they're really saying is that I'm not allowed to write about certain subjects. Well, they can go to hell. And having lived in Bethnal Green, I'm also writing from personal experience. Much of that experience was bad, and as a writer you have to work within that cocktail of truth of analysis. Many of the incidents in the fourth act happened to me in Bethnal Green, and all I've needed to do is give them a comic spin.

PW: Have you ever felt yourself in danger?

RB: There's some guy who comes to all my platforms: he came to *In the Club*, which was at Hampstead; and he came to Kingston when we did *The English Game*. Which to me is following me around. If you go to Hampstead and then you go to Kingston, then there's something going on. And he was at both question-and-answer sessions after the show.

It only worries me because the guy's dressed like you. He's obviously come from work. He wouldn't dress like that to go to the theatre, so he's obviously come from work. He looks like a really nice, respectable guy, and all that kind of stuff. But then you see the rants on the internet, and you get a bit worried. You know, because he really was very articulate, actually, in the Q&A, and spoke very perceptively about the American approach to immigration, and how that's made it easier for Muslims in America to integrate. He made a couple of good points. And then, when he gets home and does his blog on the internet, it's all 'Fucking Beano this', and 'fucking shit'. And then I think he ended one blog against me with something mildly threatening, like: 'Crying boo fucking hoo won't help ya now!' You know, a bit threatening, a bit jihadi. The sad thing is, of course, that because he's better at shouting than he is at listening, he's not aware that I'm actually in favour of Turkey joining the EU. So when he was slagging off *In the Club*, he'd missed the point of the play entirely.

PW: Do you sense that there are younger writers around who might want to take more risks – push the boat out more?

RB: Yes, I think there are a few coming through. In New York, there's Young Jean Lee, a Korean-American doing some brave and exciting theatre. Over here, too, I was at a drama publishers' dinner the other night, and there were some: one Jewish – I won't give you their names – and one black British guy who's working at the Royal Court. That was very encouraging, actually, because I've often felt like a bit of a lone voice, and you lose a few friends sometimes, as well, with what you write.

PW: Have you lost any theatre friends?

RB: I think some people have backed off a little bit, yes. I don't know about specifically: I've certainly lost a few friend-friends. That's easy to do. You've got your liberal friends who say things about 9/11, like: 'The Americans were asking for it.' And then you don't talk to them ever again. You've probably had a bit of that as well, haven't you? That's quite easy to do.

I had the 'Guantanamo' dinner party. People were discussing *The Road to Guantanamo*, the film by Michael Winterbottom. You know, that for me is an extraordinarily good example of what's wrong in British culture. We go to see the film, and immediately we're told to be on the side of these three lads, aren't we? They're going to Pakistan for a wedding, that's a given. I was sitting there watching it and going: 'I don't believe a word of this.' And I really think I'm the only one going: 'I don't believe it.' And you know, they end up in Pakistan – they get mixed up in something else, they end up in Afghanistan and all that. You know the film – rubbish. And they end up in Guantanamo. And that's the film.

And he wins the Silver Bear Award for that film! Six months later, one of the guys goes on that Channel 4 programme with the lie detector, and the questions come in: 'Did you go to Pakistan for a wedding?' – 'Yes': beep, beep, beep, lie, lie, lie. 'Did you involuntarily end up in Afghanistan?' – 'Yes, it was an accident; we didn't want to go to Afghanistan': beep, beep,

beep, lie, lie, lie. 'Have you ever been to a jihadist training camp?' – 'No, I never have': lie! And the other two guys are there, and saying: 'We're not doing it, we're not doing it, sorry!' Well, that's fine. You can understand that. But the guy who'd been in the chair admitted it all. He said: 'Yeah, we went to fight.' And Winterbottom – has he sent his Silver Bear back? Nobody's even talked about it!

PW: But what do you think motivates people like Winterbottom?

RB: I think it's hatred of America. I think that's what a lot of it's about. Take someone like Harold Pinter.[*] He's backed away from supporting Milosevic and stuff, but that, for me, was not about supporting Milosevic; it was about hating America. Here's a man whose plays are shot through with subtext, always; he can't even see his own subtext. It's just pure hatred of America. That's what it is, I'm sure.

At the moment we're still desperately trying to use 'left wing' and 'right wing' to make sense of the world of politics, and it's really inadequate. Even if you just look at the economy, the Labour party and the Tory party are just saying: 'We're the best managers of the economy.' Left, Right – it's nonsense. Doesn't help anyone, does it? Take things like the Euston Manifesto. Signing that was my last political act – if you don't consider writing to be political. And that's mainly lefties, isn't it? But there's that wonderful paragraph in it, which says: 'An open invitation to all our friends on the Right.' All it's saying is: 'We're not necessarily anti-Israel and we're not necessarily anti-America.' Which is kind of my position. But that doesn't make me right wing, just because I'm not knee-jerk anti-Israel, and not knee-jerk anti-American. But for some people it does mean that, actually.

PW: Some people think it's right wing even to say you judge Iran to be morally inferior for executing gay people.

RB: Yes, Martin Amis does that thing. I've never seen him do it, but somebody told me about it – during Q&A sessions, where he says: 'Who in this room' – it's always a western audience – 'Who in this room considers themselves to be morally superior to the Taliban?' And he says only ever about a third of the people in the room put their hands up. I mean, they stop girls going to school, they blow up religious statues! Why is it so difficult?!

PW: What advice do you have for young people who maybe want to write for the theatre?

RB: It's a tough one. I've normally said things like: 'Write about what keeps you awake at night.' But that's not going to make you a writer if what keeps you awake at night isn't very interesting. If what keeps you awake at night is how terrible George Bush is, that's not going to make you a

---

[*] This interview took place before the death of Harold Pinter.

great playwright, either... It's a tough one.

PW: Do you think the theatre will still be as important in 10 or 20 years' time?

RB: Yes, theatre's weird, isn't it? It punches way above its weight in terms of cultural debate and whatever. I think the decline in television will keep theatre strong, if that makes any sense. We have the most terrible, appalling television. *Big Brother* is considered to be a success! What kind of culture is Channel 4? Their big hit is sinfully terrible, and they're really proud of it. What's going on? What kind of culture is that?

Young people love acting and getting involved in theatre. Anybody who's ever written a film, or anybody who's ever written a television programme – they all started in theatre, as did all the actors. So in many ways, theatre is essential to the media generally. And I think it will continue. You take any provincial town: television's irrelevant to a provincial town. They're not in control of it. But they are in control of the theatre: they fund it. They can get some clever guy to run it and do something at the Liverpool Everyman, Hull Truck, Newcastle Northern Stage. So in that sense, it will continue, I think. But yeah, there's only two or three plays a year that are memorable, aren't there?

PW: I'm trying to think of a play recently that had a big impact on media discussion... Maybe your play about immigration will?

RB: Well, let's hope there is a discussion and not a shouting match.

England People Very Nice opened at the National Theatre in February 2009. The critical reaction to the play was varied. In *The Times*, Benedict Nightingale wrote:

> Who would think that unsexy subject, waves of immigration to Bethnal Green, could generate as much enjoyable ebullience as it does in Richard Bean's new play?... Will the Thames 'run with blood', to repeat a quote frequently cited in the play? It's the sort of question a genuinely 'national' theatre should be asking.

And Charles Spencer, in the *Daily Telegraph*, said:

> With great panache he has come up with an epic drama, inspired by the city comedies of the Jacobean era... Beyond the often cheap, though disgracefully funny, jokes, there is wisdom and humanity in this play.

Others were negative. Nicholas de Jongh, in the *Evening Standard*, wrote that the play

> ...although factually based, is not liberal, humane or interesting in its continual, wisecracking jocularity... It appears intent upon defaming

refugees to England in terms of the malevolent stereotypes and caricatures you find in the *Sun*.

And Michael Billington of the *Guardian* thought that the play
...leaves a sour taste in the mouth. Far from rejoicing in London's ethnic diversity, it manipulates a series of comic stereotypes like a misanthropic *1066 and All That*... the abiding impression is that Bean doesn't think much of our modern multiculturalism.

A week after it opened, I talked again to Richard Bean.

PW: What do you think of the production?

RB: I'm completely thrilled with it!

PW: And what about the critical response?

RB: I think there is a temptation to say that the intellectual class is failing us, but the truth is there's just that little niche, around the *Guardian* and *Newsnight*, which seems incapable of acknowledging the world as it is; as if they're in their own sophisticated bubble of liberalism. Most theatre critics understood the form of the play; they could see that it was Monty Python meets 'Carry On Up the Racial Stereotype'; and if you can't see that, there's not much hope for you really, is there?

If I had to define what my message is in this play, I'd say it's this: that here is the game – come here, and within three generations you should have integrated, married us! If you haven't integrated, then you're not playing the game.

PW: Leaving to one side what the various critics thought the play was saying, what do you intend its message to be?

RB: If I had to define what my message is in this play, I'd say it's this: that here is the game – come here, and within three generations you should have integrated, married us! If you haven't integrated, then you're not playing the game. Nicholas de Jongh said that it wasn't a liberal piece. Of course it's a liberal piece! And if your criticism is that the play is saying multiculturalism hasn't worked, then one could say that the play is simply in line with what the government is saying, what Trevor Phillips is saying.

PW: It's been reported that a delegation of writers and community activists from the East End, including Hussain Ismail, a playwright from Bethnal Green, is meeting the National Theatre director, Nicholas Hytner, to protest against what they regard as a caricature of Britain's racial history. What do you think of that?

RB: I'd like to know what the process was for this guy to represent the community. Was it an election? Of course not! He's like all these 'community leaders': he's self-appointed.

PW: Why is he being seen?

RB: I think Nick Hytner wants to genuinely listen to him and see what it is he objects to, because we can't work out what the problem is. He seems to be saying that the Irish act is racist, because they're all drunk and having sex with their sisters. And we kind of go: 'If that's what they're complaining about, they've missed the point, haven't they?' I think there's two discussions scheduled on the play, so Nick's going to cordially invite them to take part. I guess one complaint of this guy might be that he considers that a white Englishman doesn't have the right to write about Bethnal Green. Well, that's totally reductive, and it's the kind of approach we should always resist. I'll write about whatever I like.

I'll write about whatever I like.

The Critic – Cosmo Landesman

The rise of celebrity culture, and the fall of the critic

Cosmo Landesman is the film critic for the *Sunday Times*, a position he has held since 1997. His recent memoir, *Starstruck: Fame, Failure, My Family and Me*, described his life as the child of bohemian, fame-obsessed parents, and explored and analysed the rise of the contemporary cult of celebrity.

In the early Nineties, Landesman, together with the journalists Toby Young and Julie Burchill, founded the magazine *Modern Review*. Its aim, in essence, was to treat popular culture in a high-brow way, and, although it lasted for only a short period, its influence on mainstream coverage of the cultural scene was considerable.

Peter Whittle (PW): You've written recently about the culture of celebrity. Some commentators think it's peaked. Do you think that's true?

Cosmo Landesman (CL): No, I think this is complete wish-fulfilment. I have been watching the rise of celebrity culture since the mid-Nineties, and I could draw you up a list of people who claim that celebrity is dead – 'the whole boom is finished, it's peaked...' They would see that a magazine like *Heat* or *Hello* had a slight dip, and everyone rushed to write the 'end of celebrity' piece. I know this, because I was also one of the people that wrote the 'end of celebrity' piece. That was an article for the *Sunday Times* called 'Celebrity Fatigue', and was about how, because Elizabeth Taylor's perfume didn't sell or something, we were all getting really sick of celebrities. This was in '97. This was pre-*Big Brother*. People were tired of celebrity when it was happening then – then, after 9/11 of course, was the big pronouncement about the death of celebrity, with Graydon Carter in *Vanity Fair* saying: 'It's over now.' We will no longer be talking about *Big Brother*; 9/11 was the big wake-up call. But two weeks later it was all over: we went back to celebrity. And the latest one we've had is, of course, the Gordon Brown claim. It was crucial to staking out his idea of his kind of government, which was going to be a government of 'substance'. People supposedly wanted to talk about serious issues, and they were sick of all this celebrity thing. Yet it's been going on ever since. It is the great dream of the liberal intelligentsia, in particular, that celebrity is dying or dead. It is not – I'm sorry! It's going to be around much longer.

PW: Why do you think that is their dream?

CL: Because they hate everything it stands for. They hate the sight of all those reality television programmes, and the type of people that modern celebrity culture idealises and celebrates. And many people on the Right would actually agree with them – they don't like the Jade Goodys and the Jordans and so on. So it's not just particularly the liberal Left.

PW: Do you think there's been anything positive about it?

CL: I don't think it's a terrible thing that young, working-class men and women want to be in the newspapers, and have a kind of holiday in the headlines, away from their rather dull lives. I say, if that's what they want... I think it's rather shallow and I don't think they'll find what they want. But if they want it – fine. Let them discover. Why do we care if they dominate the tabloid press – what are we losing? You see, in a way we're focused on them, but we're not focusing on what the problems of real culture are. They are a kind of distraction. If those people want that, if they want to go on television, well, that's their choice. They're not the real problem when you look at the important cultural issues of our time. So I don't think it's that bad a thing.

PW: Why do you think that celebrity culture is so intense here in Britain, compared to many other countries?

CL: Well, it's very interesting. At one time, you would have thought that, of all the people ready to resist celebrity culture and the kind of exhibitionism at the heart of it, it would be the English, because of their culture of reticence, of restraint. We didn't do that – vulgar Americans did that, the chappies out in Hollywood and those sorts of people. Also, the English very much prided themselves on their irony and self-deprecation, and all of those qualities. So you would have thought they would have resisted.

> The gatekeepers all went, because they were pushed out, I would say, by the attempt to democratise culture that began in the 1960s, generated by people of the Left. And many of those people on the Left are now horrified.

One of the interesting things to have happened in the last few years is that American commentators constantly complain that, whereas in the old days the Americans would export rubbish to us, now it's the British who export rubbish to the Americans: the whole *Pop Idol* thing. *American Idol*, one of the biggest shows of all time – from Britain. When *Big Brother* was first mooted, Peter Bazalgette, who brought it all to our screens, said: 'This will never play in this country; it's too bad taste.' They never thought it would happen, but it did: because there's been a profound cultural shift that has let the celebrity culture rise up.

It's been allowed in the door. It had been there for a long while, but what has happened is what I call the 'seepage factor' – it has moved into new areas, where, at one time, there was a kind of resistance to it. The gatekeepers all went, because they were pushed out, I would say, by the attempt to democratise culture that began in the 1960s, generated by people of the Left. And many of those people on the Left are now horrified. Big Brother is their child, in a way. Postmodernism decimated all notions of cultural standards and hierarchy, and once you've cleared that space – well, things crawl out and move in.

PW: Who were these gatekeepers?

CL: All the cultural institutions in the 1960s tried to radicalise themselves, open themselves up. There are no real defenders of high culture anymore; they're considered really cranky people. When George Steiner goes, that's it, mate. Who else is out there? Roger Kimball, maybe, in America. But I don't know anyone here.

PW: You mentioned that there's been this massive 'cultural shift'...

CL: There are no standards. The culture club has so widened its doors, how do you keep anyone out? And, you see, it was considered a liberating thing to hear these new voices; to get away from a white, middle-class world and to bring in working people. This was always the great vision of the Left, particularly among John Grigson and the documentary makers: 'Let the people speak! Why should they be dominated?' Well, that was fine. But reality TV... The Jade generation... This isn't a cosy working class anymore. This isn't about the nice, dignified working men with those little caps and their Sunday suits anymore. And a lot of people are very horrified by that.

> **There are no real defenders of high culture anymore; they're considered really cranky people. When George Steiner goes, that's it, mate. Who else is out there? Roger Kimball, maybe, in America. But I don't know anyone here.**

PW: Do you think that the *Modern Review*, which was set up to talk in a serious way about popular culture, has helped this process along?

CL: *Modern Review* was never about celebrity culture, because celebrity culture is actually the enemy of popular culture – the two are not synonymous.

PW: How?

CL: Well, because *Modern Review* was about a critical look at popular culture. Celebrity culture isn't really interested in culture – it's not interested in great records, or great movies. It's about personal self-aggrandisement. Popular culture at its best is artistic and wonderful, and there were great books and great movies that were vital and spoke about the human experience. But these people – those of the celebrity culture – are not interested in all that stuff. They just want a platform to parade on. So it's very different from what we at the *Modern Review* were about. Do you see the distinction? I think it's a very important one: we were not about that.

Celebrity culture is exploitative; it's a big leech. The perfect example is some of these *Big Brother* people who make records, or try to make a film – they just use these forms to promote themselves. They're not interested in music or anything else: that's the key difference. Everything is a means to an end.

> **Celebrity culture is exploitative; it's a big leech.**

I never claimed that the *Modern Review* was absolutely totally original, and no one had ever done that sort of stuff. Because popular culture had been discussed before that – we all know that, we accept that. But the broadsheets still didn't take it seriously, and we wanted a third way. We wanted to discuss popular culture in a way that was between the dry, cultural-studies crowd, academics, and the kind of patronising, Sunday-supplement point of view. You have also to remember that it was still very much a literary-dominated scene, I think. What Martin Amis and Salman Rushdie and those guys said really had a lot of importance – in a way that I don't think they would have today. Despite what had happened in the Eighties, the liberal intelligentsia was still very much in power, I think. And their values and their cultural ideals still permeated the thinking, debating press.

PW: When you started, you weren't kicking against this liberal intelligentsia...

CL: Yes we were.

PW: Were you?

CL: Yes. I mean, not me so much; but I think Julie [Burchill] and Toby [Young] always hated the liberal intelligentsia back in the Eighties. They got a delight out of kicking the Rushdies, the Pinters. Do you remember that society that Pinter organised with Melvin Bragg? The Campden Hill lot? Where they tried to set themselves up as a kind of resistance *samizdat* Russian intelligentsia group? We took the piss out of them totally, and Julie had a big fight with John Mortimer on the radio. It was quite funny. Julie and I wrote this piece in the *Sunday Times* against Rushdie and that whole crowd, so we were always against them. We hated them! Partly it was, you know, mischievous: we were sort of their offspring. Toby's parents were the classic liberal intelligentsia: his father, Michael Young, founder of Open University, wrote the Labour party manifesto in 1945, and *The Rise of the Meritocracy*.

PW: So basically it was a rebellious thing – you didn't have a political agenda, did you?

CL: We didn't have an *articulate* political agenda, no. We weren't on the Left – everyone laughed at lefties in those days. And even though we knew all those other guys – those young conservative guys, [Harry] Phibbs and all those guys – and hung out with them and Dougie Smith... We knew them, but we were never really a part of that.

PW: It has had the most enormous influence, hasn't it, the *Modern Review*?

CL: Let me just go back a little bit, because I think this is really important. I think in your question earlier maybe you were trying to ask whether we regret the forces that we helped to unleash. And I was sort of denying it. But I've got to own up to this, because I think it's not just us, but a whole group of people who now say that when we all attacked the culture of good taste and high culture, we always assumed it would be there. Some are now saying: well, we think maybe we made a bit of a mistake with this populist approach. Susan Sontag basically said the same thing as well. She said: 'I still believe in standards, and the whole idea of the pop sensibility replacing everything – maybe I made a bit of a mistake there.' I think there were many people that championed a radical agenda who do regret it. They regret it because they always thought there would be two cultures: you would have your serious, high culture, and you would have your pop culture. But when the high culture kind of got decimated, they regretted it. And so, yes, partly I regret that. I regret that loss. It provided a good creative tension between the two.

PW: Do you think the magazine did transform the way that the arts were written about?

CL: Yes, I think it did. The *Sunday Times* 'Culture' section was a blatant attempt to cash in on the *Modern Review*. So I think it's had an influence. Has it transformed everything? No, not everything. But it's made an impact. For such a small magazine that was run in somebody's bedroom – yes.

PW: What has happened with arts coverage is that there's also been this influence of celebrity culture – so much more of it seems to be about famous performers, actors and the like...

CL: That's the bad side of the celebrity culture. I say let the Jades have the tabloids – fine. But please, let us have our own magazines and our own culture. But I think, more than ever now, it's about the power of the name. If you don't have a name, you're going to find it really hard. Editors and producers want a name to review, to feature, to do whatever it is. Look at that BBC series where they want to introduce people to conducting classical music. Who do they get? Peter Snow and bloody Jane Asher!

Increasingly, culture – traditional culture – adapts the methods of celebrity culture to promote itself. The BBC's *Big Read* was a classic example. It came after the whole *Pop Idol* thing, where everybody had to vote. And culture tried to play along with that game as well, and had to say 'Let's all vote for the greatest novel.' As though everyone is sitting around discussing Jane Austen versus Zadie Smith! It was a fantasy – of course it didn't happen like that. And it's sad. When people talk about dumbing down, the dumbing down isn't among the masses: the dumbing down is among the smart people, the cultural people, who should know better. That's the terrible, scary thing.

PW: Do you think it's that there was a loss of cultural confidence? The confidence to say: well, putting on an opera is essentially better, for example?

CL: Absolutely. Yes, they didn't have that confidence anymore. That was considered elitist. There was definitely a crisis of confidence. Originally, you had this group of people who did not go into television primarily to give people what they wanted. They thought people would want this or that if you educated their taste, if you provided them with new things. It was not audience-led; it was not focus group-led. It was about daring to say that this was the important stuff, and we assume that you will want to know about it. And that class had a major crisis, partly as a result of the 1980s.

PW: You've been film critic for the *Sunday Times* for many years now. What's your view on the current status of critics? Some critics I have spoken to are pessimistic about the future.

CL: The news from America is: critics watch out. In the last two years, 28 critics have lost their jobs and have not been replaced – across the board. It has to do with the power of the internet. And also, I think, there's been a cultural change now, where what the critic did – that is, his role as gatekeeper, his role as a filter – has changed. Newspapers and the culture industries are much more about 'giving the people what they want'. And you don't need a critic for that; you don't really need criticism. There's a lot of the 'should you see this film?' sort of commentary; but criticism is meant to be about something more than that. Where do you hear any, really? Even on a programme like *Front Row* on Radio 4, for example, or the *Culture Show*, there's no critical engagement. People approach culture as 'It's an event, it's a must-see'; something with which to fill their lives, to make chat, to talk. There's no real analysis, no discrimination.

> **The news from America is: critics watch out.**

PW: It sometimes seems that it's being approached as a leisure activity.

CL: Yes, and also so much of our culture is PR-driven now. That's also, I think, a really important change that's happened.

PW: Do you mean that critics have become gatekeepers of a different sort?

CL: The new criterion is no longer good or bad: it's what's hot and what's not. What generates media attention? What gets people talking in arts programmes? What generates the cover stories? That is what culture's about now. For instance, take film stars: I read a very interesting article saying that you have two types of stars emerging now. You have the stars that actually get people into the cinema, and you have the media stars, who sell newspapers and magazines. People want to *read* about Gwyneth Paltrow, her life, in a magazine, but they don't want to see her movies. She's not that kind of star; she's a magazine movie star, if you see what I mean. She can't open a movie. You can't get a movie made with Gwyneth Paltrow as the lead figure. Nobody would see it.

> **The new criterion is no longer good or bad: it's what's hot and what's not. What generates media attention? What gets people talking in arts programmes? What generates the cover stories? That is what culture's about now.**

PW: These are stars with no visible means of support?

CL: It's all media; it's all media-based. It'll keep working, because there is a perception that Gwyneth is 'hot', or whatever. But she's not hot in terms of the box office.

PW: Do you read many other critics?

CL: I don't read many film critics.

PW: What about theatre, television and so on?

CL: I still read the old guys. I'm still reading Pauline Kael and Susan Sontag and Clive James, some of his old stuff. I think what has happened is that the critic is not so urgent a figure anymore, in our culture. Remember the old days? I don't want to get nostalgic, but people really did wait for Sunday to hear what Kenneth Tynan had to say about the theatre. People really cared about what Pauline Kael said about a movie. You know, these were really important things. But who do we have now? There may be critics people like, but there's no *urgency*. And this goes back to the new 'democracy of opinion'. What is this person's opinion worth? Increasingly, I think, there's a sense that critics just have to be tolerated.

PW: Is it that they are seen as getting in the way of a process? Do media outlets just want compliant journalists who are essentially an extension of, say, the film business?

CL: Exactly. But the funny thing is, I know those kinds of journalists, and they're not even embarrassed about it! I've spoken to young journalists, and when I ask why they are in journalism, they say they want to go to parties and hang out with celebrities.

PW: What do you think of the view that, with all this 'white noise' surrounding us, the role of the critic has actually become more important than ever?

CL: I think they're more of a necessity than ever, because so much of our culture is driven by hype and PR. We need the critics to say: 'Whoa! Step back! Look at this. Stop, everybody! Let's figure this out.' But we don't have that. I don't think critics are important anymore, especially to young people. We might be possibly the last generation of critic-reading people. Young people do not read critics. Many of them, first of all, do not read newspapers, and they certainly don't read critics. I did a talk yesterday for young people who want to get into the media, and they didn't know any of the critics I was talking about.

PW: Recently there was a proposal that we should 'democratise' the theatre-reviewing process by having comments from punters on the internet posted outside theatres.

CL: That's going to happen, increasingly. That kind of 'democratisation' – more and more it will be 'let them have their say', or 'what do you think?' There's a whole new culture of 'tell us what you think'. It's kind of a barmy fascination with what the ordinary viewer or listener thinks. It's really horrible. I mean, on radio programmes now, Radio 4, every programme's full of people's emails and their phone-ins and their comments. And 90 per cent of them are completely banal!

PW: So you're saying that expertise of the type traditionally expected of a critic is a good thing?

CL: Well, no. This is difficult for me, because I don't know if it's about expertise. Because if expertise was the only criterion, there are a million people in universities who know a lot more about film than any of us, in terms of knowledge and so on. But, you know, you wouldn't want them to write the review on a Sunday. I'm not for the democracy of opinion. I recognise that there are opinions that are better, that are better expressed, that are fresher, more original, more insightful – all those traditional terms that have sort of dropped out of the critical vocabulary. They exist, and I believe in them, and I'm happy with that.

PW: So would you say that the critic is in terminal decline?

CL: Those kinds of statements always come back to haunt you, don't they? It will linger on. I met this young guy who was talking about the literary criticism of James Wood – they exist, there's one or two of those nerds left, God bless them! Let's keep them alive. But it's not informing the culture in the way it used to, and that, I think, is the change. I don't think it's a good thing: I think it's a sad thing, the way we've let go of our culture. That's the problem. We can't blame the tabloids. We can't blame all these other people. It's something that's happened within our cultural milieu.

PW: Why did this happen, this loss of confidence?

CL: Now, this is where I think we're going to disagree. If you say 'who are the guilty men?', I would say, on the cultural front, it was the Left, and on the economic front it was the Right who were to blame. The Left are to blame because, in the name of progressive anti-elitism, they championed a kind of popularisation of culture, where they said 'we're sick of all this' – this is even before the radical avant-garde and the disdain for 'dead white males' back in the Sixties. They wanted culture for the people. And later on, you had the rise of postmodernism, which said basically: all art forms are equal; let us bring in the marginalised; let's destroy the old standards, the old hierarchical standards of modernism. And so that cleared out a space. And then, in the Eighties, from the Right you had this new individualism that said: 'Celebrate the individual!' And this is something that, I think, guys like you have never really come to terms with, because you want both. You want the free individual, away from the state and whatever – you championed the Thatcher dream; but you also want the old world of reticence and restraint, where people knew their place. You can't have both. You can't have a dynamic individualism that says 'I'm going out there' – a true meritocracy, not based on class – and then get upset when it's a bit vulgar and dynamic and self-obsessed.

> If you say 'who are the guilty men?', I would say, on the cultural front, it was the Left, and on the economic front it was the Right who were to blame.

PW: So you think it's a mix of these two approaches that has led to the current situation?

CL: This is really what the celebrity culture is ultimately about. The old means by which the citizen achieved a kind of sense of self-worth, a kind of connection with something bigger than themselves, the traditional means, have kind of fallen apart. If you think of patriotism, the way that one could take pride in being English: well, today, what do we debate all the time? What it means to be English! It's not even known! The pride that middle-class people had in being professional middle-class people... Who cares if you're a teacher or bank manager these days? Those things don't mean anything anymore. You're not even allowed to take any pride in your class. The means that existed once outside of the market – things that were not generated by the market, things that gave people meaning, from which they derived worth and a sense of self-esteem – these have, one by one, been lost. Even great sporting events that we had at one time – like when England won the World Cup in '66 – we don't even have those to feel good about.

The market has moved in, and zoomed into this gap with celebrity culture, which answers the question at its most basic: 'I want some attention, I want to be looked at, I want some praise, I need these things.' These are basic human things that people have got to have. And if the public, government and society can't provide it, the market can. And by God it's done it, with celebrity culture!

PW: But America is ruled by the market, but still has a very strong sense of national identity and a national story.

CL: It's very fragmented now. It's not a national story anymore; it hasn't been for a long while. Look at America: most people would say America's the land of celebrity culture. They invented the form. The kind of coherent narrative that you're talking about – it's completely fragmented. People are Afro-Americans, people are this and that and whatever. The ideal of the melting pot hasn't quite worked, has it? I don't think so.

America's a very religious country, with God on their side; whereas we secular Europeans, we don't even have that. So that sense of self-worth, that one is 'chosen' as American, is something we are denied. I don't see what we have in our public culture. I mean, we don't even have the monarchy, post-Diana! We have them there, of course, but there's no pride. All these things that give us our worth – they're not provided anymore, especially for young people, I think.

PW: Where do you think we will stand in 10 years' time, culturally? If there is, in cultural terms, a liberal orthodoxy now, will it still be in place?

CL: I don't think it's going to be decimated. But all the signs I see suggest to me there's been a radical change in the cultural climate. That's as far as I will go. I'll give you an example: I was struck by this recently, during programmes around the 40th anniversary of the Enoch Powell 'Rivers of Blood' speech in 1968. You had the BBC raising the question – was Powell a racist, or was he expressing the legitimate concerns of his constituency? This was so radical, but no one batted an eyelid. Ten years ago, you would never have dared ask that question at the BBC. That would just not be an acceptable question. I was surprised that, in the liberal media, how tolerant they were of those questions, the fact that they were asked. Now, that is something very different.

It's going to be interesting to see what happens, because increasingly people who identify with the Left are horrified by our new cultural world – a world that they've helped create. You know, what can they champion? They championed the attack on the high culture in the Sixties, were horrified by the new popular culture, the whole reality television thing, the dumbing down, and this whole new culture we have now. So where do they go? Are they going to retreat back and rediscover the joys of high culture? Where does it go? It's going to be interesting to see what they're going to do. I think more and more people on the Left are horrified by what they see around them. They sound like the reactionaries they used to mock.

PW: Do you think that in 10 years' time there will be more right-wing films and novels?

CL: I think that's going to happen, yes. I don't think there's any more mileage out of a leftist perspective. Where do you go? The Left don't have any belief in anything. They don't have a leftist vision of a society; they don't believe in Socialism; there is no vigorous, bold leftist view outside of the Socialist Workers Party. Among the intellectual Left, what are they arguing for? I don't know: they're condemning reality television programmes, or the so-called 'war on terror' – well, of course they're going to do that, but even they don't have a coherent position on that anymore. They don't have the kind of vision anymore that underwrites those art forms. That's all gone, so what have they got left? For example, look at David Mamet. Look at that change. Who saw that coming? Who saw Sir Salman Rushdie taking the positions that he's taking now?

> **...maybe the arts, instead of being *ahead* of the times, are just *behind* the times.**

It's interesting, because the climate has really changed. People on the Left admit that, for example, the old idea of multiculturalism just didn't work. It's dead. And maybe the arts, instead of being *ahead* of the times, are just *behind* the times. It's got to turn up sooner or later, because it's out there. The arts are really lagging behind. *C*

The Composer – James MacMillan

Happy chaos in the musical world

The foremost Scottish composer of his generation, James MacMillan was born in North Ayrshire in 1959. His international career was effectively launched with the premiere of *The Confession of Isobel Gowdie* at the BBC Proms in 1990. The critical acclaim accorded this orchestral work led to more high-profile commissions, including a percussion concerto *Veni, Veni, Emmanuel*, which premiered in 1992 and has since become his most performed work. His 'cello concerto for Mstislav Rostropovich was premiered in 1997.

Among his more recent successes are the opera *The Sacrifice*, commissioned by Welsh National Opera, and the *St John's Passion*, commissioned by the London Symphony Orchestra and conducted by Sir Colin Davis at its world premiere in 2008. That same year, he was awarded the British Composer Award for Liturgical Music, for the *Strathclyde Motets*.

James MacMillan is also internationally active as a conductor, working as composer/conductor with the BBC Philharmonic between 2000 and 2009. He has been appointed principal guest conductor of the Netherlands Radio Chamber Philharmonic from 2010. He was awarded a CBE in January 2004.

In 1999, he caused controversy when, in a speech at the Edinburgh Festival, he condemned what he saw as anti-Catholic prejudice in Scotland, likening it to Northern Ireland 'without the guns'.

In an essay for the *Spectator* in January 2008, entitled 'Unthinking Dogmatism', he explained why he hated the assumption that he was a 'liberal left-winger':

> In my travels I see myself frequently described in foreign media as a 'left-wing and Scottish nationalist' composer. The latter label is ludicrous, and I just put it down to a foreigner's ignorance and justifiable disinterest in the parish-pump tedium of devolved Scotland. It doesn't bother me too much. The first, however, disturbs me much more.

Peter Whittle (PW): It was a very interesting piece you wrote in the *Spectator*, and I wondered what moved you to write it.

James MacMillan (JM): Well, there had been a build-up of comment that disturbed me. There seemed to be a misrepresentation of where I was, and what kind of person I was, especially in the United States, where there was probably a lot of old copy. I found, when I was going over there, I was being described as a left-wing Socialist and Scottish nationalist composer, all of which – well, some of which – were never the case. And there were other comments that were pretty redundant, especially pertaining to political matters. And it seemed to be skewing a lot of the discussion that needed to be had about the music that was being played.

So I decided to take the bull by the horns, really, and write an article – this piece in the *Spectator* – which charted a process of disillusionment, and certainly a process towards a state where it seems nonsensical to describe me as left wing or liberal.

PW: But your actual political background, such as it was, was more on the traditional Left?

JM: Yes, and that's why all that stuff was still in the papers, and why it was being discussed. And, to be honest, I did make reference to it quite a bit when I was younger. I still regard myself as a bit of a political animal, in a way. I'm not particularly proud of that, but I just can't help it. It's just the way my mind is wired. I happened to grow up in a culture where the context for political expression was the Left – whether the traditional Old Labour, in the working-class communities of the West of Scotland, or these various waves of New Leftism that eventually made me decide that this was not for me. I could identify with certain traditional strands of Labourism – old-fashioned Socialism maybe – that my grandfather was brought up with, but not with the New Left that has subsumed the movement.

PW: What was so different about this new group of people? Are you talking about the Sixties onwards maybe?

JM: I think so. It was difficult at the time to recognise what was going on, but certainly I was aware of a kind of conflict between values – and indeed, classes – that I had grown up with and, I suppose, a new kind of breed – metropolitan based. I was a student in Edinburgh, and the ultra-Left in these places didn't strike me as in any way connected with the working-class basis of Socialism that I'd come from. I can now see this retrospectively, but at the time it was confusing – I didn't know who these people were! They didn't connect at all with me culturally, or indeed politically. But in retrospect it was quite clear that a metropolitan left-wing class grew out of the 1968 experience and, in essence, colonised the Labour party and have taken it over; and in many ways they have dumped the old ethical values that sustained past generations of people who held those ideals dear.

PW: You mentioned in the *Spectator* piece that the arts had been particularly colonised. Can you describe how?

JM: First of all, I think you've got to look at the media in this country, which is profoundly London-centric. They are a breed, if you like, that speak only to themselves, and have no real concept of what ordinary people understand as important. I'm not talking geographically; I'm talking about people outside that particular milieu, aesthetically and ethically. And I think that a lot of the arts world are in contact with that group, and deal with them on a daily, professional basis. And they speak to each other, and they cocoon themselves in a kind of hidden charade that ignores the wider world outside. And I think a lot of what you see in the BBC, for example, can also be transferred into the cultural Establishment and those who run – command – the heights of our cultural life, whether it be theatre or television. And in other aspects as well.

They are of the same class. And they are a self-perpetuating, self-referring group. And they don't really have much contact with the outside world, with the rest of the country. I was reading a speech given by the head of BBC Religion, who said – I can't remember the exact statistics, but when asked, 71 per cent of the general populace said that they believed in God. But when it came to the people who ran the media and entertainment industries, that proportion fell to 21 per cent. And this is one particular instance of where this gulf is huge. Maybe it's because I've never really been part of London – I mean, my music's played here, and everything that makes me a public person in a sense comes through London – but I'm aware of a class and a culture, a sub-culture, here that controls the media of culture, and indeed the decision-making as to what is important in culture, and arrogantly ignores a huge and wider constituency – something which I feel very much a part of.

PW: Can you explain how this might manifest itself, particularly in your world, in music?

JM: Yes. Modernity in music, in many ways, has been more unassailable than modernity in some of the other arts. And it's because it has been given this oxygen of vitality through academia, but also through the media – through the BBC, and in Europe through a lot of the state radio stations – which have sublimated a particular kind of modernism in music to a kind of paradigmatic state, where the message has gone out that composers, and indeed the music public, should see this as not just the way forward, but the way things *are*.

And I must say that this situation is far worse in places like Germany and France, which are much more controlled by a centralised cultural view of things. The composer and activist Pierre Boulez, for example, runs a kind of personal Kremlin, in the shape of IRCAM [Institute for Research and Coordination Acoustic/Music], in Paris, which, in a very strong sense, has determined the nature of the modern music that is programmed and esteemed in Paris, and in France generally. And in Germany it's the same. I know many composers in France who, because they were not part of *L'Eglise Boulezienne*, were sidelined, and are, in a sense, outcasts from that which was seen as important and central to French modernity in music. And these composers are very interesting. I've made a point of finding out who these people are and, to a degree, championing their music; having some of it played here, and finding out what happens when you are outcast from a central orthodox modernity.

And I specifically focus on the old guard of the 'avant-garde' in Paris, and also, to a degree, in Germany. Things are not as bad as that in Britain. The British solution, the British accommodation if you like, is to value a plurality of aesthetics in modern music. That's not to say that, if given a chance, those same kinds of people here would not move in and take over if they could. There are certainly people like that around, and you can see their agendas working in some of the reviews they write about modern music in this country.

But in spite of them, there is nevertheless a plurality of aesthetics and styles in Britain. And that is what marks us out in many ways as different from the continental Europeans. And I think that's what marks us out as a healthy, modern, musical culture. Because people abroad know now who British composers are; people know who George Benjamin, or Thomas Adès, or Mark-Anthony Turnage and others are. And they also know there's no binding ingredient – no sort of false, utopian, extraneous ideology that binds us together in the same way that schools emerged according to a certain Marxist instigation in mainland Europe. And that is the beauty of British musical culture. We have this plurality and a 'promiscuous' disregard for the fundamental precepts of ideological modernism. Yes, some of them are absorbed – but a lot of them are discarded.

PW: Why is that the case here? Could it, for example, be due to the great respect for ideology and intellectualism in general in Europe?

JM: It's a fetish with ideology, rather than a respect for intellectualism. A lot of the conceit in Europe is that they have this intellectual culture; but actually, it's an intellectual culture that has been hijacked by a very stern intellectual Puritanism, which springs from Marx, I suppose, and has coloured European modernity. And I don't think we suffer from that here. In many ways, the saving grace for this country's musical modernity is the disregard for rules, and disregard for extraneous, external ideologies. We haven't allowed that to interfere in the same way that, I'm afraid, even the great continental figures – from Boulez, through Stockhausen, to Berio and a lot of the Italians especially – have allowed the fashionable views of the day, coming from politics and philosophy, to interfere with the way that they not only make their music, but decided to shape the musical culture around them.

PW: But even if it's not so bad here, would you say that the critical thrust is still very pro-modernism?

JM: There is a tendency in British musical criticism to see what happens on the continent as superior to here. And you'll find a lot of disparaging remarks about British provincialism running through the comparisons that music critics make between this island – and indeed America as well – the Anglosphere if you like, which is regarded as inferior to what happens in places where modernity has been cultivated... You'll find that an unnatural comparison, an unfair comparison between – as they would see it – a kind of provincialism and insularity at work in the UK and US, and the highest heights of professionalism and intellectual endeavour that shape the music of Germany, France and Italy. So there is that kind of self-loathing, haughty arrogance in certain aspects of the critical fraternity, which I think is a problem. Because to someone coming from the outside, it skews an understanding of what we're doing here.

> **In many ways, the saving grace for this country's musical modernity is the disregard for rules, and disregard for extraneous, external ideologies.**

And my hope is that thinkers about music will emerge in the next few decades who will counter that, and will see a broader picture; who will see modernity as something that has left its mark historically and, in a sense, may have been left behind.

PW: What has been your experience of working and maturing as a composer, as a musician, in this kind of musical orthodoxy?

JM: There has been a lot of conflict, which has surprised me in many ways, because I regard myself as part of a new music culture; and the way we saw ourselves in the past was that that culture was a radical culture. And therefore, to be seen within this culture as a conservative composer has come as a bit of a surprise to me and many others.

PW: You wouldn't think of yourself as a conservative composer?

JM: No, not at all. I find that odd. It's partly to do with this 'promiscuity' of aesthetic and style. I'm very relaxed – because I'm not an ideologue politically. I don't feel I have to make everything fit a certain plan, a predetermined plan. And therefore the music that I make can freely make references to the past, to other cultures, to modernity, to tonality, and so on. Tonality can be part of my language, unashamedly. But of course, at one time there was an attempt in music to see tonality as simply something of the past, to be dumped, unceremoniously. That seemed to me an extreme and unrealistic view. It was understandable in a way, in that traditional musical values, like all traditional values, were rejected by the new philosophical, political and cultural elites in Europe after the Second World War. There was a feeling that 'the old culture' had come to an end.

PW: European culture had come to an end?

...at one time there was an attempt in music to see tonality as simply something of the past, to be dumped, unceremoniously.

JM: Yes, that bourgeois culture had failed. Christian culture had failed. And that therefore it was a perfectly respectable position for the young artists to begin with a blank slate – a virgin field, if you like; to begin with nothing. No rules, no connection, no taint of the past. And you see that in politics, and in philosophy and everything else. But you see it in music as well, with a deliberate attempt to expunge any form of the taint of tradition in music, whether German symphonism or anything worryingly hierarchical or patriarchal, from European history. There were concerted attempts to begin again, with apparently entirely new sounds and new concepts. Exciting in a way, but with worrying unseen implications.

PW: So it really was similar to the visual arts world, where many forms of traditional learning were scrapped and now have actually been forgotten? Out of a sort of self-disgust?

JM: Yes, absolutely – self-loathing, a kind of European self-loathing of where we've come from, culturally. But the thing is, the difference between music and some of the other arts is that music *needs* a craftsmanship. It can't exist without it. So the craftsman in the composer – whether the composer was Boulez, or Stockhausen, or Berio – eventually took over. And that craftsman – the artisan as much as the artist – is what prevailed in the end. And anything that is good from that modernist phase is because of the craftsmanship and technical vision. It's a combination of craftsmanship and technique.

You know, composers, musicians, are quite rhetorical people, really. And when it comes to politics, a lot of musicians are romantics, and fall back on a received sentimental, romantic rhetoric. There's no real vibrant, principled, focused, laser-like political intelligence at work in a lot of the musicians in our time. That disappoints me, as someone who does value the political instinct. Musicians are romantics when it comes to politics.

PW: How is that expressed?

JM: Their causes are fashionable causes. And you get that right through the other arts as well, of course. I don't know whether it's better in the other arts or not. My experience is that a lot of them are from comfortable middle-class backgrounds, with no grounding in the real politics of the lives of ordinary people. The politics of whether you're thrown out of your house or not; the politics of my grandfather, who was coal miner from the 1920s to the 1970s. Politics is a comfort zone for these media trendies. I find that a lot of people I meet in arts, music and theatre or whatever have a rather facile understanding of political engagement; and it usually involves much gesturalism and rhetoric!

In music, the cultural clash has to do with the language that one uses. If one embraces tonality, that's seen as a backward-looking gesture by some. Even someone like Mark-Anthony Turnage will be regarded in certain European spheres as a reactionary composer because of his interaction with popular culture, through jazz especially. But also his modality and, to be honest, at certain times a kind of pastoralism of the sort that runs through a lot of British composers even today. That is what the European modernist mind despises.

PW: Because it's seen as being nationalistic?

JM: Yeah, and provincial, and backward-looking, with an ideal based in nostalgia. And then there's also the question of religion, which has become such a defining battleground now. I find conflict on two fronts. I have this kind of pluralism or plurality – a 'promiscuous' attitude to the past, which I value. But I have an ideological attachment to that value: there's a reason why the past is still important – not just in music, but also in politics and philosophy. And you either take the Marxist/modernist view that tradition is a tainted thing and should be stopped, so therefore you put a dam up to stop it deliberately, which is artificial. Or you take a more natural, realistic view – in seeing the past like a river, running through human history, irrigating human history at any given time, and therefore a life-giving, vibrant thing. One sees tradition as a good thing, or a bad thing, the influence of which should be halted.

In a sense, they have been mugged by history. Because their view of history – that the future is secular – hasn't happened.

What I'm saying is that the religious arguments have thrown me into conflict a lot with the liberal elites who control the commanding heights of culture and criticism, even in this country, who have an instinctive anxiety about religion, which they thought should have died out by now! In a sense, they have been mugged by history. Because their view of history – that the future is secular – hasn't happened. They are in a state of confusion about that. So they are flailing around, attacking people like me and many others. And let's face it – many composers were religious in the twentieth century, and that perplexes the cultural elites.

PW: What do you think was the high-water mark then? You just described when a dam was put up, as opposed to the continuance of a belief that somehow tradition, or what came before, should flow and should inform things. What stage are we at now? How strong is the dam?

JM: It's been obliterated. As far as these people are concerned, we live in a period of chaos. They have lost the argument. Modernism has been obliterated by the flow of tradition and many other things that they didn't see either as important or as effective in the making of the modern world. And that's why I say that they've been mugged by history. Because they haven't seen either the new things that have come into our culture, or the old things that still remain important, as being the prevailing influences that we still have today.

PW: Do you think there was an attempt to make a lot of modernist music as inaccessible as possible? Do you think that it was deliberate or do you think that that's a crude interpretation?

JM: Well, in the period after the Second World War, what the new Young Turks sought out for themselves was a laboratory culture for themselves. Because everything was up for grabs, and because everything traditional – traditional music and culture – was tainted and, in their view, finished, they had to go into a 'laboratory' to make something new. And in a sense they did value obscurantism: because if something was obscure, it wasn't connecting with those traditional and outmoded understandings of culture that they would say the bourgeoisie held dear. But to be honest, it was more than the bourgeoisie – it was the entire world. And therefore their laboratory experiment, in many ways understandable and exciting in its own right, deliberately avoided those aspects of musical communication that were primal, universal aspects of the human condition. Which is to say the profundity of melody, the profundity of the triad in western culture of a whole range of things, technical things about music that they wanted to obliterate, fragment and start again. They wanted to build a new culture, Khmer Rouge-like, out of those broken fragments. This has been the mistake that modernists and Marxists in music and politics have made ever since.

PW: So where do you stand on this new 'chaos'? You said earlier that you like the British plurality.

JM: Yes, I'm quite happy with the chaos! The 'opposition', on the other hand, view my approach as a dereliction of responsibility, whatever that means. And they see people like me as opportunists milking popular sentiment. That's the view from the *Guardian,* for example! I think that they suspect there's something wrong when music makes its connection with, as they see, a mass audience. But I never make a connection with a mass audience, in the sense that I don't write pop music – popular music. I think there's always, in the world of classical music, undercurrents and trends, but the Marxists and the modernists who do have these positions in music criticism value the obscure because they do see it as a badge of that which is above the common herd.

PW: If we have chaos now – which you're quite happy with – where do we see the practical manifestations of that chaos? Do you see it in music programming?

JM: Yes, I would say so. I think there's an instinct at large now which looks beyond 'the politburo', as it were, to see a bigger picture. If composers are exploring things now that were taboo according to the modernist aesthetic – well and good. I get the impression that people involved in the music world are genuinely interested in that. Things may be a bit different elsewhere.

To give an example: I was asked by a New Music festival in Hanover to adjudicate on a composition competition, and I agreed to it. They were all ready to send the scores. But I discovered that the deal usually was that 'esteemed professors', when they were asked onto this panel, would have their music played at this Hanover New Music Festival. But then it became clear that none of my music was being played. So when my representatives asked why, their basic excuse was that our New Music festival does not give a platform to tonal and conservative composers. Then why have you asked me to adjudicate? And there was no answer to that, so I pulled out. It was an insult, to be honest. But that kind of thing goes on, and I find that there's a modernist hierarchy that is still so powerful in places like German radio stations, German New Music festivals, French New Music festivals.

PW: You've talked before about your Catholicism. Presumably it isn't easy to be working and drawing on your religious tradition in a country that basically has an orthodoxy which is secular? That must make it even more difficult, I would have thought?

JM: Well, there's certainly an ongoing debate about it. And I'm giving this lecture for the Sandford St Martin Trust in October [2008] which will be broadcast on BBC Radio 4. I'm basically asking questions about the religious artist in our modern culture, and whether there's a place for religious artists, and how valuable and how important can the religious artist be. And it explores some of the objections to the religious principle in modern art. But it's very much from a composer's perspective. And from my perspective – I know it's different in other arts – there's a very strong, palpable strain of the religious motivation in musical modernity, in spite of what many people have tried to do to veer it away.

It all comes back to Wagner, I think, as far as the modern world's concerned. Wagner, although he was a very kind of unconventional religious thinker, his absolute ideal was a search for the sacred. And I think that has had a huge impact. Roger Scruton talks about it, and explores it marvellously in his book *Death-Devoted Heart: Sex and the Sacred in Wagner's Tristan and Isolde*. The impact of this on not just modern music, but on other forms of modernity, is an untold story. Because, if you look at, let's say, music in the last 100–150 years, you'll find a continual strain of the major figures who were profoundly religious men or women in different ways. Stravinsky, who was as conservative in his theology as he was revolutionary in the music he made, had a great love of the Catholicism he encountered in the West, and of his own Orthodoxy. He wrote masses, he wrote music for liturgy as well in Russia and the West. He was a believer.

Schoenberg, the great modernist icon, reconverted to a practising Judaism after the Holocaust and became a mystic, really, in his outlook; obsessed with the connections between silence and music philosophically. I think it's because of that that John Cage, for example, decided to study with Schoenberg. And John Cage, of course, pursued his own religious paths through a discovery of the religions of the Far East. The interesting thing about John Cage, with his explanation of silence, the philosophy and the aesthetics of silence, noise and music, was that his most notorious or famous piece, *4'33"*, which is 4 minutes 33 seconds of silence – a kind of rhetorical gimmick one might say, but a real challenge to the culture in many other ways – was originally entitled 'Silent Prayer'.

So even someone like Cage, in his counter-cultural way, really was plugged into this constant search for the sacred. Following that there was Messiaen, of course, who was famously Catholic, and everything he wrote was shaped by a theology and a personal faith. And in this country, people like Britten, of course, with his social Anglicanism, and even with Tippett, who always described himself as an agnostic – there's a deep mysticism at the heart of his work. And the fact that he chose St Augustine as one of his major texts or settings – there's another untold story there, too.

...that search for the sacred is almost part of the mainstream of modernity in music. That's a huge challenge to those people who try to rub it out of history and say that it's not important.

Since the Iron Curtain came down, there's been a whole range of composers that we've become aware of in the wake of Shostakovich. Alfred Schnittke and Sofia Gubaidulina – profoundly religious composers, embracing Catholicism, but also keeping alive an Orthodoxy, and indeed an interest in Islam as well. And of course there's Arvo Pärt from Estonia, Giya Kancheli from Georgia, Henryk Gorecki from Poland – it's almost as if there's a constant theme going through the development of modern music, that religion is alive and well. And indeed, that search for the sacred is almost part of the mainstream of modernity in music. That's a huge challenge to those people who try to rub it out of history and say that it's not important.

I got a fly-on-the-wall report from an academic board that was planning a book on music in the twentieth century. They were going through a list of headings and volumes – music and nationalism, music and gender, music and anti-imperialism, etc., etc. Someone suggested music and religion, and it was completely pooh-poohed – there was nothing to write about! Something's happened to the intelligentsia. Something's happened to academe. They can't see the nose on their face if they believe that religion can't figure in an explanation of music in the twentieth century!

PW: There are more fashionable religions, and there are less fashionable ones. But nevertheless, it's there, it's being argued over now. So they'll have to take it on board?

JM: I think that's right. They can only ignore the writing on the wall for so long. But you are right: in music it's been a constant. And in spite of, I'd say, the ignorance and stupidity of those kinds of academics I've cited, it's been there for all to see, in much more palpable ways than is the case in other arts – although I think poetry is also something where you can detect a distinct line of the numinous at work in English poetry, from David Jones, right through to Geoffrey Hill, Les Murray and many others. But the way that the arts have been appropriated by 'The Academy'... A particular kind of political class has moved in and appropriated the way that those arts are disseminated, presented and explained to younger generations. And it's those people that are culpable for having spun a particular propagandistic bias. It comes down to an understanding of not just religion, but tradition in general.

PW: I understand that a critic once said that it was a 'perilous thing' for you when you once cited the conservative philosopher Roger Scruton?

JM: Yes, absolutely. It was at a performance of my Second Symphony, in the Queen Elizabeth Hall a few years ago. They asked me up on stage to give a little bit of an introduction, and I happened to make reference to the book I've just mentioned – Scruton's *Death-Devoted Heart* – which makes a very important and powerful claim for the fact that the search for the sacred has been a constant in modern music. He is one of the most serious philosophers in this country, and it was in all seriousness that I cited his book.

There was a *Guardian* review by a critic called Tim Ashley, who described the fact that I'd cited Scruton as a 'perilous' thing to do. And it made me think: in what sense does he mean perilous? Is it perilous for me that I'm publicly associated with Scruton? Or are Scruton's ideas perilous in themselves (which seems like a bizarre idea)? But more importantly, was it perilous for me to be publicly associating myself with the other 'tribe' in this issue? That is – and I suppose I go back to a fundamental point – putting myself beyond the pale of what is acceptable to the orthodox elites by associating myself with someone who, quite clearly, was an enemy of that tribe? Was this going to damage me? And therefore, was this a threat? Was this critic threatening me that this was dangerous for me and I would be expelled from that which was acceptable? That I myself would put myself beyond the pale, beyond that self-regulating elite?

PW: You did say, however, in that *Spectator* piece, that there's change in the air. Can you say why you think this?

JM: Well you're not completely sure how cyclical these things are, and whether they'll have their day again, but I think that the whole Blair–Brown experiment is going down the drain. And it's partly to do with this that there's a change in the air. And it's given a sense of opportunity for those who have been sat upon by a certain orthodox view of what culture should be, and therefore there are all these views coming out of the woodwork. It's not just me: I've found it in many others as well. David Mamet's denouncement of his own unthinkingly orthodox liberalism in America is very interesting. They are in the middle of a horrendous culture war, and the fact that he broke ranks is very interesting.

PW: I find it very encouraging what you said about music. It would seem to me that it's therefore one of the healthier cultural areas at the moment. Would you say that's true?

JM: I would say so, yes. There are mavericks involved in music, and they're not easily boxed in. I mean, in theatre and other things they all seem to be looking over their shoulder. They know that they can get away with the basic, almost childish, childlike rhetorical flourish to gain friends in high places. I don't think that works in music. Music is more of a craft. And I think it requires deeper thought, in many ways.

From Schoenberg onwards, the New Music fraternity have formed ghettos, in which like-minded aficionados, the intelligentsia of music, were able to appreciate it without the general ignorant herd ruining it for them. That haughtiness is given oxygen through public subsidy a lot of the time. I feel in two minds about this, because the BBC is a great sponsor of the arts, a great cultivator of the arts, and I'd never want to see them damaged in that part of their work. But perhaps a reality check is required from time to time.

My hope is that there are thinkers coming forward in Britain to expand on this, to think more outside the box. It can be a bit of a lonely path sometimes. But there are some writers and critics who are beginning to think for themselves. I want to see more people like that coming through, younger figures who, in a sense, take cognisance of what's happened; see the demise of modernity and make some valuable reflections on this that we can all think about. So far, the Old Guard – the old '68-ers – just moan about it all the time, as a sign that their experiment has failed.

PW: But it seems from what you say that there's a lot of scope for what people can do now in music.

JM: Yes, I'm very optimistic, and I suppose that's the bottom line here. I think this country has always had its own sensibilities. Some might denigrate it as provincial and all the rest, but it never really has been. It's always been looking to see what's been going on elsewhere. But still, even someone like Birtwistle is regarded as a pastoralist in Europe, much to the amazement of people over here. Birtwistle and I were part of the Universal Edition catalogue, which was scuppered by its mother house in Vienna, because it didn't value the British house. And it meant that people like Birtwistle – and like him or loathe him, he's a very significant figure – were dumped, trashed by the Universal mother house in Vienna, which was, of course, the publisher of Schoenberg and Boulez and Stockhausen.

But it just didn't value, didn't understand, the British culture. I've performed Birtwistle's music, and my music's nothing like his. In many ways, he's a completely different composer from me. But I also perform Mark-Anthony Turnage's music, and Thomas Adès and I perform that in a continuum of Elgar and Vaughan Williams. And I do see a continuum. In fact, Birtwistle has acknowledged his debt to Vaughan Williams and the English pastoralists of the past. And it's definitely not a trajectory to be ashamed of. It's something that makes this country peculiar, but vibrant. And vibrant in its potential for the future. *ƒ*

The Designer –
Dame Vivienne Westwood

Culture as an antidote to propaganda

Unquestionably the most important living British fashion designer, Vivienne Westwood first came to prominence as the so-called 'high priestess of punk' in the late Seventies. Since then, her designs have often centred on idiosyncratic interpretations of traditional clothing and forms of dress. In 2004, her work was the subject of a major retrospective exhibition at the Victoria and Albert Museum in London.

Her political activity has included joining forces with the campaign group Liberty, for which she designed T-shirts bearing the slogan 'I am not a terrorist, please don't arrest me'. She has also backed the Campaign for Nuclear Disarmament, and recently announced, to some media surprise, that she was now supporting the Conservative party.

In 1992, Vivienne Westwood was awarded the OBE, and in 2006 was created a Dame.

In 2007, she launched an arts manifesto, called *Active Resistance to Propaganda*.

Peter Whittle (PW): I wanted to start with a very fundamental quote from your manifesto, Vivienne. You write: 'Every time I read a book instead of a magazine, go to an art gallery instead of watching TV, go to the theatre instead of the cinema, I fight for active resistance to propaganda.' Now, usually propaganda has some kind of point or reason, however malign that might be. What, in your view, is the propaganda that we would be facing?

Vivienne Westwood (VW): I define propaganda as being constituted of three evils. Nationalism, which might need some explaining, you may think, at the moment... And I can do that. The quote came from [Aldous] Huxley, who said in one of his essays that the world suffers from three evils – in the Thirties I think it was: nationalistic idolatry, which had taken the place of religion; organised lying, which needs no explanation – we're all aware that this is the case; and the third, non-stop distraction, which he thought was the greatest evil. I think so, too. I thought: what would I tell young people these days? And the first thing I thought of is non-stop distraction; because, if you're being pumped with rubbish all the time, then you're not thinking 'where is the future?' And what kind

40

of life do you have anyway? I've always been interested in having a better future than the one we seem to be looking at. And I mean, it's absolutely horrendous, what's going to happen!

I think that the antidote to this propaganda is culture. And so the manifesto takes the form of a search for art, which gives us culture. The question of discrimination between things – that's what culture is about. It's about recognising the difference between what's good, what's not very good, what's rubbish, and what's amazing. I define, as well, what culture is and what art is, because I think they need defining; because nobody does that anymore.

Of course, it depends which book you read. And while it isn't true, you know, that every single film is rubbish and gives us no idea of the world we live in, it really is just a passive experience that washes over us. Theatre is not: theatre is a very active thing, where you supply the imagination, and therefore you understand something – you know it. I think that film is, more or less, usually propaganda.

So I'm making a very strong statement here. And at the heart of the manifesto is the idea that when you look at art, the objective is to try to see things as they are. And I do think that culture is something that is decided by people's understanding of the world they live in. And I think that art is the only thing that shows them that. Science doesn't show it – it's incomplete.

PW: When you talk about most film being propaganda – and I make much of my living as a film critic, so maybe I'm not disinterested... When you say propaganda, propaganda in what sense? To what end?

VW: To stop you thinking. And to sort of...go along, with no criticism of the world you live in, just accepting and lapping up all the stupidities. Anything that just fills your mind and stops you thinking. It's a bit like religion, it really is! It's a panacea – something that washes over you and makes you *not* see reality, *not* understand the world you live in. You live in a dream world. That's propaganda: you're not thinking, you're not appreciating the world you live in, and you don't realise the difference between the good and the bad, and you're not anywhere near appreciating things.

In the manifesto it says you get out what you put in. That's not always true; but if you don't put anything in, you don't get anything out. And what you normally put in – when you're looking at great art – is your imagination; and if there's no chance of that, and your imagination is all sort of orchestrated into some rubbish world – well, that's not imagination; it's propaganda. It's imagination alienated. This is what I'm sort of getting at in the manifesto. It's something that comforts you and which you indulge in, but it's just your own personal little mind-fuck, really.

PW: You say this is about how you get out what you put in. But if you look at [the mid-Seventies movement] Punk, it seems that that was *not* about putting anything in; it was simply about destroying. Could you have written this manifesto then? Could you have believed what you say in this manifesto then?

VW: There's one link between Punk and now, which is that I've always been so outraged at the horrible suffering and the way the world is mismanaged. In those days, I was very against authority, because I saw all the fault coming from there. Now, I'm still of the same opinion that the world is being destroyed, and that there's all this terrible suffering in the world. But the thing that's different from those days, I would say, is that then I just thought it was enough to try to say 'we don't want this' – to put a spoke in the works. I don't believe in anarchy anymore; I think you have to have some form of government.

People think that subversion is about undermining tradition (whatever it might be), and I am really against the idea of throwing the baby out with the bathwater.

I just think that the only real subversion comes from ideas. The only things that can change a horrible world are ideas. People think that subversion is about undermining tradition (whatever it might be), and I am really against the idea of throwing the baby out with the bathwater. I think tradition is what we've got; it's who we are. It's like asking a scientist to throw away his laboratory and just start from scratch.

The twentieth century was the age of the iconoclast. You know – everything's going to be wonderful, history is bunk. That's what Henry Ford said. And today you always hear people using the most stupid expressions, like 'this is consigned to the dustbin of history'! I mean, it's like they're on another planet! To have believed all this propaganda, about how the world automatically gets better and better! And now we're faced with the result of this kind of thinking – which is that nobody's thinking at all, really.

PW: You also say in your manifesto: 'Aren't you just sick of the latest thing?' Could you explain that quote? It seems to me that it's about the fact that we are hooked on the idea that just because something is new means it must automatically be good.

VW: It has to be universal; it has to be. I mention Chaucer as an example. His characters are as alive today as they were then because they speak to us; there is something in us that relates to them. And the 'latest thing' is something that's usually just for the moment, or something which one or two people relate to.

I'm against the idea that just because something's extreme, that it's good. For example, someone once said to me: 'You've got this reputation, you could just tell us all to wear car tyres.' Of course I couldn't! That's not a good idea. But in the art world, that is what it's like: something different, you know. Wear your trousers upside down! Different, great idea! But no, no one's going to be universally interested in that.

PW: You've been very critical, have you not, of much contemporary art. On what basis? When you look around at conceptual art, for example, at much of the kind of thing that's in contemporary galleries, what is it that you object to?

VW: I think that one of the central tenets of my manifesto is that there is no progress in art. Art speaks to us. But like I say: you have to invest in it; you have to take the trouble to look at it.

You don't need to run around trying to catch the 'latest thing'. Do so, by all means. But if you start to look at great things, you will become less interested in running around looking at the latest thing – you won't have time! You'll be too absorbed. If you've got time, read a book. I never watch television; it's the last thing I could do – I couldn't bear it. It's just a total waste of my time.

> ...if you start to look at great things, you will become less interested in running around looking at the latest thing – you won't have time!

I've asked people... They go to Hoxton market, and I say: 'Why did you go down there? What did you find?' And they can't tell you. It's always something different – that's all they seem to be able to say. It's a social event, of course. There are some nice clubs and restaurants around there, and you've got people who are supposedly trendy or looking at art around there and it's a social event. But really, I don't think they're talking about what they've been to see. It's just a sort of way of grouping together there.

So I do warn people against bothering with conceptual art, because... Yes, bother with it, but you *will* waste your time. And abstract art. If you want to – yes, do so. But you have to have something to compare it with. And until you've done that, then you can't say that you have an opinion about modern art.

PW: When you say that people don't know about the tradition from which something came, do you think this is due to our culture of simply not caring about the past?

VW: I'm saying that it is the propaganda of the age in which we live, this iconoclasm. Just do nothing... The world is getting better... Politicians will sort everything else out for you... Ecological disaster – leave it to the scientists... The world is getting better, and it started getting better in

1900. Or, as I've found in fashion, most fashion editors think the world started in 1960, when they were young.

PW: In the manifesto, you have these characters – Alice and Pinocchio – and at one point there is an art conference in Paris. As I understand it, it's one that you actually attended. You make an interesting point: you say that a delegate there considered himself a 'cultured' man because he appreciated *everything*. And you also say that people such as him have mixed up anthropology with culture. Could you explain more about what you mean by that?

> **I've found in fashion, most fashion editors think the world started in 1960, when they were young.**

VW: I think what you're really trying to get at is that you would like me to say what the difference is between culture and culture in the anthropological sense. I must admit that, when I'm talking about culture, I am being Eurocentric. It is that the Greeks were humanists; the Greek mind was rediscovered in the Renaissance, and this is what Europe has had.

Anthropological culture – what's called culture now – is essentially about differences in behaviour, and it's quite a useful word to use in that sense, because otherwise you annoy people. To say 'your culture's different from mine' – it's quite diplomatic to say that, as opposed to 'my culture's better than yours', or whatever.

Now we've got this global world. But the problem that the people had with that convention was in considering how we keep tradition, and yet have all these festivals and things, and not end up with this global soup. How do we do that? They didn't know, but their only recommendation was: let's have more festivals... Let's get more tolerant... Let's get more appreciative of everybody, of what everybody can do, because everybody can be an artist, and everybody's wonderful, and we should all appreciate it. And somehow I don't think that is true.

People feel that somehow they have to – you might call it 'compromise'. That they have to somehow or other pass over to something more popular; that they should not be elitist. And what I am really claiming and defending is elitism, because elitism is the thing where you put into it what you get out. It's about somebody who has really taken the trouble to compare things, and to decide that this is better than that.

PW: Would you call yourself a cultural relativist?

VW: No, I wouldn't. I think that's terrible, that idea that 'everything goes'. I mean, when I choose music for a fashion show, I do mix things. I had some Brazilian music from the *favela*s, and then it goes into Tchaikovsky's *Sleeping Beauty*, and something else. I do that because a fashion show isn't high art anyway, and you can use things.

PW: You say that art has been conceptualised by what you call in the manifesto 'the art mafia'. Who are these people?

VW: Who are the art mafia? Well, it's everybody who's somebody on a programme called *Mixing It*, or *Front Row* or whatever they're called. It's these people who do these programmes where everything is included.

The consensus is that tradition is not good, and that new things are good, and that certain people are judges of it, and they've held onto their positions there. It's a very easy position to hold onto, because I'm talking about investing in things, really putting the effort in – it's not an effort in the end, it's a deep pleasure, to really look at things. And people don't want to be bothered; they want to be titillated with, you know – let's go to the Tate gallery and slide down a helter-skelter and all go and have a cup of tea, and look at something red – 'wow!', you know?

PW: Having just written a manifesto against propaganda, what do you think of the way in which religion has generally seeped back into society now? It is having an effect directly on the arts, it seems to me. People are frightened to write certain things and to produce certain things – even to paint certain things. What do you feel about that?

VW: The first thing is that we're all supposed to have this religious tolerance. I think there's nothing more terrible than to indoctrinate a child into a religion where they will not be tolerant anyway; and if they are, then they're going to be tolerant of all these other intolerances, so to speak. I just think it's terrible; either you believe or you think.

I've had it both ways, because, as a child, in this village... There was this lovely church – the harvest festival, Christmas and all of this kind of stuff. It was social cement and spiritual cement. So we have lost this sense of community, and we don't have anything to replace it with. Somebody mentioned – I think it was a Labour politician – that we really should perhaps concentrate more on our schools, as a community. I think that's ever such a good idea; it's something that's really been lost. And if only they would put some sort of veto on the amount that children are allowed to travel, and that they should be educated near to where they live...

Everything I do, this manifesto, is set against the world scenario that I believe we are in danger of being the victims of. There was an article in the *Guardian* by [James] Lovelock – he wrote that book called *The Revenge of Gaia*. He's a scientist. He predicts that, by 2100, four-fifths of the population will have died, and there will only be a fifth of the population left. By 2020, London will be half underwater; Europe will be half desert. We need to see a map of the world to know what that is going to look like.

But can you imagine the suffering that's going to happen? He thinks the things that will really count first of all are the disasters – like the tsunamis, the fires, the wars, the killings, the famines. He says that we are like people prior to a war – we don't do anything until the war hits us, and then it's too late. There are other scientists who say no, we have to believe in human nature, and that the one thing that is not factored into this inevitable-seeming scenario is the ability of human beings to act in an emergency. And we're not doing anything; it's all 'business as usual'.

I really would like to mobilise public opinion in some way; but my manifesto is about culture. How the hell can we be talking about culture in the face of all this? I'm saying that life is worth living, and it is worth investing in the idea of understanding the world we live in. I believe that you do that through looking at art. I believe it's the only thing that we can be objective about; that gives us a mirror on life.

I'm trying to speak to young people as well – especially. If you try to read the newspapers you will just get a horizontal view, a superficial view. You need depth; you need culture; you have to invest in this. I'm saying 'get a life' by doing what this manifesto is; it's a practice – it's saying: if you do this, your life will change. What I'm saying is: if you do this, it will give you this ballast, like a ship that won't be tossed in the storm. Yes, maybe you will be shipwrecked because of what I'm talking about; but it will give you such personal ballast you will feel that you are making progress, you will feel that you are understanding the world you live in. And I just recommend it as a way of discriminating and getting people to think. But it's terribly important that we are political as well; but do this, too, because you won't get blown away then. Young people are very idealistic and they always want to do really great things, and a lot of them are political; but I'm saying: do this as well, follow culture, because otherwise you'll be so easily disillusioned, you'll feel so inadequate in front of this terrible thing, that at least in your own life you'll start to understand something about the whole history and the genius of the human race, and what it was, and hopefully what it may still be.

If you try to read the newspapers you will just get a horizontal view, a superficial view. You need depth; you need culture; you have to invest in this.

The Shock Jock – Jon Gaunt

Class and talk radio in the UK

Considered by many to be the 'king of talk radio', Jon Gaunt has worked for many radio stations, including BBC Three Counties Radio, BBC WM, BBC London 94.9 and BBC Coventry and Warwickshire. He has won three Sony Radio Awards (one as an individual, two as part of a team).

Most recently, he was host of a mid-morning show on talkSPORT radio. However, in November 2008 his contract there was terminated after – live on air – he branded as 'a Nazi' and 'an ignorant pig' a local government councillor who was defending plans to ban smokers from fostering children.

Born in Coventry, he studied at the University of Birmingham. Before starting to work in broadcasting, he had been both the founder of a theatre company and a playwright.

As a columnist for the *Sun* newspaper, Gaunt's forthright views have brought him prominence as a commentator. He has been a guest on Radio 4's *Moral Maze* programme, and was one of a panel on BBC 2's *Newsnight* invited to discuss the channel's so-called 'White' season, a series of programmes about the British white working class.

Jon Gaunt is currently host of SunTalk, a live phone-in show on the internet.

Gaunt's autobiography, *Undaunted*, appeared in 2008.

This interview took place in autumn 2008, while he was still at talkSPORT.

Peter Whittle (PW): In America, you would be called a 'shock jock' – do you mind that label?

Jon Gaunt (JG): I don't mind it as shorthand for what I do; but I do mind it when 'shock jock' means 'thick', because I don't think people on speech radio are thick: I think they've got minds like encyclopaedias. And I don't ever say anything on the radio that I don't believe. I'd say [radio and TV presenter] James Whale is more of a shock jock, because he changes his position. I never change my position; my position is always consistent.

The first thing I learned when I got into radio was never to lie, because they'll catch you out. The audience is clever enough to catch you out. So

I just say what I feel. Of course, it's a performance, so sometimes it's an exaggeration. But the general thing: I'm anti-abortion, I'm for the family, you know. These are positions I hold. I'm not a devil's advocate, and I'm not a shock jock.

Yeah, it's shocking some of the things I say; but that's mainly because most of British radio is so bloody bland and boring, and so institutionally run by the BBC. Everyone is trained by the BBC, so everyone in this country thinks speech radio has to be Radio 4 or Radio 5 or some kind of diluted version of that. I don't think it does. I think American radio's more exciting.

I often say on the radio that when I was at university I lived this whole lie, where I thought you had to be left wing to be a playwright and to get on. And therefore all your views came out of the same filing cabinet – not just out of the same filing cabinet, but the same filing cabinet *drawer*, and in fact the same *file*. So if you were left wing, you had to be pro-gay and you had to be pro-CND, even if you thought actually that doesn't add up. I actually quite liked the way Reagan and Thatcher... I'd march around Coventry city centre precinct, when the cruise missiles first came to Greenham Common, with a bloody coffin on my back! I mean, I can't believe that's the same person I am now. At university I felt – and even after I left university and formed Tic Toc and we did these plays – I still felt that the ruling ideology was this left-wing ideology, and that if I actually said what I really felt, that somehow I'd be ostracised.

So even though I'd written these plays that had been quite successful, I only really discovered my political voice when I went on the radio.

PW: So do you think that the way our culture works is that even to be considered educated you have to be towards the Left politically? Or do you think that's paranoid?

JG: No, I think that's true. I think that has definitely been true. I wasn't going to do the interview with you until I read something where you said that the Right has won the political argument, but the Left still dominates the arts, and the media and the broadcasting world. And they do, and it's wrong. It's completely and utterly wrong.

It's like the way I get portrayed, the way I'm written about by people like Matthew Norman, when I went on the *Moral Maze* with Michael Portillo. He's not brave enough to take me on when I'm in the studio with him, because I'd destroy him. But don't forget, I wasn't in the studio: I was in Northampton, and so he slags me off. And when you actually listen to that tape, I said that if you want to say paedophilia is a sickness, I can agree with you – so long as what you're saying is that they'll be detained. And then he twisted that point.

They don't like me, that kind of person, because I'm working class. I did have a troubled childhood; my father was a copper; I was in a children's home. I think I do communicate every day with that largely working-class audience, and I'm not afraid to say what I feel. Also I am intelligent, I am educated. But they want to put you down for that, I think. It's kind of the last bastion where they're allowed to do that. If I was black, they wouldn't dare speak to me like that; or gay, they wouldn't dare speak to me like that. But because I'm a white heterosexual, happily married man, in a monogamous relationship, I'm fair game. I was on Andrew Neil's show, *Daily Politics*, and I said there: 'You may think that it looks like this, the world' – I was being rude – 'over your metropolitan skinny lattes, but this ain't the fucking real world. The real world – come to Birmingham with me, come to Coventry, let's go even further north, and I'll show you multiculturalism; I'll show you how people are living and what the problems are in this country.' London's a completely different world to the rest of Britain. And I think, if anything, that's why I've got myself a niche.

PW: You had quite a career in regional arts before the radio, didn't you?

JG: When we left university, I formed Tic Toc. We'd been to the Edinburgh Festival, we'd seen all these posh students doing plays. They'd convert a church hall, and they would then rent that out a few times to pay for their spot – if you follow what I'm saying. Me and my mate said: we'll do that more efficiently; there'll be nine spots, we'll have two of them, and we'll make money. And with that money we'll subsidise the theatre company we want to set up.

So right from the beginning, we had that entrepreneurial desire. But the moment we started doing that, the Arts Council, who were just used to giving money to people to waste, actually were suspicious of us: 'Well, these are businessmen; we can't fund them as well, we can't actually fund a business.' And we're saying (remember, this is before matched funding): 'Here we are. We can bring £60,000 to the table. Why don't you match it with Arts Council money, because we're raising this money in Edinburgh.' We were the biggest promoters in Edinburgh at one point.

So then you would get the forms, and it was like: 'Who are you going to appeal to?' It was literally like a social services form. So what we had was these big institutions that were built in the Sixties – the big rep theatres, which are funded to basically put on an Alan Ayckbourn, a poorly performed Shakespeare, and two other plays a year. Then you had 'fringe theatre' – small scale, represented by companies like 7:84 or Paines Plough, which were pretty good companies, I think, when they first started... Joint Stock, and all those people. But then, even when the original leading lights left – like, for example, John Adams had left Paines Plough – he's working in the Birmingham Rep now – but Paines Plough still got the money. Just because they were a name. But there wasn't any artistic vision there.

So I come along, and in the West Midlands there were two companies – Theatre Foundry and Pentabus – which were funded by the local Arts Council, West Midlands Arts. We come along, arguably with much better work, much more exciting work, work for predominantly white, working-class boys, going into youth clubs and doing really aggressive plays, and challenging these kids. We couldn't get any money, whereas these two other companies were doing nothing, just pissing about, basically. They were just ticking the boxes. I could always make the joke that if I was homosexual, or black, or lesbian, or whatever, they'd have funded my work; but because I was white and working class they wouldn't fund it.

PW: Why do you think that came about?

JG: Because the Left took over the arts. They took over the arts. In Coventry, we had a very vibrant youth theatre at the Belgrade, which Michael Boyd used to be in charge of for a long time. It's a tough, working-class city, but we used to do some great plays there. I think the Left took over the arts, and I think any kind of right-wing writers left were kind of – pushed out, weren't they? With, in the Sixties and Seventies, people like Edward Bond and David Edgar (Edgar's written one good play and one OK adaptation of *Nicholas Nickleby*). I was at the University of Birmingham, and I knew David quite well. In fact, to be fair to David, he gave us 12 and a half grand a year funding through a thing called the Sir Barry Jackson Trust, which used to pay Lisa, my wife, to do marketing for us. So he recognised what we were doing, I'll give him his due there. For a dyed-in-the-wool lefty, he did!

But those kind of people dominated the writing. I think Thatcher, because everyone hated Thatcher at that period, if we're talking about art, talking about theatre... I think we all hated her, including myself, I can remember. That became a rallying call, and she was slashing the arts, as well, because she was – on that level, I think – a bit of a philistine, really, to be honest. Also, I don't think anybody knew which way to go. They had the millstone of the reps, which we couldn't possibly get rid of, because they were getting half a million pounds off the local council, and the Arts Council weren't going to turn down that kind of core funding for the arts.

But yes, I think the Left just took over. And I was one of them, I think: I thought that was what you had to be. I don't think it was even a conscious thing.

PW: Do you agree with the view that the white working class has become the last group it is permissible to insult? That it's open season on them? You were on the *Newsnight* discussion recently which came at the end of the BBC season all about the white working class...

JG: I've been on *Newsnight* a few times. Robbie Gibb, who used to run it and who now runs *Daily Politics* and *This Week*, is a great bloke. I can hardly believe he's working for the BBC, because he recognises the strength of talk radio in this country. He's a big speech radio fan, both here and abroad, so he's used me on *Newsnight* loads of times.

But when I went on that programme and there was that stupid Margaret Hodge [then culture minister] and the team, chocolate biscuits... And then, of course, it was just so predictable to roll out [BNP leader] Nick Griffin. Nick Griffin doesn't represent me. You can be white, working class, English and be proud of all of those things, but not be a fucking racist – I'm not a racist. I want controlled immigration. But then, if I wheeled my mate Lincoln – who's a black guy, who went to the Royal Academy of Music, and who's now teaching my daughter piano – if I brought him in here, and you had your eyes closed, and we started talking about immigration, you wouldn't know which one of us was white or black.

> **I really hate the way they portray white, working-class people – they're trying to represent us as chavs...**

I really hate the way they portray white, working-class people – they're trying to represent us as chavs, like – I mean, God bless her at the moment – but Jade [Goody] or [glamour model] Jordan. But that isn't the working class I come from. The working class I come from is where people had a job, and people washed their front doorstep – all the clichés – and made sure their kids were spick and span for school, and wanted their child to get on.

PW: What about the idea that, in order for multiculturalism to work, there had to be a common enemy?

JG: Yes, and we were the enemy, I'd have said that. But multiculturalism doesn't work, does it?

It's about class. Rosie, my 15-year-old – she's at a private school – and we went for dinner. You know how you go to dinner at different people's houses... And we went for dinner once. They're both – one's a doctor, one's a biochemist. So anyway, we got talking about immigration. And they were very strong on immigration – said that immigration needs to be curbed, and there's too many people coming in. Now, I tell you they're both Hindus, and they were slagging off lazy Muslims. It's the same thing – it's a class thing, you know. We had vegetarian food to respect their religion, and it was beautiful and all the rest of it. But it was irrelevant. It was an interesting experience to go, and we've become friends with them, but the fact that they're Hindu is kind of immaterial, isn't it? But they live their life, and they go off to the temple, and they do what they want to do. But people try to create this problem, and I don't really think there is a problem. Of course there's white racism! I get them ringing me here and sending me emails; but I can say, hand on heart, that it's a very, very, very small minority. But in a sense, yes – the white working class, our culture was kind of denied us. I've written about this in my new book. By the same token, I used to get people – you can set your watch for when they'd start moaning about St George's Day: 'Fucking Ken Livingstone, never gives us any money, gives all the fucking Paddies money for Paddy Day!' But actually Ken Livingstone made a good defence of that, which is that no white English people ever asked him to do anything; and I half believed him, as well.

I always think that the middle class – I said this on the radio the other week... I think so many of the middle classes, they don't want working-class people to invade those citadels. They don't actually want that to happen, because they don't want us to elevate ourselves. They don't want us to be cultured or know it's our culture. Do you understand where I'm coming from?

PW: I do, but by the same token there's been a huge push in the arts to get access for audiences from a much wider social spectrum.

JG: It's lip service. I think the RSC is getting better: they stand up for Shakespeare and are using schools more. But so many people have been put off our culture, you know, by terrible productions when they were at school, or being forced to do it... But I do feel that our culture, it's kind of been denied us, yes.

PW: Do you think you are a safety valve for people's sense of anger and frustration? Do you think that's a fair description?

JG: I think it can be, yes. But I think you can effect change as well. I think you can change people's attitudes. I think I've got immense power, immense responsibility. Maybe I'm unique, because I can do it in the column in the paper and I can also do it on air, but I think I *have* got power, and I think I *can* influence, and I think I can change policy.

I've seen people like David Cameron sit in my studio – the first time he came in, I saw him petrified when he had to take these calls. And then I saw him come a second time – he's been four times; he loves it now. He comes in, does an hour's phone-in, no notes – you must listen! They just ring up and have a go at him, or agree with him, or whatever. They ask him any question. And he's the best politician at the moment at dealing with it – Jack Straw came in, and he had dossier after dossier in front of him, all marked.

So I think I can influence; and I can effect change; and I think I can effect change in my audience as well. When I had my theatre company – I didn't set up a theatre company just to do plays: I wanted people to believe in my world view. And although you're probably not meant to say that, in terms of Ofcom, that is what I'm trying to do still on the radio. I want people to realise that the people who control them, you can make them accountable; it isn't just through the ballot box.

So am I a valve? Yes, on one level. Because people can moan to me rather than actually do anything. I wish they would do something more than just moan, of course. But also I think I can give an expression to people. I don't want the Radio 5 audience – I want *my* audience. Again, they can be characterised – 'Oh, the white van man!' And again, that's another derogatory term. I tell you, sometimes people phone up, and they might go: 'Gaunty, I think this, I think that...' But actually, if you listen to some of them and what they say, it's absolutely tremendous stuff, what they're thinking about. They just might not be educated or articulate to do it in a Radio 5 or Radio 4 way.

It's interesting, when I was on the *Moral Maze* and I got home, there were loads of emails from Radio 4 listeners: 'You're brilliant', 'I agree with you, Jon'. I was on Central Weekend TV years ago, and I did a debate. I can't remember what it was about, and I came away thinking: oh, I went down dreadfully there, because the audience wasn't with me, the panel – Yasmin Alibhai-Brown was on it, and Darcus Howe. The next day I went to town, and I was getting stopped in the street by loads of people: 'Thank you for saying what we think!' And that made me realise: when I'm in the TV studio, it isn't what Michael Portillo, or Yasmin Alibhai-Brown, or even the producers or researchers think about me – it's about me staying true to my ideals.

> So I suppose I am a safety valve, on one level. But I also want to be a conduit, because these people don't want to write to their MP.

So I suppose I am a safety valve, on one level. But I also want to be a conduit, because these people don't want to write to their MP. They probably don't know who their MP is!

PW: Have you read this book by Peter Oborne called *The Triumph of the Political Class*? He explores how we have got into a situation now where the ruled and the rulers are so far apart. Do you think they are, compared with when you were growing up?

JG: Definitely, yes. But I think things were slightly different then, because the political class then came either through the trade union movement on one side, or on the other side were entrepreneurs and business people, so they actually met working-class people and heard their views on the factory floor. Then I think on the factory floor, they had ways of organising themselves, and ways of talking, and ways of addressing their problems through the unions, through the shop stewards; but I think that's disappeared, as communities have been destroyed. I mean, I couldn't be an MP, could I? I wouldn't get selected, because they know I'd be too much of a maverick, and you don't get those.

Dave Nellist, who was the MP for Coventry, a militant Labour man, got kicked out of the Labour party for being a Socialist. But he was a great man. I disagree with more or less every political point he has, but he was a great constituency MP, because he only took the wages of a skilled tool-maker – and he actually lived by those principles. Now I think he's stupid – I would take the proper wage! But that's what he did. There aren't those kinds of mavericks and those people there. I think that's why the politicians today are disconnected: because they live in a totally different world.

I always tell the listeners a great story about Livingstone and Steve Norris. When I first came to London, I thought: I've made it, got a job on BBC London. There were those two as mayoral candidates. They rowed on my show for about an hour, and at the end of the conversation, Norris said to Livingstone: 'Are you going back to the House?' And Livingstone says: 'Yes, do you want to share a cab? Have you had any lunch? Shall we go for lunch?'

And I see this as Mr Naïve: I've come there, I've got all the Sony Awards, and I've come to London. I see this, and I realise it's all just a charade, a club.

PW: Do you think that the liberal elite is stronger here than in America?

JG: Here, you've got the big political programmes like *Question Time*. When I watch *Question Time*, it's like: I can't believe this! They did one on the death penalty. It was Greg Dyke, and – I can't remember who the others were. The question of the death penalty came up – there must have been some terrible murder – and not one person on the panel agreed with the death penalty. I just wanted to throw things at the TV! How is that representative?

Well, in America there's a great middle section. It's such a massive country.

PW: The shock jocks are terribly powerful in the US, aren't they? Why do you think it's not the same here?

JG: It will be. This isn't BBC bashing, by the way, this next bit (although I'm quite fond of bashing them normally). We're all trained by the BBC; the only way to really get into speech radio is through local BBC radio, because we haven't yet got a load of speech radio stations. So everyone's trained in the BBC way. There's this idea of impartiality and balance – which, of course, doesn't exist, especially in the BBC, because it's stuffed full of those very people we're talking about. So therefore, how do you ever break that mould? Everyone says they listen to the *Today* programme, which is a bit like saying everyone's read *Ulysses*. They think they should say it, when actually they haven't. The BBC dominate everything. They also dominate the management structure.

I think there's a massive pent-up desire for interactivity among the working class of this country. As you know, I write for the *Sun*. Since we've developed the interactive side of things, the amount of hits I get after I write a column...! People can react to the columnist's page; they can send me emails, send me texts. People want to do it.

So I actually think it will grow. I don't think people tune into my show to say: 'I hope he's talking about abortion tomorrow.' They're going: 'Fucking hell, did you see this? Jon Gaunt's going to go mental tomorrow. I can't wait to hear what he says about this!'

The BBC don't understand that. They don't get the fact that when I was a lad, you didn't listen to Radio 1, you listened to Noel Edmonds; then you turned over to somebody else. So talk radio is going to have its day. I think it will take off massively, and I think the people who are good at it – and there isn't anybody who's any good at it, apart from me and a couple of others – are going to have great careers. We need regulation to be relaxed as well.

You can't be impartial. Nonsense. It's nonsense.

PW: Do you think that the whole concept of 'impartiality' is a bit ridiculous?

JG: You can't be impartial. Nonsense. It's nonsense. I was talking to someone at the BBC and they said: 'You know, we could never employ you, unless you stop saying "I think".' I said: 'Well, I don't want to fucking work for you then!' They said: 'Oh yeah, but there's cleverer ways of doing it; I used to work with someone who developed a whole load of grunts and sniffs that made it clear to the audience what he thought.' I said: 'That's fucking impartiality, is it?' Because it's not, is it?

And you see that with James Naughtie all the time; that line 'are we going to win the election?' is the most blatant. But you hear it all the time in the way they interview. Paxman, actually, to be fair, plays it both ways. Nowadays, on the BBC, I can't believe how many of them – Nick Robinson, prime example. Why is he allowed to editorialise? Then they pretend he's impartial! He's clearly not impartial, so let's scrap the rules. The sooner we have Fox News over here, the Fox version I want Sky to make... But the people who run Sky – again, trained by the BBC – don't want it. We need Fox.

They used to try and give me vox pops – interviews with members of the public – to play out, and I said: 'You don't need vox pops! It's a phone-in!'

'Oh yeah, but on a phone-in, Jon, you might get nine people saying "Hang the bastard", and only one saying "no".'

I said: 'Yeah, but that's alright then, isn't it? Everyone's got the same chance to pick up the phone and ring.' But no, they thought balance was two for, two against.

I stood in for Edwina Curry on Radio 5, years ago. I said: 'What time do you want me there?'

'Three hours before the show.'

I said: 'It's a phone-in!' But you want to show willing, don't you? So I went in and a man came over to me and piled this big thing on me. I said: 'What's that?' And he said: 'It's the script.' I said: 'What do you mean it's the script? It's a phone-in!'

It listed the bullet-points. Then he got this big sheet out, and I said: 'What's that?' And he said: 'That's how the discussion's going to go.'

I said: 'How do you mean, "that's how the discussion's going to go"?'

He said: 'We're going to start out here, talk about da-da da-da da-da... and we'll end up here.'

When I watch *Question Time*, it's like: I can't believe this!

I said: 'You can't do that! You've got to see how it goes! You might get somebody come on, a phone-in guest, or a guest, they might say something so brilliant, we want to go on that.' No, no, no... And that's what's wrong, in my opinion.

They don't really want that audience. That's the other thing: that's why people in the media love voxes – because they can go back and edit the vox and make it all neat and tidy. They don't actually want real people. And when they do have them on, it's with Jeremy Kyle, so they can look down on it. If we had real debate... Why can't *Question Time*... The *Question Time* audience, for example: it probably never crossed their mind that we always get the same audience. But of course it is.

PW: 'Real people' have disappeared from the airwaves, in a lot of ways. Certainly in the area of news.

JG: That one about the death penalty was a prime example of that. You can look at the audience, in that first shot, and you can go: 'There's the two Muslim girls who are going to talk about the veil; there's the black educated guy who's going to talk about black working-class kids, boys, not getting on in education. But where's the black kid who fucking isn't in education, who can really give it large? They haven't got him onto the programme.' And I think: well, that's why Robbie Gibb was being quite good when he was on *Newsnight*, because he said: 'I want Jon on.'

And the guy he said this to, [Sky anchor] Colin Brazier, he said to me one day: 'You're the genuine voice of the white working class, dispossessed.' And I said: 'Oh, fuck off!' And he said: 'No, I mean it. I can't think of any other way to say it, Jon. I really value what you do and what you bring.' He was the first person in the media who ever said that to me.

I don't think I'm unusual; I don't think my views are unusual. I can't say that I represent everyone's views, because I don't. But I don't think I'm unusual. But you don't see me on telly. Though they have me now a bit on panels – in a sense as the tame puppy dog.

PW: Do you think that's how they see it?

JG: Yes, I think there's a danger of that. But I try not to do it. You can fall into that trap, can't you? Pick up your 150, 500 quid, whatever it is. I want to go on *Question Time*: twice they've asked me, but they've always asked me last minute, knowing I probably wouldn't be able to do it. They won't have me on *Question Time* because I would disturb that little thing, where they all go for their dinner afterwards, don't they? I accept they wouldn't want to have dinner with me, probably. And I wouldn't play up. I would just say what I feel, because again I've got over that. I'm not scared of the television lights. I would just be the same as I am on radio, and the same as I am in real life. But they don't invite you. They control it, they are controlling it. And it's their own downfall in the end, because they're not representing the working class. You don't hear those views.

> They control it, they are controlling it. And it's their own downfall in the end, because they're not representing the working class.

PW: But isn't it progress that you were on *Newsnight*, instead of Peter Hitchens, say?

JG: Yeah, that was a great step forward. I think, again, what surprises them is that I then turned round and agreed with the black geezer, who was a councillor, and when I agreed with [trade union leader] Bob Crow, you see – and me and Bob Crow were laughing afterwards. Because there are lots of things I'm opposed to that Crow stands for; but he's a similar bloke to me, and his real view is right in terms of his experience. He knows what he's talking about, because he does work for those tube drivers. And yes, he's a militant and all those things; but at least he stands up for his boys, so I respect people like him. So I think that surprises them. What also surprises people is when I talk about art and culture and theatre, because they say: 'You did all that? You wrote for telly? You wrote plays?' They can't believe that, because they want to portray me as white, working class, bit of an oik, bit of a hooligan.

Now, I'm trying to talk to an audience that isn't traditionally part of the media Establishment, so in a way you make rods for your own back, really. I could have just slipped back, because I'm clever enough; I could be on Radio 5 now, doing the Nicky Campbell gig. But then that wouldn't be me. And so is it better that I'm now getting on the telly? Yes, that's good. Will they ever give me my own show? If I had a tenner for every time they said: 'Jon, we want to give you your own show; we're going to push the boundaries. Late night, you do a controversial – basically, do the phone-in.' But they never do, when push finally comes to shove. Even Channel 4. Ridiculous – they wanted me to do some documentaries, but in the end the top man said: 'No, you're too popular.' Too populist is what he meant.

The Sculptor – Alexander Stoddart

Stilling the will

At the end of 2008, Alexander Stoddart was appointed Her Majesty's Sculptor in Ordinary in Scotland.

Born in 1959 in Edinburgh, Stoddart attended the Glasgow School of Art and began work as a sculptor in Paisley in 1983, working for private clients. The first architectural sculptures he made were in strict neo-classical style. From this he went on to develop a heroic-realist style for historical costume works.

In 2008, his statue of the economist Adam Smith was unveiled in Edinburgh, joining his portraits of Robert Louis Stevenson and the philosopher David Hume in that city.

The recipient of two honorary doctorates and an honorary professorship, Stoddart also completed a programme of sculpture for the new Queen's Gallery at Buckingham Palace in 2002. Among his sitters have been Tony Benn, the philosopher Roger Scruton and the architects Robert Adam and John Simpson.

Shortly after his appointment in 2008, he strongly criticised the National Galleries of Scotland, claiming that they were pandering to populist appeal by purchasing and exhibiting 'modernist rubbish' by such artists as Damien Hirst and Tracey Emin, whom he has described as 'the high priestess of societal decline'.

Peter Whittle (PW): There has been an ongoing discussion about what should occupy the empty fourth plinth in Trafalgar Square. Now, a system of temporary installations has been settled on: at the moment we have Thomas Schütte's *Hotel for the Birds*, and before that *Alison Lapper Pregnant* by Marc Quinn. What do you think this says about the way that sculpture is regarded at the moment?

Alexander Stoddart (AS): I think it's interesting, because everything that's happening there is reactive. If that empty plinth were sitting in a field, or even in another street, it would be different. The magic that the context affords that plinth lies in the fact that there's a body of sculpture there that two fingers can be lifted to. And that's really fundamental to what's happening there. In his recent TV programme about sculpture, the art critic Waldemar Januszczak urinated on Mount Rushmore; the activity on this plinth is a form of urination on the surrounding statues.

59

The other statues are critical to that. It's a formation of the cocking-a-snook culture that the modernist imperium has insisted on for a full century; [Marcel] Duchamp drawing a moustache onto the Mona Lisa began what this continues.

Without the presence of a dominant culture, this kind of thing cannot obtain. This is true, for example, of all satirical magazines – they depend on the thing that they oppose. And it's exactly the same with the fourth plinth. It has to be there with Nelson; it has to be there with George IV; it has to be there with all these people, because, if it's on its own, the outrage cannot obtain. That's the key.

What you see on the plinth there is really the triumph of a bastard child of the modernist movement.

Now this is very different, of course, from the way that the old modernists proceeded. As Roger Scruton has correctly pointed out, there was a certain nobility in the modernist project, the project of Ezra Pound, T. S. Eliot and Hugh MacDiarmid.

But the failure of the high modernists was that they cut themselves off – in an act of snobbery, really – from the rank and file of people. What you see on the plinth there is really the triumph of a bastard child of the modernist movement.

PW: Have you ever done modernist work?

AS: I did extremely modernist work when I was still at school – Perspex panels, for instance, screen printing. Looking at pop art. I was very interested in Yves Klein, the auto-destructive 'artist' of the 1960s, who used to photograph himself falling off buildings, and then he'd exhibit his X-rayed broken bones; or he'd get a girl he fancied, cover her with paint – naked, of course – and drag her across a canvas on the floor! I was very keen on this sort of thing, and doing a lot of it. I was in on that kind of ticket: I was going to be a real 'wild child', you know. And it's a lot to do with bravura in the end. I have a window through to the soul of that person, me, who was doing that – and that's why I'm so confident of where I stand now. Because I see myself as the showing-off, talentless upstart that I was then. And I see it everywhere now, among all these ones that still do it.

So, if you ask me what the underlying trend is, I'd say that one of the trends of modernism is a failure on the part of most people to actually engage in plastic accomplishments of any sort. They can't draw, so they pretend not to *want* to draw. And of course there's a small child in the heart of these people that's really crying out to be able to draw like an angel. (We use the expression 'draw like an angel' – we don't say 'draw like the devil'. You can *run* like the devil; you can *fight* like the devil; but you *draw* like an *angel*. So many of the simple vernacular platitudes –

clichés – are so useful in telling us the true nature of things!) So, that's one reason for it: it's the simple resentment argument. They hate the artist who can draw.

PW: So what's their reaction to you?

AS: When I get modernists coming to my studio, they look around and their body language is hilarious. They

They can't draw, so they pretend not to *want* to draw.

fold their arms – they're looking up and down – and they say, every one, 'wonderful space', with a lingering emphasis on the second word. They 'valorise' the space in a furious attempt to overlook the astonishing objects contained therein! The will in them instinctually wishes to applaud that which is not there (in other words, the opposite of the art works), because art – as any student of Schopenhauer will recall – 'stills the will', and the will in them doesn't want so to be stilled. Then these people say to me: 'Isn't this kind of art so boring?' And I say: 'Look, stupid: the kind of art I make is intended to send you – especially you – to sleep!'

And of course, at this they smile, because in their eyes I've condemned myself. They grin in that Voltaire way. Yet this was possibly one of the wisest things that was ever said to them. The modernist imperium has turned this entirely around, so that the kind of art that calms you – what might be called 'hypnotic' art – is really only to be found being attempted at the heroic amateur level, in provincial painting exhibitions, for instance. The official arts, on the other hand, have gone all 'stimulative', and that's why they are so intimately associated with barbaric behaviour.

PW: There seems to be an awful lot of explaining around much contemporary art...

AS: For so long now we have had a text-based arts culture. Ian Hamilton Finlay pioneered this for the late-modernist era, and it has declined from there to be the resort of [Tracey] Emin and such-like strugglers. Having no credibility in the purely perceptual line, the works of such people depend upon the catch-all, but necessarily crude, *modus* of the Word; 'the handmaiden of the concept', as Schopenhauer identifies it. No matter how badly drawn, spoken or even spelt, the Word always conveys its meaning. But one slight slip of the pencil can make Ingres's Odalisque appear to be suffering a bowel cramp. As Mendelssohn said: 'I use music not to express ideas that are too vague for words, but rather to express ideas that are too *precise* for words.' The Eminites are distinguished in the vagueness of their ideas, so this perpetual chatter is their comfort. And, of course, the works themselves need to be talked about. They exist in an amniotic fluid of dialectic – they're nothing without people speaking about them. Great art, however, has the delightful habit of shutting everyone's gobs, which is why we still, in gross disobedience to our arts-mandarin masters, lower our voices when entering museums.

But take, for example, Paul Delaroche's *The Execution of Lady Jane Grey* at the National Gallery; it exists completely in silence. Now this is a type of art that really is art; that actually has the effect of stopping the dialectic – stopping speech. This is why there's a leftist antipathy to that kind of art. The Left is predicated upon the dialectic imperative – that

Great art, however, has the delightful habit of shutting everyone's gobs, which is why we still, in gross disobedience to our arts-mandarin masters, lower our voices when entering museums.

is, People Making Speeches. Putting a sock in it, and paying attention for once, is what makes some loathe both the opera and Sunday School; nothing else, really. Conservatism, on the other hand, has a capacity to brave all sorts of silences – and stiff, studded collars, too! I mean, such objections to the experience of culture can have not only a psychological, but also, in fact, a *physical* source. In this respect, [Richard] Dawkins is quite right when he insists that biology is not so much a scientific discipline as a branch of philosophy. Schopenhauer had thrashed all this out a century and a half before 'the only saint we have' came stumbling onto the scene in his clown outfit.

PW: I've always found portraiture to be quite satisfying in its 'stilling' effect...

AS: Well, it's a noble thing. Portraiture is a noble calling, and most of the great artists have done it – in the modern age at least. A good portraiture artist has, in some respects, to outrage two constituencies. The first is the constituency of the sitter's vanity (it never will look like Catherine Deneuve in her prime). And then he also has to outrage his own egotism by subjecting himself entirely to the image of another. But the first impertinence is the really telling one, for it happens that certain subjects conceive a mighty terror of being 'caught' by another – just as primitives (rightly, in my opinion) fear the camera. In civilisation, of course, the artist mediates, as a kind conductor of this alarming process, with soothing tones of speech and perhaps music – over a long time – so that the sitter declines into a state of amnesia, lulled into distance-gazing as the image slowly forms. It's all so calm. In photography, the modernist's crutch, the subject is 'shot'!

But I have a story for you about portraiture. One of my favourite Scottish galleries is the Scottish National Portrait Gallery. It was designed by Robert Rowand Anderson, the great Scottish architect – a beautiful piece of national romantic architecture. And I'd really like to have a portrait in that collection, as a real honour. Every couple of years, I get in touch with its director and say: 'James, I really think it's odd that I haven't done a portrait for the collection.' And each time James Holloway says he'll commission me to that effect, and nothing comes round. Anyway, one year, remarkably, he got back to me. He said (in rather a hushed tone, as I remember): 'We believe that we should commission you to do a portrait of Gordon Brown.' Brown was chancellor then. Now, I don't want, really, to do a bust of Brown, his head being quite unsuitable for the noble art of sculpture. But I have a sense of duty, and if the National Portrait Gallery of Scotland commands you to do something in the national cause (within limits), you put your personal feelings aside. If they asked me to do a portrait of a footballer, I might draw the line – because for every footballer that is admitted into that Carlylian Hall of Fame, a poet remains out in the cold.

So I said I would do it. Well, they sent a letter to 11 Downing Street and waited for a reply. Nothing was forthcoming, though. So someone – who was a friend of a friend of a friend in the government – had to make an informal inquiry on the state of this, and was told that Brown was 'not minded to sit'. But no formal reply was ever received by the Scottish National Portrait Gallery, which seems a kind of snub, don't you think? How does one explain this extraordinary behaviour?

Well, it is intimately related to his refusal – remember? – to wear white tie at the Lord Mayor's Banquet. It's the same thing: the poison of what they sometimes (but I believe wrongly) call 'cultural Presbyterianism'. Often hiding behind a kind of pretended modesty, in fact there really lurks in this a 'will to power' like the South Atlantic; petrified of any form of objectification which might render it 'seen'. Thus Heraclitus: 'Nature loves to hide.' And this, too, is the source of the primal act of fury of the world's first dialectical iconoclast, Moses himself. Do you know, really, why he takes such umbrage at the dancers around the Molten Calf? It's simple. The Children of Israel (you can read the story in the second sura of the Koran), by setting up the image, have settled; that is to say, they have *stopped*. Next they are dancing, which means that speech, too, has *stopped*. Furthermore, a beast has been represented, which is an objectification of the 'will in nature'.

In other words, these Children have betrayed the forward-thrust imperative obeyed by all barbarians and Trotskyites. The 'perpetual revolution' of their wandering has been arrested. A profoundly Conservative little moment in Hebrew mythology! Added to this, they have tamed nature (the will) in the representation of one of its more vigorous forms. They have stopped Hegelian dialectics through want of breath, and have engaged in some sort of *grace*. Now, Moses, in high fury, comes off the mountain wearing horns (I am not in the slightest convinced about the 'rays' theory – it makes no sense) – real horns to oppose those represented on the calf. And he is wielding a mighty *text*, with the prime command 'Thou Shalt Not Sculpt!' emblazoned upon it. He destroys the calf, much as the Taliban destroyed the still, graceful, silent and harmless Buddhas in Afghanistan. In its initial besmirchment of the represented human form, followed by its wholesale outlawing, the modernist movement declined into just such a Mosaic, Talibaneering outlook. Really quite diabolical, if you think about it.

Recently, some maniac was commissioned to run about – or to direct runners to run about – Tate Modern. Did you hear about that? Again, this is merely a visceral reflex, Mosaic in character, to oppose the still (art) with the vital (modern art). The two, art and modern art, stand in fundamental opposition: the first in defiance of the world, the second in outright collaboration with it. Modern art, then, far from being 'brave' and 'heroic', is, in fact, a supine toady, giving up entirely on the resistance commenced, in modern times, by dear little Cimabue and his Madonna.

PW: Do you know of any other people coming up who believe what you believe, or work the way that you work?

AS: Well, I don't see any. And the problem is that I don't have a school. I can't take my time away to teach young people, because I live only by what these two hands can make. If we lived in a culture where we didn't have health and safety legislation, we didn't have employers' tax, I would have a school going by now. I'd school assistants, and then I'd school pupils as well. I've got people who come to the studio to help. There's a young 15-year-old who helps. I give him the odd twenty-quid note. And he's desperately interested in the stuff that I do; but if I wanted to have him work full time, then goodness knows what 'safety checks' I'd have to submit to. And then there's health and safety measures, because of the dust, and also lots of ladder-work. And then, of course, I won't allow certain things in the studio – you know, rock music. Not allowed. So that might be an infringement of his human rights, although he'd grow out of it soon.

> If we lived in a culture where we didn't have health and safety legislation, we didn't have employers' tax, I would have a school going by now.

So this boy comes and helps periodically. After one morning I had him welding, unsupervised. A beautiful weld, his first. He's cutting steel. He's mastering rude joinery, providing things needed to make monuments – the James Clerk Maxwell monument for Edinburgh's George Street. You know, he's *part* of that project; he's suddenly been given a role in the real world. His parents tell me that the transformation of his character has been unbelievable – he's chatty, he's interested in things, and he's cheery, because he's being integrated into the adult world; the world of *men*. He goes back to school after the holidays, and it's back to the world of children again. This boy, like so many boys these days, really needs to be integrated into the real world, as opposed to nannied in the infantilising world of the school. So then he's told he should go and study for a degree somewhere. Maybe to get a Golf Course Management Studies degree. And yet, within two years, he could actually be modelling drapery for statues for me. He wishes to go to art school, where they will thrash all his talent, and his goodness, out of him.

PW: Do you think there's less resistance to figurative art now than maybe there once was?

AS: Sometimes people say that I am accompanied by other 'figurative' sculptors, and so in that sense 'belong'. But I never allow myself to be described as a 'figurative' sculptor. What other sort of sculptor *is* there?! No, my view is that such a description bears witness to the hegemony of the modernist clampdown, just as art history, for instance, lies when it declares that, in 1910, cubism rules painting (in fact, only three weirdos in Paris are up to it, while the rest of the bleeding world is carrying on in the symbolist line – full of technique, and philosophy and Wagner!). Also, the description 'figurative' fails to make the distinctions so crucial to aesthetic apperception. After all, Miss Emin is, in her horrible way, a 'figurative' artist, too.

But if we mean that there are other sculptors around, employing traditional techniques – yes, certainly such exist. But the vast majority of them show no knowledge of, or capacity to imitate, the styles of the past; none of them have any interest in being anything other than original. But I am a *stylist*, working in many and varied idioms: heroic realism, domestic realism, verism, neo-classicism, neo-Florentine classicism, *beaux-arts* style – even, sometimes, in something rather Soviet! And this can happen because of my lifelong work with architects (real, traditionalist ones, I mean). For they – like [William Henry] Playfair, for instance – can work in neo-Greek, then Greek revival (subtle difference); they can work in the Gothic (or Gothics), in the Jacobean, Arts and Crafts, neo-Renaissance, romantic classicism, national romanticism and so on. A vast scope. Some of the most advanced even manage to produce pastiche modernist works, as follies for the policies of grand estates! Currently I'm designing a vast neo-*beaux-arts* scheme for Chicago, in a distinctly American accent. We need to ditch modernism so that we can begin, once more, to discover our capacities to discern such differences. Modernism, like leftism, really worried about the way discernment picked holes in its blanket policies. That's why it worked so avidly against drawing, since drawing is the apotheosis of discernment: absolutely based upon what is, and what is not, so.

PW: Your work is very popular, and I don't mean that in any pejorative sense...

AS: Well, I was told once by a very rich and influential man that the arts in Britain are governed by 12 men. They decide what is and what is not to be countenanced. And they do it as an administration. So they issue a command, and it goes down to smaller bodies. Eventually, they have people in the Scottish Arts Council making recommendations that no local museum is to acquire work by Sandy Stoddart. That's been written just so, believe me! But the very widest scope of people gather round to support me, for they see in what I do a kind of hope for a return from Bedlam, and the tyranny of the ugly. At root, these people have a desire for peace, and they see its manifestation (or is it its potential source?) in the works I get to make. I am often anxiously approached by students who wish to join in this effort with me. They come secretly, from the art schools. When I suggested to one such, from Edinburgh School of Art, that he get his tutor to invite me over to speak to the students, he told me he had indeed made that suggestion, but had been told that over the tutor's dead body would Stoddart ever lecture in this art school! The public hopes I can do something to end this most savage junta's stranglehold over the national, and indeed hemispherical, culture.

PW: You haven't taken part in this boom in public art over the last decade?

AS: I never do public art. All the work I do eventually sits out on streets, true, but I never do public art. I make monuments. Public art is a terminology that's relevant only to what? Private art. What is private art? Formally, it tends to be the kind of stuff that best exists in the incubated territory of a white-walled gallery, surveyed by a snooty bitch, with a mouth like a pussycat's bottom, sitting at a desk and making sure that she's looking down her nose when you walk in. She wears those 'sneer specs' – very horizontal, so that even if she herself gets exhausted with constantly sneering 24/7, she can take a break while the specs sneer on for her. Private art is when the artist pipes up with: 'I kind of like the way that, when you look at a teabag in the sink, you can kind of say that that's a model of life as a whole, and so I made this installation.' This is so often the level of it. Garbage dragged along with words, for ideas too vague to be represented in any 'music' medium.

> **What is private art? Formally, it tends to be the kind of stuff that best exists in the incubated territory of a white-walled gallery, surveyed by a snooty bitch, with a mouth like a pussycat's bottom...**

And you might say it's a very private art, that. I mean 'private' in the Greek sense of the word. When you talk to an ancient Greek, and you say the word 'democracy' to him, he hears 'mob rule'. Likewise, when you say 'he's a very private person', the Greek hears 'he's an idiot' – because privacy is identical with idiocy in ancient Greece. The Greeks were so dedicated to the social question that to be 'private' in your behaviour was to be idiotic, stupid. So you could say that this private art is imposing a kind of artistic idiocy upon the public lawn. The concept 'public art' seems to confess, and thus establish, this idiocy. I'll have none of that.

PW: You talked earlier about the uncomfortable reaction in some people to your work – that they resist having their will 'stilled' as it were. Could you explain this more fully?

AS: If you read Schopenhauer (and he is the informing philosopher of my entire career – how can I thank him enough?), what you discover is that the negative sensation felt by such people – wets and modernists mainly – in the face of, for example, classical architecture is the feeling of the intimidation of their will. In fact, their will is being calmed, or soothed to sleep. And this will in them strenuously resists. The will – which the Christians call, quite simply, the Devil – then starts mocking the lullaby idiom in a frantic effort to remain awake, for in sleep no mischief can be done. This is the way of the world. But art – in particular classical art – exists to subvert that way. A very great architectural historian once asked me, rhetorically: 'Why are all modernists such odious people?' It is clear to me at least that the cause of this tendency (which all observe) is their hopeless indenture to the 'will in nature', from the penal servitude of which they know no Sabbath.

> **The modernist is like the toddler who never grew up. He's rubbing his eyes, but now he's running around in his nappy, giggling.**

Just like toddlers at bedtime, they'll do anything to delay going to their cot. So the last thing they are going to do is voluntarily take the sleeping draught of high Occidental art! The modernist is like the toddler who never grew up. He's rubbing his eyes, but now he's running around in his nappy, giggling. Next the wind has changed, and he's crying. Now he's bitten his Daddy, and Mummy's had to give him a smack. What time is it? Late! Roughly 2009. Well past his bedtime. But soon things will be quiet, and we can all sit down and have that *belter* of a gin and tonic – and a smoke! You get my analogy? It's not merely an analogy, especially the smoke bit! For the smoking ban, and all the other bans, are also part of the modernist project. Do you seriously think the governments give a damn about health? No, they hate the idea of anybody enjoying that soothing, Balkan Sobranie moment!

Schopenhauer said that everything that is noble, cultivated and refined in the world is an expression of the denial of the will to live. Now, this is very hard for us to accept, because life has propagandised us into believing that it is, fundamentally, a good thing. Pessimism offers a less unscrupulous alternative: life involves, at any given moment, one animal being eaten alive by another; but when the lights in the auditorium fade, and the curtain opens, the crowd hushes and the music starts, something extraordinarily un-natural starts to happen. The killing stops, and all the savagery and sex. This is why modern operatics often engage modernist directors and designers – to keep the slaughter going, despite the art; to keep the children awake.

PW: You were recently appointed Her Majesty's Sculptor in Ordinary in Scotland, by the Scottish Government. Could this have happened even 10 years ago?

AS: Ten years ago? Well, I do think this has come about because of my work for the capital. Four major monuments in Edinburgh over the last decade or so. I must admit that, when the letter came through, I sat down cross-legged on the floor, weak at the joints with joy! The post is fundamentally that of a monumentalist, having been created in the 1840s for the great Sir John Steell, who made a greater personal impact on one city's monumental profile really than any other sculptor. Latterly, sculptors less devoted to that branch of the noble art were appointed to the role. Of course, it's unpaid and without duties. Eduardo Paolozzi was the previous man. I fully expected that a further development of the modernist inevitability would inform the eventual decision as to his successor. So it has been a startling reversal for an arch-traditionalist to be picked out for it. A reversal in forward gear, you understand! I was very critical of Paolozzi in the past, and this appointment has not in the slightest altered my opinion of him. He was, of course, a Titan – but in the strictest, mythological sense of the word. Do you know what I mean by that? The Titans are aboriginal, established for aeons beyond counting, superstitious, consuming of their children, earth-serpent-like, obscure, without history, hurtling, energetic, utterly solipsistic – and modernist! They are opposed by the Olympians, who make, among other things, the Occident. For myself, I am simply trying to shore up that Occident, for I believe it is the only place in Creation where gentleness is even considered – apart from the Orient, which is still permitted to be, in its own way, its Occident. *€*

The Novelist – Lionel Shriver

Anti-Americanism and the difficulty of talking about immigration

Lionel Shriver's seventh novel, *We Need to Talk about Kevin*, was a major critical and commercial success, winning the Orange Prize for Fiction in 2005. The book, an exploration of a mother's ambivalence towards a teenage son who has perpetrated mass murder at his high school, was universally praised, the *Daily Mail* calling it 'a vocal challenge to every accepted parenting manual you've ever read'.

Born in North Carolina in 1957, the daughter of a Presbyterian minister, Shriver published her first book when she was 30. Her most recent, *The Post-Birthday World*, appeared in 2007. She has lived in the UK for 20 years, 12 of them in Belfast. She has also had spells in Israel, Nairobi and Bangkok. She currently lives in London.

Lionel Shriver has written for, among others, the *Guardian*, the *Wall Street Journal* and the *Economist*, and has been a regular guest on BBC 2's *Newsnight Review*.

This interview took place in the latter stages of the US presidential election campaign.

Peter Whittle (PW): Do you think that anti-Americanism in London is greater now than when you arrived?

Lionel Shriver (LS): I think it's been much worse during the Bush administration. You know, I've not only lived in London for the last nine years, but for 12 years previously was in Belfast. So that's over two decades of exposure to being an American in the UK. If Obama wins the coming election, maybe anti-Americanism will grow less acceptable. But meanwhile the Bush presidency has given Britons – and Europeans generally – a good excuse to let their natural envy of the US and its political and economic role in the world run rampant. And anti-Americanism doesn't come out, of course, overtly as envy. It comes out as disparagement and condescension.

PW: But it is envy?

LS: Ultimately, yes. And then – given what's going on right now with the financial implosion, which is spreading to Europe – a certain amount of *Schadenfreude*. I think my personal experience of anti-Americanism has been fairly subtle. The Brits are rarely overt about these things; it's more a tone of voice or an intangible attitude. I'll always be a little self-conscious whenever I open my mouth, in social or even commercial circumstances. I immediately brand myself as an American, and I know that I'm calling up a whole file of attitudes that I may have to contend with in this exchange – in one fashion or another. I think my accent often elicits a kind of eye-roll. After all, Americans are commonplace in London. They're everywhere. So we're not exotic. It's like 'Oh God, another one!' I think the initial reaction is suspicion and a willingness to think badly of you, right? Or being on the lookout for confirmation of various stereotypes.

PW: Do you think Europe actively values its own culture, as opposed to just valuing it in that it isn't American?

LS: Actively values its own culture... I certainly think that, on a political level, Europeans use the United States to feel morally superior. They're under the illusion that what drives European politics is virtue, and what drives American politics is self-interest. This is dubious. And an awful lot of European virtue is all talk, right? Europeans are great on talk, but they don't put their money where their mouth is. They don't put their troops where their mouths are. They're big on diplomacy, because diplomacy is cheap.

Culturally, you know, obviously Europeans consume American cultural products voraciously, so there's a lot of resentment that many of the books and films and even plays that Europeans consume are from the United States. But I guess, you know, I'm sympathetic with that. I understand that resentment. I'm one of the Americans who have colonised the UK, the British literary scene. And there's a lot of attitude about me as a consequence.

PW: Do you think anti-Americanism is strong among the intelligentsia, on the literary scene?

LS: In the literary community – insofar as you can ever speak of a 'community' with a bunch of back-biting writers and publishers and editors... It's got that usual contradiction, because there's a lot of envy and even admiration of American writing. And the worry over here is that the subjects that many British fiction writers, for example, choose to write about are too small, too domestic, too contained, too quiet. Whereas the Americans write the big books, the panoramic books, the books that capture a whole era or generation. The British don't have the same tradition of the 'great American novel' (which is hard to say with a straight face). But we don't ever talk about the 'great British novel'. It's not an expression.

But at the same time, there's also a lot of pride in Britain – in being the originator of the English language, having all of these classical, wonderful writers like Shakespeare and the canon, and really being the home of writing in English, the birthplace of writing in English. And certainly, there are many fine fiction writers in this country. So I think that this sense of sheepishness is not fitting, and people here do write big books sometimes. A novel like *English Passengers* by Matthew Kneale is a huge book, a mammoth book, and hilarious, and great. I tout it all the time. So there's no reason for British literature to have a sense of inferiority to American. But it's there a little bit. And the British writers I know don't feel that they've really succeeded unless they've got a publisher in the United States. That's still the Holy Grail. That's still the definition of your having made it.

PW: There was such a thing as a sprawling social novel in the nineteenth century, when we were in the same position America is in now.

LS: Yes.

PW: Do you think that the American cultural scene is more dynamic than the European one? The sphere of the high arts seems to be pretty healthy in America.

LS: Yes, I think it's pretty healthy. American culture has got an awful lot of influences acting on it, and it's never at a loss for material. Something's always going on; it's a big country. So it's got a lot of the same problems that Europe has, writ large: the financial problems hitting right now, and the immigration situation, which is so much more extreme in the United States than it is in Europe. It's difficult in Europe, but the United States... The literal complexion of the United States is in a state of total transformation.

So I think that does produce a dynamic culture. The thing is that, in the US, there's much less distinction made between high art and popular art. It's all one big mush. And most artists, you know, film makers, or writers like me, don't just want to be admired or given a prize. They want commercial success: that's the real prize, commercial success. And Europeans still seem a little more involved in that high art–popular rubbish distinction.

PW: Do you think that America has stopped caring about what Europe thinks, culturally?

LS: Yes, I think that Americans are much less inclined these days to idolise Europe. There's a small sub-section of left-wing Americans – they're always left wing – who have clung to that idolatry, and start talking about moving to Europe if McCain wins, or were saying the same thing (although they didn't move) if Bush got in, or if Bush got in a second time: 'We're going to go to Italy.' Although they never say that they're going to go to the UK.

> **I think that Americans are much less inclined these days to idolise Europe.**

PW: I don't get the feeling anymore that Americans think that Europe is the benchmark...

LS: Well, that's why this story that broke this past week... Did you read about the – what's he called? The general secretary or something of the Swedish Academy... He's the head juror for the Nobel Prize for literature, and he did an interview with AP this past week, saying that, basically, Americans were not in the running for the prize this year; that American writers were too insular and ignorant; and that the centre of the literary world is still Europe. I did a little piece for forbes.com last week that made light of that opinion, because it's farcically untrue. And I think this is standard European bitterness. It's almost as if he thinks that if he says it, he makes it true.

The truth of the matter is that American writing is translated into European languages *en masse*. The whole literary top tier ends up coming to Europe; but it doesn't work in the other direction, and Europeans are annoyed about that. I think understandably annoyed about it. But Americans do not read Europeans in translation in any serious quantity, and they're not interested. I think that's actually where publishers are probably judging the American commercial appetite well, because as soon as you say 'It's translated from French', it's just: 'Oh!'

PW: The British talk about the 'special relationship', but we're pretty much lumped together with Europe, aren't we, in American eyes now – culturally speaking?

LS: You know, with writing in particular, there's a lot more connection with the US, for the obvious reason that we write in the same language. So the Brits have a better chance at the American market than anybody. There is more of a sense of relationship with Britain than with the continent. Wouldn't you have found that yourself?

PW: I don't know the literary scene particularly. The *New York Times* bestseller list, for example: how many British books get onto that?

LS: Not too many. But you'd have a crack at it, if you were really...if you were Ian McEwan. I don't know how well a book like *Atonement* did there, but I certainly wouldn't fall off my chair if it made the bestseller list. It's a very fine book.

PW: And you were talking about left-wing Americans who cleave to the European ideal in some way...

LS: Yes, there's some thin political envy of the way Europeans do things, because of this association with virtue. But I think it's more a fascination with the idea of exile. The attraction of moving to Europe is partly petulance – as if the United States is going to miss you! And the primary attraction of Europe is not cultural, but aesthetic. This is where they really know how to live, they still appreciate beauty, they have wonderful food, they have beautiful architecture – 'We would have a nice life there.' It's more a vision of a nice life, a pretty life.

PW: Do you think that group of people, the left-leaning, metropolitan liberal elite, have become more or less powerful, in terms of the way in which they shape American culture?

LS: Since I don't live in the United States, except in the summer, that's the kind of question that I find hard to answer. And also, it's so general that I might have a hard time answering it even if I lived there. My general feeling about the US is that it's shifted, sneakily, to the right; and so, yes, the left wing has reduced power. They've still got control over a lot of the media, but that media is now polarised. And because of the atomisation of the media itself, what's happening in the United States (which is also happening here) is that, increasingly, everyone is preaching to the converted. People seek out information which validates the views they have already. And so we've got what looks like exposure to more information than ever, and actually people's real exposure to information is more narrow than ever. Because you can now fine-tune where you get that information so specifically to wherever you fall on the Left–Right spectrum that you go through the day never hearing anything that might change your mind.

PW: Overall, this tends to help the Right more than the Left, doesn't it?

LS: That's because the Left used to have much more of a lock on sources of news and other information, because there were fewer television channels and people read newspapers. There wasn't an internet. Because mainstream news sources have historically been controlled by left-leaning metropolitan elites – yes, now that it's more split up, the Right has its own mouthpiece. Many, many mouthpieces – you know, Fox News. So that now conservatives can watch conservative newscasting all day long, and all these radio shows have cropped up with 'shock jocks'. Yes, I think it has helped the Right. I was never very comfortable with the left-wing controlling of news and information in the United States, and so – to a degree – it's good that it's been broken up, that monopoly. But I am a little despairing that it's actually the more moderate voices that get lost in the shuffle.

PW: People in Britain don't seem to believe that. They think the US media is part of the 'military–industrial complex'. But when I was in America, I never met a single Republican journalist or editor.

LS: Journalists aren't Republicans. In fact, interestingly, at the *Wall Street Journal*, where I have worked a total of about nine months on the edit page, the edit page is all conservatives; they were all Republicans, except me. And yes, they're driven ideologically. But the news people are all left wing. The people who do the reporting – they may cover it up, but they're Democrats. It's so weird; there's a complete split. And that's because journalists in the United States are not Republicans. And you're right: I think people over here don't understand that. And of course, as you know, the *Wall Street Journal* is the conservative mouthpiece of print journalism.

PW: Do you feel that, unlike the US, the British media, the cultural establishment, is of one mind?

LS: Yes, of course it is. And in that way the United States is healthier than Britain. Here, the media speaks with one voice, especially on television. The BBC, and Channel 4 and ITV all share fundamentally the same political perspective. Every once in a while you're going to have a departing voice on a single documentary; but that's the exception. Even in the political sphere here, the Tories and Labour occupy a very narrow political band. They differ on precious little.

PW: In your journalism, you tend to talk about quite touchy subjects.

LS: I like to get myself into trouble.

PW: Yes, but isn't it frustrating, that writers on the whole don't?

LS: Because they might get themselves into trouble. My favourite example is immigration. I did a whole article for *The Australian Literary Review* [ALR] about the difficulties of writing about immigration; and it's a subject where you can really put your foot in it fast. I think the tendency therefore is either just to write the company line – that is, immigration is wonderful, end of story; a fine influence on the country; brings in new blood; makes places like London so much more interesting; they do the work that we don't want to... You know, just straight-down-the-line orthodoxy. Or else they don't write about it at all. If you have misgivings, keep them to yourself; write about something else. Because otherwise, you're going to get pigeonholed as BNP. You'll not just be anti-*immigration*; if you want more restricted policies, you'll be anti-*immigrant*. It immediately becomes personal, and, rather than walk into that kind of a minefield, it's understandable that people would just avoid it. I haven't entirely avoided it, and I suspect the book after the one I'm writing now will be about immigration.

PW: I can't think of any other writers who really talk about it. Did you have any fallout from the piece you wrote recently?

LS: It's entirely possible that I had fallout from it, and I didn't go looking for it. I protect myself from responses to articles I write. I don't ever read blogs that run after them. Occasionally I get posted a letter, and I'll generally read that – most of them from people who are completely out of their minds. But no, I can't tell you... I'm sure, for example, if you went to the piece I did recently for the *Sunday Times* 'News Review' – I think that must be what you're referring to – about population? It's entirely possible there is a blog after that, but I wouldn't have read it. If there is, then there will be people who've taken offence. Actually, it's a piece that was written with a studious neutrality. I was putting some facts out there that you should know, if you live in Europe.

That is, what's happening to the population of Europe, and what's happened to the population of the countries which immediately abut Europe. And it's shocking. Native Europeans have a severely under-replacement birth rate, and their populations are beginning to contract. Meanwhile, all the countries immediately to the south and east of Europe still have incredibly high birth rates, and their populations are going through the roof. These are also countries with high unemployment, with poor prospects for a growing population that is also – in contrast to Europe's – very young. And virtually all those countries are Muslim. So get ready! It's going to turn into a huge influx of Muslims into Europe. That's just going to happen. Now did I say anything about whether that's good or bad? No. It's just going to change things. It raises certain questions. What is the impact going to be on the culture? Do you think that means there's a higher risk of terrorism? I basically didn't say anything. Though obviously you can infer that I think that having that many Muslims coming into Europe is...an issue.

But then, my true feelings about immigration constitute one big cognitive dissonance. They're full of contradictions. I guess I do believe in stricter immigration policies, in both the US and Europe. But I also believe that stricter policies won't work. Desperate people are very resourceful. And especially countries like the US aren't going to control the influx – like scads of students and people flying in on tourist visas and then melting away so you never hear from them again – without so restricting travel that it would have a deadly influence on the economy, as well as on freedom of movement for citizens.

Or another contradiction: on the one hand, I do feel – well, a little mournful about the dwindling and dilution of traditional western culture. It's my culture.

I also believe that there's something deeply wrong with cultures that cannot be bothered to reproduce themselves.

And I get a little exasperated that it's all very PC to defend the Inuits or something, and establish Inuit Studies departments in universities; but defending German culture, for example – I'm German on both sides – is outrageous, is neo-Nazi. On the other hand, I also believe that there's something deeply wrong with cultures that cannot be bothered to reproduce themselves. That there's something wrong – I've written on this at some length – with people like me, who won't abridge their personal happiness in order to have children. So that maybe the cultures that still value procreation – still believe in family, in lineage, in nation, in the persistence of those cultures – *deserve* to take over the world.

I feel profoundly conflicted about the whole thing. I *do* think heterogeneous countries are more interesting to live in, and I *do* think that the US has benefited from immigration. After all, I myself am an immigrant twice over: my family immigrated from Germany to the US and now I've more or less immigrated to Britain. But the United States has become hoist on the petard of its own mythology: 'nation of immigrants'. Hoist with its own bullshit. Just because the country has benefited from immigration, that doesn't mean you can't have too much of a good thing. The rest of the world has bought the mythology, too. The option to emigrate to America is now regarded internationally as a *human right*.

We still can't say anything about immigration, but we can now denigrate multiculturalism, which was a response to immigration. We lived through a funny little watershed when suddenly it was OK to diss multiculturalism; when Brown started promoting Britishness, and all that nonsense. Which for some reason is distinct from BNP nationalism, I don't know why. Suddenly we could say – well, this multicultural approach is not working. We should start promoting assimilation. We should start recommending that people who come to this country learn English.

PW: In 1987, Ray Hunniford, a teacher in the Midlands who had a majority ethnic class, said that they should learn English, and he was hounded from his job. But now that's pretty much mainstream thought.

LS: That they should learn English?

PW: Yes. Some have gone further than that, and said that newcomers should adopt our values. Why do you think we don't really discuss what's happening in Europe, in terms of population and demographics?

LS: Everyone's afraid of seeming racist. It means talking in terms of self-interest instead of virtue – apropos of the polarity that I brought up at the very beginning of this interview. This embrace of virtue is very important to the European identity. And that involves mouthing tolerance and open-mindedness and colour blindness. Everything has got so awkward, it's so politically mixed up, because the immigration rate from the Middle East gets confused with race and religion, and a very long history, right? Of being divided between the Crusaders and the Muslim world. Political leaders face the same risks that writers do: of putting their feet in it, of seeming Nazi, as you said, because World War Two was not very long ago, so there's even more sensitivity to anything that might be associated with

76

a German brand of nationalism, a fascist kind of nationalism. Nobody wants to be associated with that.

PW: It's astonishing that, as a writer, you would have to approach the topic of immigration with trepidation, isn't it?

LS: Well, the nice thing about doing things in fiction is that you can put anything in other people's mouths, right? What I wrote in that ALR piece, about writing about immigration, also applies to politicians. That is, fiction writers have historically found it very easy to make the immigrant sympathetic. The immigrant has always been sympathetic. That is because the immigrant is the weaker party, has the much harder task, and is in the conventional hero's position of having to triumph against the odds and surmount difficulty. It's a classic quest structure, which is actually a way of describing virtually all fiction. What's really difficult is to make the native population sympathetic – especially anyone in the native population that isn't welcoming immigrants with open arms. Because the native population is in the advantaged position to begin with, the position of strength – generally is regarded as having more money, understands how things work, is already accepted, is already part of the society. No quest, it's all defensive. It's not attractive, there's nothing attractive about that position. In fact, if it interests you, you should look up that article, because I put it better in the article. *The Australian Literary Review.*

Governments have the same problem. Politicians have the same problem, in terms of story. Sticking up for their own populations is not, especially in European moral terms, comfortable. It seems mean, it seems closed, it seems fascist, it seems racist. You know, what's wrong with more people? Why does it make any difference whether your growing population is from your own stock, or from elsewhere? And therefore you get into – well, what does it mean to be 'an Italian'? Of course, we all keep talking about 'European culture', but there's no such thing, is there? And that's one of the problems with European culture.

> **Of course, we all keep talking about 'European culture', but there's no such thing, is there?**

A little diversion here: we should probably stop talking about 'European culture', because there never has been a European culture, and maybe there never will be. There's French, Italian, German... It's one of the charms of so-called European culture – the fact that there's no such thing. It's many cultures, all of which vary in their permeability, and their insularity, and to what degree they regard themselves as the Japanese do, for example, who hate immigration, despite the fact they've got one of the lowest birth rates in the world, and pretty soon are just going to disappear. They're going to really put themselves in a pickle.

PW: The narrative of multiculturalism is that racism is always perpetrated by white people, but the Japanese...

LS: They're the most racist people in the world!

PW: But isn't the fact that you're going to be writing about immigration, and that, for example, there is a new Richard Bean play, *England People Very Nice*, opening at the National Theatre – isn't this encouraging? Gradually things are becoming sayable?

LS: Maybe gradually, bit by bit. And if I'm lucky, the book that I have in mind will hit at the right point. And things have changed in Holland. You can get away with saying all kinds of things in Austria (Austria's always been a little bit of a special case). You've always been able to get away with saying atrocious things in Austria. And things are beginning to change in France.

PW: But it hasn't happened here yet?

LS: No, I don't think it has happened yet. If I ever did a piece on immigration for the *Guardian* – and I have touched on it on occasion – I'd get in huge trouble. People would jump all over me. Unless it was just the orthodox line. I've written very gently on immigration for the *Guardian*, arguing, actually from the position of an immigrant who has gone through channels and recently had my husband go through the whole nonsense of getting residency. You have to jump through hoops, and you actually have to pony up a lot of money. Basically, Britain is selling residency. It's selling passports. Residency and citizenship now cost thousands of pounds. It's outrageous. And the fees go up, not just every year, but, you know, three months from now, it'll be more. Immigration has become a real – a nice little earner.

So the lesson of this is: cheat. Illegal immigration is easy, and free. Generally speaking, you can get away with it, and they'll never kick you out. Britain doesn't deport anybody to speak of. This is true in the United States, too. Statistically speaking, we don't deport anybody either, not compared to how many people get in. Actually, one of my main concerns with immigration is that, because governments in Europe and the US can't control illegal immigration, they then turn the screws on *legal* immigration. So it gets harder and harder to get in when you follow the rules, and more and more expensive. And we exclude more and more people of the sort that we should want: PhDs, scientists, doctors.

You know how long on average you have to wait for a Green Card in the United States right now? *It's 10 years!* They can't handle the caseload. Meanwhile, you know, if you have no education, don't speak the language and can swim – right across the Rio Grande. Nobody will ever come after you. And if you then have children in the United States, then they're Americans. Which is another one of the, you know... You're never supposed to question that in the United States: it's in the Constitution. But most of the world doesn't operate that way. In most countries, for a child to be considered a citizen at birth, at least one parent has to be a citizen, too. This is one of the reasons we've got such a bad illegal immigration situation. We have motivated them, powerfully, not just with better-paid jobs, but with this business that all you have to do is have your kid on this side of the river, and he or she is an American for life, and their children. Well, that's a real inspiration.

PW: Do you think that Britain will essentially buckle under just to keep a quiet life, or will it change, in the next 10 years?

LS: I could see it changing. Actually, Europe is far less tolerant than the United States. And European identity, or Europeans' identity, is much more racially and religiously defined than it is in the US. Italians are Catholic, and they're white. And they don't have an idea of themselves that they could be Muslim, could be originating from Morocco – no. The people from Morocco are not from here, and they're not Italians. And they don't have a whole ethos of: 'Oh, but you can become Italian because you eat spaghetti now.' You're not Italian! Your mother wasn't Italian, you don't look Italian and you're not Catholic – so you're not Italian. It's not an assimilationist culture.

And most of Europe is like that. Most Europeans don't think of national identity in terms that are completely apart from race and religion. Whereas at least the United States has an identity framework – which is now under enormous strain – which can accommodate all kinds of incoming difference. Or at least that's the conceit. The US thinks of itself more as a white Western European country than it pretends, so that once the white European population is a minority, in what it would like to think of as its own country, there's going to be a little reckoning, a little tremor.

PW: Isn't that coming around 2050?

LS: Yes, actually that date has now moved down. Don't quote me on this, but it's now closer to 2045, something in there. It's coming down – in other words, the trend is down – sooner. Immigration is so high, and the immigrants are having much larger families. The once dominant Western European element is having far fewer children, so the ethnic makeover of America is accelerating. There are several states now that already have 'majority minority' populations, turning the whole word 'minority' into, well... When we're all minorities, there's no point in using it anymore.

PW: Turning to radical Islam, we've recently had the controversy over Sherry Jones's novel about one of Mohammed's wives, *The Jewel of*

Medina. Publication was dropped here, after the publisher's home was firebombed. There is this ongoing discussion about what can and cannot be said about Islam. Do you think that you would write about Mohammed?

LS: As a matter of fact, I resent the fact that I should probably be thinking about writing something to do with Islam. I mean, one of the things that's disturbed me since 9/11 – and, of course, subsequent terrorist incidents – is how effectively they have put Islam at the top of the agenda.

Suddenly, we're supposed to be talking about Islam, and caring about Islam, and concerning ourselves with the differences between Sunnis and Shia. Now we're all becoming much better educated about Islam and what they believe, and how easily offended they are. I don't like what propelled them to the top of the agenda, right? In the same way that it angered me that the Irish Republican Army [IRA] were so effective at getting attention and support for their cause because of what they did. I don't like it when terrorism pays. And Islamic terrorism has paid huge cultural dividends in the West. We talk about Islam all the time, and Islamists, and the Middle East, and we concern ourselves with their concerns. Not because we're tolerant, but out of a sense of fear. It's as if we should start knowing the enemy. We don't put it that way, and a lot of the documentaries that come on television are all very understanding. But they wouldn't be on television if it weren't for an underlying fear.

> Islamic terrorism has paid huge cultural dividends in the West. We talk about Islam all the time, and Islamists, and the Middle East, and we concern ourselves with their concerns. Not because we're tolerant, but out of a sense of fear.

I mean, we've been bullied into being interested in Islam. I resent it. No, I'm not going to write a book about Islam. It's not one of my interests. I may, some day, write a book which concerns itself with religion; but it will be broader than that, because yes, I think some religions are more obnoxious than others. But basically I throw them all into the same obnoxious pot. So no, I'm not writing about Islam. But that larger issue of terrorism paying dividends – I have concerned myself with that for years. And with the worst of behaviour paying dividends.

PW: Do you agree with the view that, in Europe in the post-war years, it has seemed that we celebrate people who try to destroy us – a form of nihilism, almost?

LS: Yes, it's a *faux* sophistication. It's certainly been the case in the States for a long time.

PW: And similarly in the case of Northern Ireland – that somehow right was on the side of the IRA...

LS: Which it wasn't. They were outrageous. In fact, in talking about terrorism – I don't catch these people on as often as I ought to do, but every once in a while you should listen to journalists talking about terrorism these days, and compare it to the way that they were talking about terrorism in the Seventies and Eighties or Nineties. Before 9/11 in the UK, basically, terrorists were sympathetic. Especially the media elite's relationship to the IRA in Britain was dumbfounding. And it was dumbfounding for decades. It was like: 'These people seem great: they're trying to blow us up.'

It is self-hatred. And also a warped sense of chic. It was cool to support the IRA. And they marketed themselves that way. They were the cool people. They were always the cool people in Belfast. I was one of the only recalcitrant, uncooperative blow-ins they ever had to deal with, to the point that, for years, I may have been the sole American Unionist on the entire island! But it was just assumed when I came into town that Sinn Fein would take me under their wing, because here was another American writer who was obviously going to be on-side. Other Americans who did come through town – whether they were journalists or fiction writers – pretty much always took the company line, too. Because, you know, the Catholics were a lot more fun, and the dreary SDLP [Social Democratic and Labour Party] people were middle class and a drag. So the ruling dynamic had to do with a raciness, that the Provies were more risqué. They were on the outer edges, and that was in a cultural, as well as a military, sense. You know, they were the people you really wanted to get in with. I wonder if the same dynamic doesn't operate among Muslims these days: that the jihadists are the cool people.

Anyway, it's worth keeping an ear outside contemporary newscasting and commentary about 'terrorism' in Britain. What were these same people saying about terrorism during the Troubles? And was IRA terrorism any different, any nicer? Then why was it so bloody sympathetic? Honestly, with so much understanding shovelled in Irish Republicans' direction, so many ideological contortions contrived in their defence by the very people the IRA were targeting, and so many concessions made in the 1998 Belfast Agreement to these assholes in the name of 'peace' – including, no less, letting them all out of prison!.. Well, you've got to wonder whether, in relation to the next wave of the same tactics, from Islamic fanatics, Britain has asked for it. *

The Artist – Jonathan Yeo

The return of substance and the revival of portraiture

Born in 1970, the son of the former Conservative cabinet minister Tim Yeo, Jonathan Yeo has become one of the most prominent portraitists working today.

Self-taught, he has painted some of the best-known figures of our times, from the artist Grayson Perry and designer Ozwald Boateng to Andrew Lloyd Webber and the Duke of Edinburgh. In 2006, the National Portrait Gallery in London acquired his portrait of Rupert Murdoch for its permanent collection.

During the 2001 British general election, Yeo was commissioned by the House of Commons to paint the leaders of the three political parties. The paintings now hang in Portcullis House in Westminster.

His portrayal of George W Bush, a collage made from pornographic photographs, caused some controversy. He later used the same method for a portrait of Paris Hilton.

Peter Whittle (PW): I came to the [Southbank Centre] discussion on whether all modern art is left wing. Why do you think they were asking that question?

Jonathan Yeo (JY): It's a nice provocative statement. It has a ring of truth about it, and therefore it's a good premise. Maybe it's a more interesting thing to discuss because it isn't as true as it once was. In that discussion, my position was that it's such an orthodoxy – the left-wing bias in the contemporary art world – that it's pointless questioning whether or not it's there. What's more interesting is that it's perhaps not as strong as it once was, and it may be even less so in the future. That could be partly due to the fact that western governments have become more centrist than in the past. In this country, we are 12 years into a notionally left-wing government and a lot of the creative people are saying it couldn't be any worse under the Tories now – which, for them, would have been an unthinkable position 20 years ago. So there's a shift which is probably connected to the political cycle. The only trouble with the Southbank discussion was that the 'left wing' tag was never properly defined. Ed Vaizey chose to interpret it as the art market and art as a business.

PW: It seemed to me that he made a fundamental error, which was that somehow, because something makes a lot of money, that somehow renders it incredibly right wing.

JY: That's right. The implication was that any successful artist is right wing because they're part of a capitalist system in which they're allowed to make a lot of money. There's a kind of undertone that artistic integrity is either anarchic or left wing, by nature, and anti-conservative; while any sort of capitalism must be right wing.

PW: Do you think, as an artist, it's assumed that you'll have a certain set of views?

JY: Yes, but I get other assumptions made, too. As an artist, it's assumed that you'll have an underlying philosophy – probably a left-wing, anti-conservative point of view. It's true that artists tend to question the status quo, or conservatism with a small 'c'.

At the same time, my father was a Conservative politician and people sometimes assume that you take on the values of your upbringing. In my case, I would say the opposite is probably true. I grew up with someone who would encourage you to disagree with him, and to test your arguments all the time – which was sometimes great fun, sometimes quite hard work, but a good introduction to both art and current affairs. It may also have been helpful from the point of view of not wanting to accept the conventions in the art business. But going back to that left-wing bias we discussed, even though it comes from a place of doubt, challenging the way things have been done before and questioning the status quo, it's still an orthodoxy in itself, and therefore is a status quo of its own. So there's a paradox there. And while I think people are aware of it, it still exists, and is slightly problematic, because it means that most art, if it does attempt to say anything politically, is quite predictable.

PW: You said in an interview that contemporary art has become more figurative. That doesn't make it left or right wing, but isn't there a perception that it makes it *conservative* – that that's somehow a step backwards?

> **What's happened over the last decade is that far more artists are using figurative art because they want to make art with a narrative again.**

JY: I know what you're saying. But it hasn't gone backwards, in the sense of reverting to the figurative art of the past. What's happened over the last decade is that far more artists are using figurative art because they want to make art with a narrative again. Obviously that includes figurative paintings and drawings, but I would say also photography, video and even a lot of conceptual art.

In a way it's conceptual art that started the whole thing. Charles Saatchi, a genius at advertising, encouraged a movement of artists who treated contemporary art almost as though it was advertising. The technique was very similar: make a quick, obvious, punchy, unexpected, witty, immediate visual point, whether it's an installation, painting, photo... What mattered was not the medium or style but the idea. It had been done before by many artists, from Marcel Duchamp onwards, but what the YBAs [Young British Artists, or Britart] did differently was to make it accessible, and to provoke a reaction. The method was really not very different from the one you'd use if you were trying to do an effective advert in a newspaper or on a billboard. Art was basically taken by a skilled marketing person and put in galleries – that was the start of it all.

Up until then, for most of the twentieth century, art had largely been about style, about the medium and its own place in art history, rather than the message. It had become completely solipsistic. Basically, from the point photography became widespread, it's almost as though art had a crisis of confidence. From Picasso and the post-Impressionists onwards, it was about pushing the limits of style until it went into abstraction. Movement followed movement: cubism, futurism, surrealism, abstraction, minimalism, pop, etc. The narrative content of pictures became relatively unimportant, because it was really about what the artist was doing, the manner of depiction, which conventions they were breaking with. This became the subject matter of the art. Anyway that all changed, I think, in about the early Nineties, when art went into the mainstream. And in a way, what's happening now is an extension of that: it's figurative again. If you go to any of the contemporary art fairs, such as Frieze and Zoo in London, most of the work you will now see is art which you don't have to have studied in order to understand at some level. It's become more accessible again. But at the same time, it's not something that you're going to confuse with the Old Masters. It's not the Royal Society of Portrait Painters, or the Royal Watercolour Society, harking back to an era when life was safe and comprehensible, and when paintings were more straightforward. The figurative work emerging now is necessarily twisted, ironic, critical or weird – or all of the above. There is some other level to it. But you can read it as easily as if you were watching a film.

PW: Are you saying that art has again become more what something is actually about, rather than its style? From about the early Nineties?

JY: The roots of it were in the YBAs, even though most of them were conceptual artists, so they weren't making figurative paintings. They changed the way people talked about and looked at art. It's also becoming apparent that the artists whose work is proving enduring are those whose work is figurative, or at least where there's a narrative to it. We're now getting a generation of even more interesting painters who are making figurative work, albeit with a deliberate knowing twist to it.

PW: You can mention some of these, if you want...

JY: John Currin is one of the most successful artists in America now and a good example. He paints what are superficially very beautiful, neo-classical paintings; but he takes kitsch Seventies magazine photos, adverts and pornography as his subject matter – the fun is in the contrast between the two. In a way it's the reverse of what I'm doing with my collages.

But what's interesting is the way contemporary art has managed to maintain its veneer of being edgy and daring, despite the fact that it's actually turned into a massive global luxury-goods industry, with international art fairs now becoming the ultimate upmarket shopping malls for wealthy people.

When I was growing up, modern art seemed to be something impenetrable, to be understood only by a very small bunch of people who were closely involved. Everyone else was outside it. Over the last 20 years it has become a mainstream thing, discussed on news programmes and in lifestyle magazines. Yet it has somehow managed to keep this pseudo mystique of being experimental and risky, when actually, if you survey the big art fairs and contemporary galleries, most of the work you see is very similar to most of the other work there, and it is calculated not to actually offend anyone who might buy it. The work has become largely derivative and entirely safe. Even the galleries all look the same with their white boxes, efficient staff, and tasteful, bland modernity. And there are orthodoxies in the work, too: things you are and aren't allowed to do.

PW: What sort of things are you and aren't you allowed to do?

JY: One example, which was referenced in our Southbank discussion, is the fact that artists are presumed to be anti-war. No one raised an eyebrow at Mark Wallinger's 2007 Turner Prize exhibit in which he criticised British involvement in the Iraq War, even though it was shown by a state-sponsored gallery just a few hundred yards from the centre of government. Now I'm not arguing that they should, but it's hard to imagine any artist at the moment daring to adopt a pro-war stance. It has become such an orthodoxy that they'd struggle to retain their contemporary art credibility.

There's not much art made outside America which uses pro-American standpoints as its subject matter at the moment, either. I made a collage that was a two-fingered gesture at George W Bush. It received a lot of worldwide interest and its popularity seemed to hinge around the idea that it was daring to be cheeky to such a powerful authority figure. Yet the reality is that I'd probably have been lambasted if I hadn't criticised him in some way. In fact, there's a lot of work out there which is explicitly critical of him, and often implicitly of American values, too.

> *...contemporary art has managed to maintain its veneer of being edgy and daring, despite the fact that it's actually turned into a massive global luxury-goods industry...*

85

PW: Do you think Saatchi has been enormously important?

JY: It might not have happened without him. I don't think he's politically motivated, but his patronage early on was a huge factor in determining which artists did well, and which ones had their careers progress quickly. He opened his new gallery, and he's opened it with Chinese art. As some reviews have already said, the Chinese art is a funny thing, because it's superficially daring – a lot of it is using mainstream images of Mao and their leaders – yet it doesn't have a very sophisticated message underneath. It's almost as though they're just getting used to their new freedoms; they still can't quite believe that they can make fun of the system and of authority figures, but have yet to work out where they want to go with it. I don't think Saatchi himself is trying to do anything 'editorially' in his curating of the exhibition, other than show what he thinks is the current trend. I hadn't found the Chinese contemporary scene particularly interesting so far, but the fact that he's pushing it so hard means that I will reassess it. I may come to the same conclusion again, but he's so good at spotting which artists and movements are agenda-setting that it's usually foolish to ignore him.

PW: Do you think, as Brian Sewell has said, that there's almost a cartel of critics and gallery owners who maintain the orthodoxy?

JY: There's an element of people playing pantomime roles, Brian included. I recall he was very critical of Nick Serota in particular. But we should remember that Serota comes from a time when it was a struggle to get people into a modern art gallery in London, and so it's been a crusade for him. I think he really believes in contemporary art and has a sort of missionary zeal. I respect him for that, and the fact he has been so successful with it. It could be said that the area of art they focus on, in the Tate and the Turner Prize, is probably a little narrower than I would like to see and that there's more in the art world than they focus on. But they've been enormously successful in widening the audience for art in this country, and that is good for all artists.

The Turner Prize fed off Brian's splenetic outbursts and the outrage of the tabloids. The *Daily Mail* questioning 'How can Tracey's bed be an art exhibit?' was the oxygen that kept it alive and the sponsors happy. Maybe it made people curious to form their own conclusions. Either way, they flocked down there to see it. The prize became a caricature of modern art in this country and it became more fashionable to be interested in it than to take the reactionary tabloid view. The success of the Frieze art fair and the establishment of London at the centre of the global art scene might not have happened without Serota – and Sewell for that matter – playing their roles.

PW: I'm not sure what people are thinking when they're walking around the Tate Modern. What do you think? Do you think they're genuinely curious about contemporary art, or do you think they almost feel that they're buying into a world view? Do you think that's too jaundiced?

JY: No, but I think there's several things going on, really. For a start, fine art is very different from other areas of the arts. You rarely get reviews of a contemporary exhibition saying 'It's shit, this is rubbish', in the way that a bad play, album, concert or film gets no stars out of five. You might, occasionally, see it in relation to a blockbuster exhibition or someone who's already an established success; but it doesn't happen very often. Art critics tend to say very balanced things rather than make value judgements. And the people who visit are even less likely to have a critical view, or to dare to declare a show a success or failure. They usually see themselves as being there to learn.

The Tate Modern has a very wide remit: it's supposed to represent a huge number of different art movements that have happened in the last hundred years around the world, and contemporary ones, too. And it's a massive job to do. You wouldn't go to a concert hall or somewhere to listen to all the genres of music for the last hundred years... You're not going to like them all! If you're very interested in music, you might have the time and patience to give each one the benefit of the doubt and really explore it. But you probably wouldn't. You might think on the first sound: 'I don't like that.' I think people think they either like art or they don't, or at least that used to be the case. I think people are starting to understand that it's a wide thing, and you can like lots of different areas. I like Old Masters and the best contemporary work equally, and I hate rubbish Old Masters and rubbish contemporary work; I listen to some very contemporary music and some classical on the same day, while I'm working, quite happily as well. I think you can bounce around. But you know the sort of thing you like after you've spent a bit of time exploring it.

I think in this country we've taken longer than the Parisians and New Yorkers to get into – to be comfortable with – contemporary art. But we're embracing it very fast, and thoroughly, and we're getting more confident of our tastes. In time, the people like Serota and Saatchi, who've been big cheerleaders for certain areas, will become less influential, because, as a generation, we'll become more sure of what our own views are and what we want to see, and we'll have a louder voice in ourselves.

PW: So they've been midwives, in a way: helping people become more literate?

JY: Exactly. We may look back on it and say: 'Wow! It was very myopic, the stuff the Tate was buying at the time.' Or it may be spot on. But above all, it's given us a chance to react to it, good or bad. People are much more sure: they know more about it now than they did 20 years ago. Hopefully, we'll know a lot more in 20 years' time. Hopefully, there'll be enough good art around to support that. There's obviously a lot of bad art around, as there always is at any point in history – most of the stuff around at any one time is not very good. Hopefully, we'll spot the good stuff, buy it and put it in our museums.

PW: Why has there been a re-emergence of portraiture in the Nineties? You would have thought that this is one form that would fall by the wayside.

JY: I grew up loving portraits and the National Portrait Gallery. Good painting never really goes out of fashion and, while you also see some bad painting there, there's more amazing painting in there than anywhere else. The hardest thing to paint well is a face, because you're trying to juggle many different considerations all at once. And that's always impressed me; it's always been something I wanted to know how to do. When I started off in the early Nineties, portraiture was the most out-of-fashion and uncool thing you could possibly choose to do. It was liberating in a way: it meant that I wasn't trying to compete with anyone to be cooler than them. It meant I could concentrate on doing something difficult and try to get the hang of it. In retrospect, it was probably quite a good training as a painter, for someone who hadn't been to art school to try to do the most difficult thing first.

> **When I started off in the early Nineties, portraiture was the most out-of-fashion and uncool thing you could possibly choose to do.**

PW: Were you the only person you knew who was concentrating on portraiture then?

JY: No, there were other people doing it, too. But it had been so battered into a subservient role in the art world, or seen as a lesser art form, that most people were forced into a role which they might not have chosen otherwise. The main tendency was this one for harking back to the classics – society paintings in the style of [John Singer] Sargent, or in the style of the Old Masters. They mostly weren't executed very well either. Even if you're brilliant as an artist and do it as well as it was done in the past, it's still a bit of a wasted exercise, because why not direct your energies at doing something new? But it seemed worth exploring and I felt that, once you got good at it, you could turn it into something of your own.

Also, there was Lucien Freud out there who was basically a portrait painter, doing something absolutely his own way, and who was finally getting completely reassessed. In the Sixties and Seventies he had been totally out of fashion and seen as an anachronistic old fart. Yet as he turned into an old fart, he actually became more fashionable, with people finally seeing him as being a great single-minded genius. So it wasn't like there was no encouragement at all. Good artists have always used portraits as subject matter anyway. I couldn't believe it would stay sidelined for very long.

PW: Do you think it might be anything to do with the cult of individualism and celebrity? That we're interested in images of people, politicians and tycoons and so on?

JY: We're used to seeing certain very stereotyped celebrity images – the photos their publicists put out, or in glossy magazines – and we're assailed by those every day. By lunchtime you will probably have already involuntarily seen dozens of these images while watching television, going on the internet or reading the newspaper. Even just riding to work you'll have seen some on billboards. They've become a massive part of our lives, and consciousness, and in doing so their currency has devalued – they've become so disposable. But a painting forces you to stop and look at it differently, possibly because time has been taken over making it, and you see far fewer of them in a day than photographic images.

PW: So they've become more powerful?

JY: I think they force you to look at them in a different way. Another sort of image you see a lot of are the satirical newspaper cartoons, depicting politicians, royalty and other celebrities in an obviously caricatured way, for comic effect. The point of those images is to reflect current perceptions of people. Political cartoons in retrospect tell you much more about the orthodoxies and prejudices of the time than they tell you about the subject of the cartoon. They date incredibly fast. But when you do certain portraits, especially political ones, you're often aware of an expectation that your painting will be similar to the newspaper cartoons of the time. But portraits are designed for the long term, so they have to work beyond the current news agenda. I think they have to be as true as you can make them. But that doesn't mean you can't also make them symbolic or tell a story. With the portrait of [Tony] Blair, I used the poppy as a way of symbolising war. I'm taking a gamble with that, but I think he'll always be associated with the Iraq War, first and foremost. Even when people are looking back in 200 years' time, I think that'll be the single most massive decision he went anywhere near in his time in office. I might be wrong – maybe he'll be seen as the man who rescued something we haven't even thought of yet.

I think it's OK to do that sort of thing, if that's the long-term reference. But on the whole, I think with portraits their value lies in the fact that you've had first-hand experience of people who don't necessarily give anyone access. All kinds of people have given me their time, talked to me and let me observe them in a way most people don't get to see. It would be a waste of an extraordinary privilege not to depict exactly what I see, and for there to be a consistency to the work. The best portraits tend not to make any single obvious overriding point, but are more considered. Perhaps because of that, everyone projects onto them how they feel about those people, and so, again with the Blair picture, I had people who thought he's a war-monger saying: 'Ha! Great! You got him! Look at him with blood on his hands' – or who thought he was 'looking remorseful for the terrible things he's done'. The people who are still fans of his, admittedly in a minority, but there are some – one in four or one in five of the people who reacted to it said: 'You got his decency; he's reflecting on what he's done; he thinks he's done the right thing; you're using the poppy to show that he regrets some of it.' People project their prejudices onto the image.

PW: Your pictures in Portcullis House are arresting, in that they make you still; they 'still the will'; they somehow make you consider them.

JY: That particular project was an unusual one. They were supposed to be portraits, but they weren't really done like portraits. I was trying to do several things with those pictures: one was to show the images as we were seeing them at that stage in our history – an election which most people experienced through the television. Two hundred years ago, your experience of an election would have been very different. It would have been the week or the day a politician came to your town. You'd have gone along and tried to hear him make a speech on his soapbox. Two hundred years from now – I don't know: there may be holographic images in your living room; there may be some way of cloning these guys so that they can actually come and meet you! It'll be different. Whatever it is in 200 years' time, our experience of the most important thing we do as a democracy won't be via a rectangular box in our living room. So the widescreen format, flat metal frames, TV colours and flat newsroom lighting were all designed to make you feel a bit like you were looking at them on a telly. At the same time, I was trying to show what sort of faces these guys were making to me in private, when they were thinking about how it was going. William [Hague] was, for the most part, in good spirits and had great gallows humour – he knew he was going to lose by a mile, everyone knew it from the start, as Blair was so far ahead in the polls. But actually, when you stopped him and made him think about what was going on, you could see him reflecting and being a bit sad he wasn't having a better chance at it. He knew that if he'd been doing the job five years or 10 years later, he might have had a proper chance of winning.

PW: Do you think you'd be painting like this if you had gone to art school?

Would the ability to paint have been drummed out of you?

JY: It's not so much whether the ability would have been drummed out as the will to do it at all. I certainly think it would have been a struggle, and I'd have needed huge self-discipline to pursue something which was the opposite of the prevailing mood. I was an instinctive and relentless rebel at school and was very bad at doing anything I was told. It might therefore have been helpful being told not to do it, because that might have made me want to. But I fear that, if I'd gone to art school, I might have got fed up with being made to do things, and ended up doing a different job entirely. One of the people I painted recently observed: 'You did portraiture when no one else was going to do it; now that everyone wants to do it again, you're messing it up by doing collages!' My next project involves painting portraits again, but this time focusing on people who have had cosmetic surgery. Some of the works will be diptychs showing the effects of the procedure.

PW: Before and after sort of thing?

JY: Yes, and I think when I look back in years to come, it will have been the most serious thing I've attempted. It's really quite insane when you stop and think about where we're at now: the things people are doing to themselves voluntarily, for vanity; the medical danger, the risks they're taking doing things they don't need to; the expense, and the discomfort of it when it goes wrong. Even after all that, there's the fact that a lot of the time you can tell straight away when someone's had work done, which rather undermines the impression they are seeking to create. And they still bother doing it! It's a weird, weird time.

> **...vanity is such a massively growing industry that it will develop very fast and, in another hundred years, it will be much safer, less painful, and much quicker. You'll take a pill in your lunch break and almost instantly have bigger breasts or a smaller stomach.**

PW: You have said that people will look back on this time with horror...

JY: Yes, exactly. It's barbaric. Like the way we look back at the way they used leeches and other primitive medical things in the past and think: 'How did it not seem obvious that it was madness?' Clearly cosmetic surgery is not something that's going to go away. On the contrary, vanity is such a massively growing industry that it will develop very fast and, in another hundred years, it will be much safer, less painful, and much quicker. You'll take a pill in your lunch break and almost instantly have bigger breasts or a smaller stomach. But at this point in history, while it's still risky, messy and obvious, it feels like the obvious subject for some paintings.

PW: Do you see them as portraiture?

JY: Yes, I do. But they will potentially also have a contemporary angle, a historical angle, and also a bit of a conceptual angle.

PW: Would you say to people that they should teach themselves, and shouldn't bother with art school?

JY: Not necessarily. I think I'm possibly a bad example in this respect. There seem to be some art schools now which are running good painting courses. I think the Slade has probably always done it; but there are plenty of others, too, now. I can't be specific because I haven't properly investigated this, but I think you're probably better off, if you can, going and studying somewhere where you've got the chance to spend your day painting models.

It's true that I taught myself, but I was fortunate. I just didn't know any better. I chanced into doing portraiture and got a handful of commissions early on that kept me going through all those early years. When most people had to give up and go and get a proper job, I was able to keep indulging my hobby. A huge part of that was luck. I couldn't responsibly say to someone now: 'That's a good way to do it.' It would be safer to go to art school.

In retrospect, one benefit was that it gave me total independence, and it meant that I wasn't indoctrinated by the prevailing fads, interests and obsessions. I also wasn't told what I wasn't allowed to do. I think it's important to believe that anything's possible, not only in terms of being able to create any illusion or idea within the work, but also the way you want to see the world, and what influence you can have on the world.

I've also been lucky with timing. We've had an extended period in which art has been more about the idea than about the craft of making it. Not that that is any better or worse than work which is well executed but has nothing to say. But I think ultimately it's better still if you have something which is beautifully made and also communicates a great idea. Because, as a viewer, part of you does want to have that bit of wonder, where you look at something and ask yourself: 'How did a human being make something as beautiful or as brilliant as that?' Like someone playing an incredible piece of music – part of it is enjoying the music, but part of it is watching their hands on the piano and going: 'Oh my God! How can someone be that brilliant?' You want to be in awe of the quality of the work. And I think the artists that emerge over the next few years will be ones that do both.

PW: Are you optimistic about that?

JY: Yes, I think I am. Obviously you don't get very many in a generation like that, but in recent years the talent for making things hasn't been so important. I think Grayson Perry is a good example of someone who's benefited slightly later in life from people valuing the craft as well as the ideas. For a long time there were a few insiders who knew what he was doing, but he is much more widely recognised now, and rightly so.

PW: I was talking to James MacMillan, the composer, and he was very optimistic. He said that the dominance of the atonal movement had come to an end.

JY: I think there's a similar thing in the art business, but lagging a bit behind, after a protracted period of breaking all the rules for the sake of it. Almost like an adolescence. As if art history started with a childhood, of conventional western art, getting increasingly skilful – the twentieth century was like an adolescence, sticking two fingers up at the parents, saying: 'We want to break all the rules, test all the limits.' Having done that now, we've had almost the left-wing, student days of having to be anti-Establishment; everything is studiously rebellious and unconventional. I think we may move out of that soon and see art more as grown-up entertainment, as something to be experienced and enjoyed, rather than feel that every single thing you see in every gallery has to be kicking against the system.

> ...the twentieth century was like an adolescence, sticking two fingers up at the parents, saying: 'We want to break all the rules, test all the limits.'

PW: One of the important points you make is about being awed by someone's sheer skill.

JY: For me the most exciting thing about where contemporary art is going is that there's a sense of industry that wasn't there before; and a great deal of energy is being applied to the actual making of things, to make them beautiful. At the same time, there seems to be a realisation that it's a waste to just make things beautiful and not have a point to them as well. So there's wit, there's fun, there's subversion going on, too. So I think the next 20 years or so are going to be really enjoyable for someone like me who likes that kind of work. And I'm lucky that I got started a bit earlier than most, otherwise I'd have a much harder time getting noticed.

The street art movement is interesting and is something that I think will run for a few more years. Banksy has been its cheerleader, a representative for feelings of anti-globalisation and suspicion of politicians and other authority figures. He also wryly manages to make fun of the art world, so he has his cake and eats it. But in this period of international, economic and environmental insecurity, he seems to speak for people's fears and suspicions in a way that most mainstream contemporary artists fail to do. Why aren't more artists tackling the unholy world domination of politics, religion and PR? They are too solipsistic and obsessed with their own place in art history. That's not to say even Banksy is taking any real risks with his statements. But then I wasn't really with my Bush or Blair pictures either. If one of us had mocked radical Islam in a punchy and conspicuous way, that would have been far more unusual and brave. It's perhaps exactly what someone needs to do.

Even with my piss-take of George Bush – my little jokey riposte was really what it was – I'm sure he'd find it funny if he saw it. I don't think he'd even be offended. Hopefully, some of his more loony right-wing middle-American followers might have been mildly offended or irritated by it; so it was worth doing, because I think they're very dangerous. But it's not really a personal risk to do that. I risk getting strip-searched and held up when I go to America, which is a bore, but I think that's the biggest risk I take. The thing we're afraid of, the real challenge to our freedom and our own lives – if it's anyone at all, other than the capitalist system, which is crumbling and is going to cause us trouble in other ways... I think Islam is an interesting one, because I think a lot of people are afraid to tackle it at all.

PW: Isn't it a problem for the arts that it is exclusively Islam that is making threats?

JY: A couple of people suggested doing a pornographic depiction of one of the Islamic leaders, but I'm not interested in sending up people's religion, because I think that's a very different thing. Nor would I do it to Christianity, either. As it happens, I think some of the Christian fundamentalists in America are nearly as dangerous as the radical Muslims in the long term. But I don't see it as my job to impose my religious beliefs on the world, any more than I think they've got the right to. It would be hypocritical of me to do that, but I do think there is a way of exposing these people we're scared of as being sad, inadequate people, desperate to follow something. That would be a useful job for the artist.

I think part of the problem is that we've made this situation, or we've fanned the flames of it – there are a lot of interested parties contributing to the pantomime. If you really didn't want fundamentalism spread, you wouldn't give these people the oxygen of publicity. You wouldn't have the 7/7 bombers up there with their teenage bedroom suicide video messages. You wouldn't put them out in the media, because you're effectively showing that these guys have succeeded at their objectives. You wouldn't mention their names in the media, because they were after martyrdom. Don't give it to them! What that is doing is telling a whole new generation of disaffected and inadequate youths that these tactics work. But of course, it makes good television, because everyone wants to have baddies and to believe in the struggle of good and evil. And the news media are not going to be the ones to stop it – certainly the newspapers aren't going to! It sells a lot of papers. Can you imagine a newspaper headline saying 'Everything's not that bad' or 'We're not going to talk about that because it'll make the situation worse'? Fear is what sells papers.

It's the power of nightmares. The politicians certainly aren't going to stop you being scared of terrorists, because they want to be able to stand up to the terrorists and look tough. Most of the politicians in Britain, America, Australia, Spain, Israel and elsewhere said it's in our interests to go to war in the first place. So they are hardly going to play down this invisible threat of terror. In my view, the Tories made a massive strategic mistake by supporting the Iraq War so unreservedly, and the Democrats did so, too, in America. So there's no one there with a vested interest in saying: 'Actually, there's less of a threat than we thought and we can make the threat smaller by talking about it less.' Certainly, the police are unlikely to talk it down, either: they get a bigger budget for the extra security needed. The security services, MI6, all those people who were struggling to justify their existence in the post-Cold War world suddenly have massively increased budgets, not to mention the bonus that more secrecy and less accountability can be justified, too.

It's like the guys who invented the millennium bug to give themselves a bit of work on computers. They need the threat of terrorism to keep happening to justify their existence. Commercially – even the airports benefit from terrorism, because you have to get there two hours before, so you've got much longer to spend shopping. I'm not for a second suggesting that any of these groups exaggerate or deliberately contribute to the threat. But the problem is that there isn't a pressure group, there's no vocal lobby, for doing the logical, sensible thing – which is ridiculing these extremists or, better still, ignoring them altogether. Ridicule would be very powerful, because they're doing it to seem serious and to seem important, and because it seems like such a noble purpose. Comedians should be our weapons in this, yet they're not. Or if they are, they are denied the oxygen of media exposure because the BBC and everyone are scared of the possible reaction. So in the vacuum there is an opportunity for artists to show the way. Assuming they are not too scared.

PW: People generally seem to be more cautious in what they'll take a risk with.

JY: It's funny it has taken so long, really. But I think there are other things going on which are more damaging to society. I'm fascinated by what's going on with the financial side of things. I've felt for a long time that capitalism has a shelf-life as a system, and needs to evolve into something else now, because, having made everyone slightly wealthier for a bit, the divide is clearly – so massively – increasing between wealthy people, who can pay themselves what they want and avoid paying tax, and the people on the other end of it. That isn't a sustainable situation, so that's all going to fall apart. But we don't have a replacement system ready yet.

The Director – Sir Richard Eyre

The UK's growing cultural apartheid

One of Britain's most important cultural figures, Sir Richard Eyre was director of the National Theatre between 1987 and 1997. His diaries from this time were published in 2003 under the title *National Service*.

Among his many notable theatre productions, over a career spanning four decades, are *Guys and Dolls* at the National (1982), *Hamlet* with Jonathan Pryce (1980) and then again with Daniel Day-Lewis (1989), *Richard III* with Ian McKellen, and numerous new plays by, among others, Tom Stoppard, David Hare, Trevor Griffiths and Alan Bennett.

In the late Seventies, Eyre worked as both a director and one of the producers of BBC's *Play for Today*. In 1988, he directed the Falklands War story *Tumbledown*, for which he won the BAFTA award for best director.

For the cinema, he directed *The Ploughman's Lunch* (1982), which won the *Evening Standard* award for best film, *Iris* (2001), starring Judi Dench and Kate Winslet, *Stage Beauty* (2004) and *Notes on a Scandal* (2006), again starring Judi Dench.

In 1997, he received the Olivier Lifetime Achievement Award. He was knighted the same year.

From 1995 to 2003, he was on the board of governors of the BBC.

Peter Whittle (PW): I wanted to start by asking you when, last year, you talked about a cultural apartheid...

Sir Richard Eyre (RE): I've been saying that for about 15 years...

PW: You pretty much put this at the door of the television, the BBC and education – I think you pointed out that you had been brought to the arts by teachers, and by television as well. Why would you say that these two particular factors are to blame?

RE: What I was saying was this: if you believe – as, of course, I do and apparently the government does – that it's worth giving money to the arts, or if you're genuinely interested in investing money in culture, there is a corollary. Money for culture always comes with riders, and the riders are to do with forms of access, and obliging the institutions that receive government grants to provide access, outreach to broaden the base of their public. So, if you believe in the virtue of giving that money, then the corollary is that you must believe in educating – in ensuring that those people who are disenfranchised from the arts are actually able to experience and understand what is being offered. And that's where I think there's been a huge breakdown, and there's been either reluctance or ignorance on the part of government. Because it can only be done from the centre – it can only be done by an initiative from the top – to oblige the DCMS [Department for Culture, Media and Sport] and the education ministry to get together and work out some method of mutual benefit.

PW: Why has there been that breakdown?

RE: I think because of an implicit and probably unconscious indifference from Cabinet to the arts – the amount spent is very small, if you look at total government spending. Although it's quite a substantial figure, it's comparatively small. To its credit, the Labour government has, over the past 10 years, upped it – slightly above inflation. But still, it's small, and I don't think at cabinet level it's ever discussed. It's an anomaly that people in the arts have a very large voice because they have access to the media – and by definition they tend to be articulate and in the public eye, so they have a means of making themselves felt – yet still they're just pinpricks against government.

I think that's always been the case: I remember when I was running the National Theatre – and the whole time I was running the National Theatre it was a Tory government – going to Alistair McAlpine, who was then chairman of the Conservative party and who had organised a dinner. He's something of a philanthropist, an art lover. He had organised a dinner, and there were a number of Tory ministers there. I was there, and Nick Serota and Jeremy Isaacs; there were people who were running big arts institutions, and there were probably heads of museums there, too. Geoffrey Howe was there, too, and he said: 'You've all got a problem.' And we said: 'Well, what is the problem? Convincing the Treasury?' And he said: 'No, no – the problem is convincing anybody in the Cabinet.' He said there was simply no interest; that the arts lobby has absolutely no purchase on central government. So you need a prime minister who is prepared to say: 'Look, we give this money to the arts, we trust the culture, this is an entirely proper thing for a government to be doing, but we must look out for the corollary of this: education in the arts, in order to widen access.' This should be a basic line of Labour policy. It's absolutely in line with everything the Labour party's always believed in.

PW: The implication of what you're saying is that this has come about – that no one listens in Cabinet – because they aren't interested. Does that mean that once they would have been?

RE: No. I think politicians... Harold Macmillan is always quoted as being the last prime minister who read: he used to, allegedly, go to Chequers on a

Friday night and read novels over the weekend. But I just don't think they have the time. I suppose Churchill had an interest in the arts – but they simply don't have the time, and they don't have the passion. It's just not something that is there, that anyone in power feels has to be instituted.

Harold Macmillan is always quoted as being the last prime minister who read: he used to, allegedly, go to Chequers on a Friday night and read novels over the weekend.

PW: When it's about funding or education – or indeed TV or arts programmes – what's your view of the idea that just as important as the financial aspect is that there's almost been a collapse in cultural confidence? The idea that cultural relativism has made it pointless to find out about the high arts? There's a lack of confidence about saying now to kids: 'You really should know about...'

RE: You're right, it's interesting... On the front page of the *Guardian* today there's a piece on exactly that subject. I never thought I'd hear myself say I admire something that Boris Johnson said – but actually this is his cultural advisor, Munira Mirza. I entirely agree when she says that it's presuming that young people will only like art if they can immediately relate to it: 'Working-class students may be steered towards popular culture, new media and film, on the basis that they will find older art forms such as opera or ballet irrelevant. It's extremely patronising.' I absolutely agree. That's exactly in line with my point; in the end, the only thing that can convert people, persuade people... The only way in which art can make an argument is through art itself. It's only through being exposed to something – you think: 'Oh, I see! I understand this, I *receive* this.'

But if you're never, through your education, exposed to it, then you're going to end up with the crap. And the crap is served out to people in this awful, patronising way. I mean, it's perfectly possible for high art and low art to exist in perfect mutual compatibility; most of us are perfectly happy [with that]. I did come from a financially privileged background, but there weren't books in the house. We never went to the theatre, ballet, opera, looked at paintings – ever, in my childhood. I only became interested in it through being exposed to it when I left home, when I was 18. So I feel that's the big chasm. It was when I was at the National that I first described it as 'apartheid'. It's ironic that nobody picked up on it at the time. And then it's just chance, years later, because I have been repeating it like a mantra.

PW: My parents were working class, but had an aspiration to learning, took us all to various places. And the difference is that they, as working-class people, had a basis of knowledge, which they had from school, and it went on to me and my sister. There came to be a trend for middle-class teachers to feel they were being 'bourgeois' by pushing a certain culture onto children. To me, it seems to have come from the Left, that view. But it tends to have always been the 'philistine' Tories who have been blamed.

RE: I wouldn't say that at all. There's not much to choose between them. Probably the Tories are marginally better – because of this patrician element, the inheritance of a kind of ownership of high culture. Actually, I had to deal with about eight different ministers when I was at the National. The only one who had a real sense of culture – its usefulness – and an intelligence about how it should be funded and managed was Peter Brooke, whom I loved. Wonderful man. So I wouldn't for a moment say that.

I think there's a lot of head-banging nonsense talked by the Left. And desperately patronising, and coming from virtuous motives of empowering people who are, in other ways, deeply without a sense of ownership of their own lives. There has been the blind alley of multiculturalism and also of speaking down to people.

> **There has been the blind alley of multiculturalism and also of speaking down to people.**

PW: Do you think that we're now past the stage where teachers, taking their class to see *Swan Lake* – maybe a class of predominantly ethnic kids – might have imbibed a sense that it's not those kids' culture; it's not relevant to them; that this was almost 'imperialism'?

RE: They may have, and it's up to teachers – it's putting a lot of responsibility on the teachers, but why not? That's exactly what I think has to start at primary school. And in some places it's done and done brilliantly. And so often, as with the El Sistema [youth orchestra programme] in Venezuela, it actually works! Give people credit, and treat people as if they're capable of the best and of understanding the best. It takes really strong leadership, in all directions.

PW: You said that you were concerned that the next generation might turn its back on the world of classical art and entertainment. [The tenor] Ian Bostridge wrote an article recently saying that he sensed that people no longer feel that it's quite good to like classical music, even if you don't understand it. He said that, in a funny way, it's dangerous when people no longer feel that they have to pretend to like it.

RE: You could only deal with that through education, through simply exposing people to the thing that is admirable. One of the bizarre things about the way that the arts are treated is that they aren't treated like sport: I mean, there's participatory sport that is encouraged, but actually what people admire is really gifted people doing something quite extraordinary – doing something that the rest of us can't do. And that element, I think, should be encouraged in art. Now, of course, that's a view that is often completely mistakenly described as elitist. What's elitist about it? It's only elitist if, in some way, you're organisationally barring people from experiencing that extraordinary gift of expression, of making music.

Give people credit, and treat people as if they're capable of the best and of understanding the best.

PW: An example of that is the way the Olympic gold medallists were feted. Is the reason that this isn't the case in the arts because it goes against the idea that we are all born with equal talent?

RE: It could absolutely be. Have you read Malcolm Gladwell's thesis about genius? He's just published a book, and his argument is that really there's no such thing as genius – it's hard work. There's pseudo-science attached to it – that it's 10,000 hours of practice, as it were. Nigel Kennedy is a brilliant violinist because he practised for 10,000 hours. It's a slightly specious argument, I think, but I think that people don't resent the gifted. Actually they feel it enriches them.

For all the supposed crap of 'anyone can be a star', actually the interesting *Strictly Come Dancing* argument is fascinating, because, in one sense, the whole basis of the programme is that anyone can do it; but I think the public can and do distinguish between people having a go, having a laugh, and people who are supremely talented at something that is expressive, that is about opening their eyes to the world. What is art but a means of making you see with somebody else's eyes, or listen with somebody else's ears? Understand somebody else's feelings? So there is a massive appetite for fiction and for metaphor, and I don't think people want to be talked down to.

PW: Has the same thing affected television? Do you think that people there have lost their obligation to educate and inform as well as entertain?

RE: I absolutely do. That comes from the top. Of course, they have a really difficult job, squaring the circle between the BBC's Reithian remit and pulling in a large audience. They've got a responsibility to x million licence payers, and any number of surveys show that a substantial number of licence payers feel that the BBC is not for them. So it's entirely legitimate to make programmes for the whole span of the audience, but it's extremely hard. So they agonise internally about how to reach that audience; and of course mostly they end up by mimicking stuff that appears on the other channels. In the course of the agony, they actually just ignore the higher remit and feel uncomfortable about embracing the two, so they generally end up in a sort of uncomfortable middle ground.

PW: Where do you think this will lead us? What state do you think the BBC will be in, in 10 years' time?

RE: I was a governor of the BBC for nine years, until just before the Gilligan affair in 2003. Even then there would be debates, initiated by the BBC executive, about whether they could justify the existence of Radio 3, and precisely about the mix, the responsibility towards licence payers. I thought there was a sort of gravitational shift towards a – perfectly understandable – slipping away towards the middle ground and appeasing the mass audience. And it wasn't so much ratings; but it was, of course... The BBC always express themselves in a rather pious, sanctimonious way; would always be talking about the 'obligation to the licence payer'. Well, it comes to the same thing in the end. But there was nobody with the vision or courage to stand up and say: 'Look, we should be doing this, we should be doing *Strictly Come Dancing*; but at the same time we have a responsibility to the other end of the spectrum.' And although they say – do you know the concept of hammocking? – in the old days, when you had three or four channels, you would have a programme, and they'd say: 'Oh, nobody wants to watch that'... I mean, there was a fantastic ballet on a Saturday night, so they would put that between *Steptoe and Son* and the Lottery show. So you 'hammock' it: it just slings between. This pre-dates the remote control, and people were too lazy to get up and change the channel, and they didn't have the choice of 60 satellite channels. So you can't 'hammock' anymore, which is why they have niche programming. It's further diminished their reach.

PW: I would say Radio 3 is exactly what they should be doing, and in fact it's harder to justify Radios 1 and 2.

RE: I agree. That's precisely the argument that I made. But it would be interpreted in quantifiable terms, so they would say that less than a million people listen to it, so the cost per hour of Radio 3 is disproportionately high. Well, that's the decision... The people who run the BBC – that's what you do, you rob Peter to pay Paul; that's what making policy is, and don't be feeble about it.

PW: Do you think our culture is in a worse state than when you began your career?

RE: Do I think it's in a worse state? No, I don't at all. I think it's rather healthy. I'm always dazzled by the fact that the audience isn't diminishing at the Proms. Actually theatre audiences – I think probably in some [theatres] are as large if not larger than they were 10 years ago. I'd say the film industry is rather a poor index, because that just fluctuates wildly and is a satellite of the US film industry. Look at the figures from the Tate – absolutely fantastic! And for the big showcase exhibitions at the National Gallery and the Royal Academy... So I don't see a falling off, and I don't see any cause for despair. I think that's precisely why

– it's one of the few success stories in this country – that's why a prime minister should get behind this and create an initiative to make sure this is perpetuated for future generations. But they're very wary of making public pronouncements about the arts, the PR people always – it's a no-go area.

PW: But isn't there a difference between appreciation – the number of people going to things – and the actual health of the thing?

RE: The area that I'm aware of particularly is theatre – there's a lot of good new writing; there's a whole swathe of very gifted directors and designers. So I feel that in theatre there's a lot going on. And there are a lot of gifted film makers. It's very difficult to get a film made in this country, but some of them are working in television, and I think there are some very interesting things happening with young people in the visual arts, and also in classical music. And I'd say that the pop world is quite lively: it's not inert. All of these things are like sunspots: you can't predict when or where the next eruption is going to take place, because, by definition, you're waiting for the emergence of talent, and then for the talent to be educated and nurtured and then exhibited. It's the same as in sport. I'd say that the network is there, and is probably in as good health as it's been for a long time.

PW: So what we need is for somebody to stand up, as the sports minister did after the Olympics, and say we are going to put more money into this, to get more gold medals. You think that's what we should have in the arts?

RE: I think it would be admirable, yes. And the analogy with sport is very good, because they've made the same analysis: that if you're going to create great sportspeople you've got to start early; you've got to inculcate the desire to compete at an early age. And of course there's so much nonsense about child-centred education... So many sports facilities have been dissolved, sold off, put to other uses. So they've got a lot of work to recover.

PW: You once quoted this [from John Ruskin] in an article you wrote: 'Great nations write their autobiographies in three manuscripts – the book of their deeds, the book of their words and the book of their art.' What would it say now, then, that book?

RE: You can't say at the time, can you? You can only look back...

PW: But if we were reading it in 50 years?

RE: Well, it would certainly speak of a collective restlessness and self-doubt – surprisingly, I would say not as pessimistic as perhaps it ought to be, if you believe in climate change and in recession. Of course, everything in the world goes in a wave pattern. The financial wave – one can see that for every up there's a down. But surprisingly there seems to be... I would say, collectively, the mood is not one of universal despair. It's not a dystopian universe in the arts.

PW: So are we in denial?

RE: I think we don't know, and I think this has been the case increasingly, with the twentieth century and the horrors of the twentieth century. What we've seen in the last 20 years: we've seen the collapse and total exposure of the nullity of Communism. So you've had the collapse of Communism, and recently we've had the collapse of capitalism, or of market capitalism. And so I don't think we've yet absorbed the fact that the two great ideologies of the past 100 years have been shown pragmatically to be unworkable. No one has evolved anything yet. No one's yet come up with an ideological middle way; an idea to which we can adhere, that's going to take us through the next decade. We just somehow muddle along. But then that's true of the majority of people in all societies at all times: you just somehow muddle through. One of the ways that help you to muddle through is that you have artists who put the bits together for you, make it possible for you to understand, give some sort of narrative to the muddling through. *☾*

The Editor – Daniel Johnson

Cultural threats to the West in the post-Cold War era

Daniel Johnson is the editor of *Standpoint*, a centre-right cultural and political monthly magazine, which was launched in 2008. *Standpoint*'s stated core mission is to 'celebrate our civilization, its arts and its values – in particular democracy, debate and freedom of speech – at a time when they are under threat'.

Son of the author Paul Johnson, Daniel graduated with a First in Modern History from Magdalen College, Oxford.

He made his name as a leading journalist when, as German correspondent of the *Daily Telegraph*, he covered the fall of the Berlin Wall. He was a leader writer for both *The Times* and the *Telegraph*, as well as literary editor and associate editor of *The Times*. The journals and papers he has contributed to include *The Times Literary Supplement*, *Prospect* and the *New Criterion*.

In 2007, his book *White King and Red Queen: How the Cold War Was Fought on the Chess Board* was published.

Peter Whittle (PW): Could a magazine like *Standpoint* have appeared 10 years ago?

Daniel Johnson (DJ): No, I think until the whole world was alerted to this global threat to western civilisation – and that really only happened with 9/11 – I don't think most people would have seen the need for a magazine like *Standpoint*. As Tom Stoppard said in his speech at our launch last May, if the end of the Cold War really had been the end of history, as we were told at the time, there would be neither a need nor a purpose for a magazine like *Standpoint*. But as he said, we all know what really happened. And I think we are in a situation now which is, in many ways, comparable with the Cold War – except that I think the threats to the West come as much from within as outside.

PW: What is the biggest threat from within?

DJ: I'm not sure whether I want to have a sort of hierarchy of threats. I think a number of different factors have come together. Most obviously, the intellectuals in our society – who overwhelmingly identify themselves as on the Left – seem to have become deeply disenchanted, deeply alienated from the values and the principles – the traditions – of western civilisation. And I think it is very difficult for a civilisation to endure when

104

its own intellectual elite has become so cut off, if you like, from those roots. So that's one factor.

Another factor, clearly, is that our societies have fundamentally changed, here in Western Europe and in the United States, over the past two generations, in the sense that they have ceased to be monocultural. They've become, whether we like it or not, what is known as multicultural. That is, of course, a misnomer, because there is no new high culture to replace the Judeo-Christian Enlightenment culture that we've inherited from past centuries. That's still the only show in town. But our societies have become multicultural in the sense that large numbers of people have no historic connection with that high culture, and cannot, in many cases, be expected to integrate into it because they haven't even been given the basic tools required. They haven't got the language, or they haven't got the value system that would enable them to integrate. And that's our fault. That's the fault of the host societies. So that's another factor: the multicultural thing.

But of course, there are more problems than that. I would cite the fact that our society has, to a very great extent, quite wilfully turned its back on the higher spiritual intellectual values that any society in history has always needed – the kind of idealism that I think sustains any successful civilisation. And instead, we have gone whoring after false gods: whether extreme forms of materialism, greed, the kind of thing that everyone's suddenly woken up to with the current economic crisis. Or strange kinds of ideology: a sort of worship of the wackier forms of scientific utopianism – eugenics, effectively. The idea that we can live forever. The idea that we can somehow replace religion and morality with something else – something better or more modern. All these ideas, it seems to me, are knocking around. And what we're lacking is any firm basis, any anchoring in a kind of metaphysical and moral framework. Such a framework has never embraced everybody, but it provides a sort of bulwark. Something that, if you like, people can rebel against. But if there's nothing to rebel against – if the whole of society becomes a society of rebels – then you have a real problem.

PW: You say the intellectuals are broadly on the Left...

DJ: Sorry, I just want to say that it isn't only the intellectuals. Initially, I identified the intellectuals as part of the problem. But I think that the deeper problem that I was just speaking about applies right through society. I think you find this sort of confusion and chaos right down to the lowest levels of society now: you find it in the poorest housing estates, no less than on the campuses.

PW: But the existence of *Standpoint* and the people I've interviewed for this book seem to indicate that there is a quite healthy non-left-wing intellectual class. And if these people do exist, have you – or did you at some point – lose your nerve?

DJ: Well, what I would say is that there was a revolution – if you like, a cultural revolution. I think it's too simple to say it started in the Sixties. I think it probably began a long time before that. And if you really want to trace back the genealogy of ideas, you can usually go back at least to the French Revolution or thereabouts. But certainly, there was a cultural revolution here in the West, which, if you like, was one of the last great twentieth-century nihilistic upheavals, along with Fascism and Communism, and various other 'isms'. But this was not so much a political as a cultural crisis, and I think we're still in the grip of its consequences and its aftermath. The generation that brought this about is still with us, after all. They're no longer dominant, but the spiritual progeny of that cultural revolution is dominant.

I think it is true to say that there have been various attempts at counter-revolution against it – some more successful than others. On the political stage, of course, there was the Thatcher–Reagan phenomenon in the 1980s. And intellectually, again, there have been a number of rather brave attempts to re-establish some kind of moral compass, to coin a phrase. But these are invariably dismissed or demonised. A term like 'neo-conservatism', for example – that's only one example – is intended – certainly the way it's used now, anyway – to delegitimise what was, in fact, a perfectly reasonable and mainstream reconsideration by people who had considered themselves on the Left of the political spectrum... A realisation that they did need to rediscover moral absolutes.

PW: Do you think the Reagan–Thatcher years might come to appear merely as a deviation from a historical process that is still going on?

DJ: Well, I think western civilisation is still alive and kicking, and I think it's got much more profound resources than that. By the way, when we mention Reagan and Thatcher, I think perhaps we should throw in another name – John Paul II. Without him I don't think one would have had that great uprising in Eastern Europe, which is, for my money, the most hopeful and extraordinary phenomenon of my lifetime. And that gives us great grounds for hope: societies that had become spiritual deserts, and were intellectually dead, are now among the most interesting parts of Europe. And also, incidentally, politically among the most robust regions of Europe in standing up to the enemies of the West.

But to answer your question: no, I don't think these were a blip. But I don't think that the political level is the deepest level. When the pendulum swings back in a genuinely liberal direction – liberal in the true sense, and conservative in the true sense – swings away from totalitarianism in all its different forms, then I think that, unless it is anchored in areas like education and the media and religion – unless, in other words, it embraces the whole of society – then it's bound to be ephemeral, it's bound to be temporary. And I think that may be partly what we have seen. We've seen it much more recently with Tony Blair. Tony Blair did understand some of the problems of our society, and did try to do something about them, and did try also to show solidarity with leaders of other countries who were trying to resist threats to the West. But, in a sense, he neglected the cultural dimension, too – just as Thatcher had done – and the result has been that those forces have reasserted themselves very quickly: they proved to be too strong for him.

PW: What were your reasons for calling the cultural section of *Standpoint* 'Civilisation'? It seems that, in our culture, that's become rather a definite thing to do.

DJ: Yes, I think it has. And, in my case, quite deliberately so. Yes, one or two people wondered if it wasn't a bit bombastic or a bit overambitious or a bit pompous, to be claiming to defend and celebrate western civilisation with a little magazine. What can a magazine do anyway? Well, the answer to that is, obviously, that you have to start somewhere. The battle of ideas – it's become a cliché, an overused trope, but it still has to be fought. And, of course, it isn't really the ideas that do the fighting: it's the people with the ideas; it's what you *do* with ideas that matters. Ideas in themselves are often morally neutral: they can be for good or ill.

No, civilisation is a concept that had almost fallen out of our vocabulary. When 9/11 happened and people suddenly remembered this idea of a 'clash of civilisations'... Now, I'm not sure that's what we have got – that that is the best way to describe what's going on in the world now. It's more of a chaos than a clash. And I'm fairly confident, too, that what western

> **...what western civilisation is fighting against is not another civilisation but really a form of barbarism.**

civilisation is fighting against is not another civilisation but really a form of barbarism. Nonetheless, because there is a very important religious dimension to all this, it's quite easy for our enemies to mobilise thousands of years of history, in order to try and depict – to dramatise – the struggle in that way: as a clash of Islam and the West. And I think we have to explain why that's an oversimplification.

But in any case, the kind of Islam that threatens us – a particular kind of Islam, perhaps – is not the Islam that is celebrated in great books and works of art. Unfortunately, the Muslim world has not been very productive of great books and works of art for quite a long time now. And there is a deep malaise there, which many scholars – Muslims and others – have written about. But what is clear is that, while some may seek to resolve those problems by finding a common enemy in the West, this is a delusion. Attacking the West, attacking the modern world, attacking modernity itself is not the solution to the problems of the Muslim world.

PW: Do you agree with the view that the situation we find ourselves in now is actually a reflection of a crisis in the Muslim world?

DJ: I think there's a lot of truth in that. But that's not to ignore the fact that we have an internal problem here, too: we have our own Muslim presence now, in Western Europe. That's one factor. But I'm trying not to allow this conversation to get steered down the track of thinking only about Islam and the West, because I do think we would have a big problem even if Islam didn't exist, even if there were no terrorists, even if there had been no 9/11.

I think our problems are much deeper than that. We are uniquely self-destructive, I think, as a civilisation. And I'm not here thinking so much about things like climate change – although, obviously, we do need to husband our resources; we do need to be good custodians of our physical, natural environment. Of course we do. But unfortunately, that, too, has become a pathological phenomenon of our intellectual malaise. Because the obsession with climate change and the catastrophist interpretation of environmental problems has become a sort of pseudo-religion, which is itself now quite a serious threat to the West. If some of these policies were actually implemented, life as we know it would become impossible.

PW: What do you think of the view that the environmentalist movement has a strong element of self-hatred in it?

DJ: You are absolutely right to say that. Like most of the pathologies of the modern West, it does feed on self-hatred. I mean, the environmentalists themselves are not necessarily self-haters. I think they are often rather smug and anything but self-critical. But they certainly do appeal to a public that is consumed with self-doubt and that often falls into a kind of guilt-ridden self-abnegation. This is one of the problems of the West: if we compare ourselves to the age of the Victorians, that was a self-confident, hopeful, outward-looking and very idealistic period. Ours, in the twenty-first century (not surprisingly, after such a terrible century as the twentieth century turned out to be) is a much more self-denying culture; a culture that is, perhaps, to a great extent, in denial about its own problems; which is inclined to abjure and jettison some of the best things about our history, and our art and our way of life; and which is also afflicted with a very debilitating kind of amnesia about where its basic principles and motives come from. We've sort of lost the plot.

PW: Do you think that, as James MacMillan has suggested about music, in the post-war period there has been a desire to wipe away and negate what has gone before in our culture? Was it as nihilistic as that, or was it based on offering an alternative?

DJ: Well, like so many movements, I think the modernist movement in music and art and literature began as an exciting avant-garde experimental attempt to push the boundaries, but ended up as something rather different – something, unfortunately, rather destructive. This is the kind of art that I grew up with, and in many ways still feel a very strong affinity with. But the evidence is too strong, and I can't now ignore that it has left behind again a kind of – I have to resort again to the metaphor of the wasteland or desert. If we look at present-day high culture, there are good things in it. You mention James MacMillan: he's one of a number of very fine composers and performers who deeply value the western tradition, and have continued to develop it, and are managing – very brilliantly in some cases – to combine twentieth-century impulses with much earlier ones.

So it's not all gloom and doom, by any means. But I think, if we're honest, we have to admit that this is not a great time for western culture, in almost any branch. We're much better at rediscovering the treasures of the past than we are at producing new ones. And that is not nothing – I mean, I think there is a lot to be said, if you have a small talent, for devoting that talent to the reinterpretation and rediscovery of the great works of the past, and wait for better times to come. I think, if we can survive the onslaught that we're undergoing at the moment, then we may well have a great future here in the West. And by the way, the West is itself an abstract concept. I mean, the West is wherever people who preserve these traditions happen to be. We are now scattered all over the earth. And I think we can reassemble, if you like, the jigsaw at any time.

> ...if we're honest, we have to admit that this is not a great time for western culture, in almost any branch.

But there's no question that – as a society, as a collective entity – we have rather lost our way. And certainly, almost all our political leaders seem to me to be very confused indeed. In a way, this is not surprising. If you really do attempt to throw everything into the melting pot; if you follow Nietzsche's advice to live dangerously, to attempt the transvaluation of all values, to turn everything upside down, to say that good is evil and evil is good and all the rest of it; if you abandon the standard of truth; if you take a completely relativistic view of cultures – say that all cultures are equal, none is better than any other, there is no special privileged position of our culture (for ourselves, I mean: I'm not talking about imposing our culture on other societies; I'm simply saying that, within our culture, we will not privilege the core texts, the core works, the values, the things that make our culture unique – if we simply treat them as interchangeable with any other)... Well then, I think, you must expect that ordinary people will become both confused and, in many cases, rather angry.

PW: How far do you think that the popular idea of multiculturalism was naïve and well-meaning, and how far do you think it was an attempt to devalue our culture?

DJ: Well, I don't want to go into some kind of conspiracy theory, but I think there is some truth in that old Gramscian idea of the 'long march through the institutions'. I think that when the great political revolutions that many people hoped for didn't happen – because essentially capitalism was very, very successful and really resilient, and survived all the crises, just as it will survive this one, I have no doubt at all... This was not what the Left had been led to expect. And when they realised that the political revolutions that they were hoping for and expecting were not going to happen – because essentially people were much too content with the rising standards of living that they enjoyed – then they embarked on other strategies. Take the universities: I think that's a very interesting example of the problem. Universities emerged in the West right at the dawn of our civilisation, really, in the early Middle Ages. It was actually the Church that really originally encouraged them, because it needed them. And universities have, for most of our history, been not just an ornamental, but an efficient part of our civilisation: they've been an absolutely essential training ground. And they continue to be that. I mean, universities still teach and conduct research that is immensely valuable.

But in the humanities – or, shall we say, in certain branches of the humanities – it does seem to me that the universities have lost that utility and instead have become almost a threat to the society around them. They seem to take an almost perverse delight in undermining the economic, the social, the political and the moral foundations on which they are built. To put it crudely, they are sawing off the branch on which they sit. They're almost a luxury we can't afford anymore. And I think the universities are in urgent need of reform. But I can't see that coming from any quarter at the moment. There's nothing on the horizon – certainly not in this country.

PW: Do you find yourself torn, with institutions like the BBC and the universities – perhaps we are too weak now to support these institutions, which are biting the hand that feeds them?

DJ: Well, I think what you're really asking me is: should we abolish the BBC, for example? Replace it with something else? The trouble is, it would be the same people – wouldn't it? – that would be running whatever successor institution you might want to create. I mean, there is a lot to be said for breaking up monopolies. And I think that goes for the education system, as it does for large media organisations like the BBC – well, there isn't anything like the BBC, it's *sui generis*. And its institutional structure pre-dates the cultural transformation that I've been talking about. The two don't go together very well. I mean, there was a time when, as you say, it was probably a rather impressive embodiment of the best of British culture. But those days, alas, are over.

When is it a matter of impartiality to say 'We can't possibly call these freedom fighters "terrorists"? And when does that simply become another symptom of the inability to distinguish between good and evil; or between a threat to our way of life and something we must tolerate?

There are still, of course, bits of the BBC which are very fine. And when you talk to, for example, its director-general, Mark Thompson, as I was doing the other day, you have the impression of a civilised, decent, honourable human being. And then you start to think: but how can he preside over so many terrible...excrescences? I actually said to him: 'If there is a dictatorship of relativism, aren't you the dictator?' He laughed, and he said: 'Of course I don't believe in relativism; I believe in impartiality.' Well, it's a very interesting philosophical debate: where does impartiality end and relativism begin? When is it a matter of impartiality to say 'We can't possibly call these freedom fighters "terrorists"? And when does that simply become another symptom of the inability to distinguish between good and evil; or between a threat to our way of life and something we must tolerate?

PW: As you point out, we're good at appreciating past achievements, but are going through a rather arid time culturally. There are retrospective exhibitions which draw many thousands of visitors, but this does not mean we're living in a culturally vibrant time, does it?

DJ: Well, there is a paradox there. Of course there is. In many ways, these great exhibitions are a very positive phenomenon. They're enjoyable, they do bring a huge number of people into contact with great works of art and literature and cinema and so on – whatever kind of exhibition they are. People who otherwise might not ever see these things. And that's obviously a good thing. There is, however, a downside – or perhaps many downsides. One of them is that, quite often – not always, but quite often – the curators and organisers of the exhibition have an agenda. They're not interested in just showing you the past, but in reinterpreting it, in a tendentious way, to try and prove something, which may or may not be true.

One example might be the exhibition at the moment at the V&A about the Cold War. I mean, in itself it's a good thing, because the Cold War, although it's very recent history, still is history. And there is a very young generation growing up now who have no first-hand memory of it. Even those who did live through some of it at least, as we did – as you and I did – we have only a very, very partial view of it, and our memories play us tricks, and so on. So it's great that we're being reacquainted with a chapter in our own history, not just that of our society. But if the aim of the exercise is a kind of moral equivalence – to show that the West was no better than the Soviet Union; that both sides had much to be said for them; that the only thing really wrong with Communism was the way in which it was put into practice; that there was nothing wrong with the ideas, they were very well intended, and there was much to be said for that way of life... If that's the sort of interpretation that's on offer, then it's a pretty mixed blessing, I think. Because that sort of tendentious interpretation of the past can be almost worse than actual ignorance.

I said earlier that I thought one of the great problems of our society was amnesia. And yet that amnesia can coexist with a sort of eclectic attempt to give you a little bit of knowledge about everything. You know, books about everything are very popular at the moment. And the internet is another very powerful tool, which again gives people a smattering of knowledge – a kind of illusion of knowledge. They feel that, because they have Wikipedia and other instant reference books at their fingertips, therefore they don't actually need to read very much. They don't really need to have much first-hand acquaintance with the past. They don't need to actually learn anything. Why stock your memory when it's all there in a computer? That seems to be the attitude. I find this is infiltrating our schools and universities and our museums and all those institutions that are there really to preserve the collective memory, and to keep it alive, and to re-use it. Not just keep it there as a sort of artefact in a glass case, but as something that's a living part of our culture.

Now, why is it that our schools, for instance, don't dare now to teach children about writers from long ago, who are, in their eyes, not relevant to people's lives? Why do they think they can only teach – I'm talking, I suppose, mainly about English here – why do they think they can only teach contemporary writers, who may be quite mediocre actually, and who may not exemplify the best of what's on offer even now, but certainly not of the whole history of our culture? It's easier, and superficially, I suppose, they have a sort of instant appeal. But we are producing generations of children now who, unless they're lucky enough to have parents who will make up for those deficiencies, or who somehow, by some miracle, acquire a real appetite to learn more than they're being offered in the classroom – I think these are going to be very shallow human beings, who are not going to resist when they're confronted by a threat to the West. Because they're not going to realise how precious the things are now that they have to defend. If you don't know what you're losing, then why should you fight to defend it?

PW: Do you think there's a chance that there could be people coming along who won't know about the Cold War and so on? And so, having watched the government step in during this economic crisis, could turn back to a form of Marxism? The government's stepped in on these occasions, why not all the time?

DJ: 'Jolly good idea!' they'll say, of course. Well exactly, if those who know nothing about the past are condemned to repeat all the same mistakes again... This is why *Standpoint* tries very hard to reacquaint people who may not have known anything about it in the first place with books and ideas that will help to inoculate them against making those same mistakes again. For example, we've got a series called 'Overrated and Underrated', and in our next issue there is an 'overrated' profile about Slavoj Žižek, who is a very fashionable, kind of neo-Marxist

> **If you don't know what you're losing, then why should you fight to defend it?**

philosopher who, on many campuses, is a great name to conjure with, and whose idea is startlingly original: it's called 'egalitarian terror'. Basically, he's recycling every form of left-wing egalitarianism since Robespierre, only he's adapting it to the sort of twenty-first-century lifestyle. So, for instance, he advocates, apparently, that you should be punished for using more than your fair share of energy resources – you know, off with your head if you leave your light switched on overnight, or you put out too much rubbish in your recycling sack. It's sort of at that level.

So we need to puncture those sorts of windbags. And, conversely, we have an 'underrated' one about Leszek Kolakowski – another figure from Eastern Europe, but this time a man with real achievements to his name, above all as a critic of Marxism. You know, the man who really took on, took the trouble to wade through the great Marxist theoreticians, and show what was wrong with them, and who was speaking from first-hand experience of Poland. But a man who also has tried very hard in his life to grapple with religious ideas from a sort of very postmodern perspective – someone who is fully abreast of modern thought, but who nonetheless – not, perhaps, from any very orthodox standpoint – but nonetheless tries to take seriously the spiritual heritage of our Judeo-Christian tradition. So that's somebody who might have been in danger of being forgotten. Because people think: well, the Cold War's over, why should we need people who attack Marxism? Well, we might need them again; we might need to remind ourselves why those ideas failed.

PW: What do you think of the idea that one of the problems was that there was no victory parade for the Cold War?

DJ: Yes, not that I think a victory parade would have made a huge difference in the long run. I mean, we had VE Day and VJ Day after the Second World War; and yet, unfortunately, some of those ideas carried on. But I think there's a lot in what you say. I think we – perhaps because it was a bloodless victory – we took it too easily for granted, and perhaps didn't sufficiently reflect on the true significance of what had happened. If we had, then perhaps some of the idols that continue to be worshipped in our cultural institutions would have been smashed at the same time, along with the political.

I mean, what collapsed – with the Wall – unfortunately was not so much the ideology, as the visible manifestations of it. You know, we knocked down all the statues, and things like that; but some of the ideas continue to haunt the West as well as the East. I think totalitarianism is not dead. The desire to control everything is still very much around, and it takes different forms. It can even mutate into, as it were, apparently very ancient forms. You could argue that the kind of Islam that someone like the ayatollahs and Ahmadinejad profess, is a kind of bastardised form of Marxism, combined with a very archaic form of Islam. Because they try to use all the tools that were developed under Communism and Fascism, while dressing it up in a sort of religious guise. They, in particular, are reinvigorating anti-Semitism, which is perhaps the biggest lie of all, and which actually both the Nazis and the Communists used in different ways, and which has now taken very deep root, unfortunately, in the Muslim world.

PW: You say the ideas are still drifting around. Does this account for the way that, in our culture, we do not seem to have had that much criticism of communist history? Do you think it's because of the general philosophical leaning of the people who produce our culture?

DJ: I'm sure there's a good deal that one *could* say about this, but one point I would like to make is that, if you are completely ignorant about the way in which Socialism originally emerged, and you've never read any of the texts, you don't really understand either about the way in which those ideas were then put to work on human beings – beginning with Lenin and Stalin, but then moving on to vast tracts of the world. And there are still vast tracts of the world where these ideas have their grip – I mean China, most notably. If you simply don't know any of that, then I suppose getting a kind of proper moral grip on the sheer enormity of these crimes is quite difficult. And they are simply – they're literally – mind-boggling! And I think it's a very natural human instinct to turn away from these things, and to perhaps make excuses for them.

Now why hasn't that happened with the Nazis, in the same way? Well, perhaps because this country was very directly menaced by Nazi Germany, and I think we have a folk memory about where that came from, what the nature of it was – we've made damn sure that our children are taught a great deal about Nazi Germany. Now, it is true that a lot of that teaching is bad, and sometimes tendentious, and is manipulated to prove all sorts of things that have nothing to do with it. But overall, there isn't the same level of ignorance. There is, at least, a sort of skeleton, a framework, within which you can try to explain what happened. That doesn't begin, of course, to get to grips with the scale of the Holocaust, and indeed all the other crimes that Hitler was responsible for. But it seems to me that when you get onto Communism – which, after all, was a genuinely global ideology – people simply give up. Life is too short, and they'd rather think about pleasanter things. And they'd rather believe that man isn't quite as wicked as history tends to demonstrate.

The strange thing is that even the sort of rather noble by-products of that era – I'm thinking of the dissidents, the literature that emerged from it – even that has tended to be somewhat marginalised in our culture. An educated person doesn't necessarily have to have read the important Russian writers of the twentieth century. In fact, they're much more likely to have read Tolstoy and Dostoevsky than they are to have read Bulgakov or Solzhenitsyn.

The truth is that we're still in the early stages, actually, of coming to terms with these phenomena. And I think that the societies in which they happened have not come to terms with it, either. That's another big difference. I mean, the Germans, for better or worse, have made a pretty determined attempt to come to terms with their past. It took them some time, and it's far from perfect, and so on. But they tried, at least – many of them – to be honest with themselves. There's no equivalent at all to that in Russia. And even in Eastern Europe, it's still only in the very early stages. Just this week, there was a story – wasn't there? – about Milan Kundera, and what he may have committed. I don't know about the truth of it, but it sounds as though he, too, had feet of clay. [Kundera was accused of denouncing a western intelligence agent to the Czech communist authorities in the 1950s.]

PW: Is it to do with an idea that the motives behind Nazism were clearly bad, but with Communism somehow the heart's in the right place?

DJ: Oh yes, that's clearly a very big part of it. Insofar as people know anything about Communism, they know that it was supposed to be all about sharing, and goody-goody things; whereas Nazism was all about racism, and we know that's meant to be bad. That's about as far as most people get with the moral dimension of this.

They tend to overlook, by the way, that some aspects of the Nazi project have not completely gone away. You know, the idea that you can kind of create a perfect human being, who would be a sort of 'master race'. I'm not sure that idea has completely vanished from our society. But that's a whole different story. I think the communist idea is still very present in many nooks and crannies of our culture, and the assumptions on which that was based. And to that extent, it goes against the grain to face up to the sheer horror of what actually happened: the 100 million human beings who were killed in that period.

> **I think the communist idea is still very present in many nooks and crannies of our culture, and the assumptions on which that was based.**

PW: Do you think that when we look, say, from the middle of this century, there might be more perspective on it? The Cold War ended less than 20 years ago...

DJ: It's very recent, isn't it? Think back to how little we really understood 15 years after the Second World War. People didn't talk about the Holocaust 15 years after the Second World War: they were only just beginning to fully comprehend the enormity of that crime. So I am hopeful. I think these matters will be scrutinised more intensively in the future.

116

Scene from *The English Game* by **Richard Bean**,
as performed at the Yvonne Arnaud Theatre, Guildford, 2008

Scene from *England People Very Nice* by **Richard Bean**,
National Theatre, London, 2009

Adam Smith
statue by
Alexander Stoddart,
unveiled Edinburgh, 2008

Scene from *Sons of York* by **James Graham**,
as performed at the Finborough Theatre, London, 2008

Bush. Collage by **Jonathan Yeo**, 2007

Tony Blair.
Oil on canvas by
Jonathan Yeo,
2008

The New Black
by
Sarah Maple,
as shown at the
SaLon Gallery,
London, 2008

Haram
by
Sarah Maple,
as shown at the
SaLon Gallery,
London, 2008

The Arts Politician – Lord Smith

Government and the arts...and hating Cool Britannia

Chris Smith became a Labour MP in 1983, and was made national heritage secretary when the party won its election landslide in 1997 – an appointment that also meant he became the first openly gay cabinet minister in political history. His department was renamed the Department for Culture, Media and Sport soon after. He held the post for Labour's first term, before being replaced by Tessa Jowell in 2001.

Perhaps unlike many of those who have held that particular office, Smith had a reputation for being someone with a genuine interest in, and connection with, the arts. His long interest in the performing arts began when, as a schoolboy in the Sixties, he saw Ian McKellen in *Richard II* and *Edward II*.

Chris Smith stepped down from the House of Commons at the 2005 general election and was created a life peer. He became director of the Clore Leadership Programme, an initiative aimed at helping to train and develop new leaders for Britain's cultural sector.

In 2006 he co-wrote (with Richard Koch) a book entitled *Suicide of the West*.

In 2008, he became chairman of the Environment Agency.

Peter Whittle (PW): Do you think that, compared to when you were in government, the arts are now taken more or less seriously?

Chris Smith (CS): It's something that I've thought about quite a lot both before and since. One of the things that's always disappointed me about Britain as a political culture is that we don't take the arts seriously as part of the central purpose of government. It's always regarded as something that's a bit off on the side of politics. Occasionally, you get a government that's prepared to put some investment in – that sees it as something that's worth nurturing. But it's still not part of the centrality of what they see government as about. Now, contrast that with, for example, periods in French government, when Mitterrand was president, and Jack Lang was the minister of culture, and culture was part of the central purpose of what government was all about. It was essential to the Mitterrand presidency. Take New Zealand now: when Helen Clark became prime minister of New Zealand about eight or nine years ago, she said: 'I'm going to be prime minister and I'm going to be minister for the arts, personally.' Which sent a real signal through the whole governmental system in New Zealand that this was something that the government took seriously. Now, I suspect we'll never get that in the UK. What I think I was able to do, when I was secretary of state, was certainly bring the arts up the agenda; to make a bit of a fuss; to twist the prime minister's arm – and sometimes the chancellor's arm – to put in extra investment; to see it as something that was part of what the government was about. Still, I always felt that I had a bit of an uphill struggle. But I was able to make, I think, more of a splash than perhaps had tended to be the case before or immediately afterwards. I think the job of culture secretary in government really does need to be done by someone who loves what they're doing: it's not just another government job that you do on the way to something else – it has to be something that you really feel passionately about and engaged with, if you're going to make a real difference with it.

PW: Would you say that your engagement with it was atypical?

CS: I think, yes. There are some people in the role who have had a genuine enthusiasm for it, like David Mellor, for example. He really got it, but sadly didn't last for very long, because of reasons we all know. I think both James Purnell, briefly, and now Andy Burnham have a genuine respect for the arts; but there are others who, I think, have seen it more just as another part of being a politician.

PW: There's the view that countries where culture is not at the centre of politics – like the UK or USA – are actually more artistically dynamic than somewhere like France, which, despite the apparent centrality of the arts, is far less creatively dynamic.

CS: The dynamism of French culture comes and goes. I wouldn't label it as permanently undynamic. I happen to think that currently, here in Britain, we have a period of exceptional dynamism, and engagement and flourishing of artistic endeavour. Mostly that's down to the artists, but it is also partly attributable to the additional investment that we – that I – was able to secure and to put in place.

> **I happen to think that currently, here in Britain, we have a period of exceptional dynamism, and engagement and flourishing of artistic endeavour.**

The job of government is not to create art. The job of government is to put a platform in place, on which artists can thrive. And there are some governments that set about putting a good, robust and useful platform in place. I hope that that's what I was able to help to do. There are others who set about knocking it down, and can be rather unhelpful. But I think, more specifically in relation to your question, we've never had one single model of funding and support for the arts in the UK. We've always had a mixed economy of funding: some of it coming from central government/the Arts Council; some of it coming from local government (and some cities have been fantastic over the last 20 years, some haven't); some of it coming from private patronage; some of it coming from corporate donation; some of it coming from people paying to attend performances or going to exhibitions. And we haven't had the huge reliance, for example, that you have had to a large extent in Germany, on state and regional funding. And you haven't had the huge and exclusive reliance on private donations that you have in the United States. We've tried to combine all of these elements, and I think that's helped to keep us going – through ups and downs of government commitment, through ups and downs of economic success, through ups and downs of private giving.

PW: The UK and US seem to have thriving popular cultures, compared to other countries in Europe, and yet also seem to produce people who become known worldwide in the high arts. Why do you think that might be? Is it just a language thing?

CS: I think why British popular culture and (what one might call) British 'high culture' — why they are both successful and flourishing... I think part of the reason, yes, is the English language, which reaches much more easily worldwide than any other language. This is an accident of history which is incredibly useful to us. Secondly, it is due to a number of key institutions which themselves bridge the divide – the most obvious of which is the BBC.

Take, for example, the under-sung role of Radio1 in the development and support of popular music. If you're a young group creating new music in the US, there is no nationwide vehicle by which you reach an audience. Here in the UK there is. Part of the reason for the existence of Radio 1 is that it doesn't just play the things that people are familiar with. It breaks new ground, and it gives an opportunity to new groups coming into the popular music genre – it gives them the opportunity to reach a big audience. And we should never underestimate the importance of that. But exactly the same goes across the whole of the rest of what the BBC does.

So, having a number of key cultural institutions that carry respect and have huge audiences, but are also prepared to do new things, is part of the reason. And I think the other element I'd put into the picture is: never forget the importance that traditional and 'high' culture have for the success of popular culture. If, for example, we didn't have a really vibrant regional theatre in the UK, enabling people who are actors, who are stage designers, who are lighting directors, who are artistic directors – enabling them to cut their teeth, to learn their craft, to experience being in front of an audience, to create good work but to do it at a place near them... If we didn't have that, we wouldn't have that area of engagement feeding through into the great national companies, like the National Theatre and the Royal Shakespeare Company. And if we didn't have that, we wouldn't have the people feeding through into film and television work, using the skills that they've developed in a stage setting.

You could say exactly the same about music, and the way in which the music training that people get at school and at college feeds through into their ability to become popular music successes. The links between high culture and popular culture are really rather important. And if we didn't have the success and the investment in high culture and traditional culture, I don't think we would have anything like the same vibrancy of popular culture that we do.

PW: The director Richard Eyre has talked of his fear of what he called a 'cultural apartheid' in this country. Do you agree with that?

I worry particularly about what one might call the celebrity fascination and the sort of 'tabloidisation' of the range of cultural experiences which young people are exposed to...

CS: I worry about it, as a danger. And it's one of the reasons why I helped to put what we called 'creative partnerships' in place – linking schools, especially in particularly deprived areas, with artistic organisations, performers and creators, in order to try and raise the excitement of cultural experience for kids who simply didn't have it. And I think we need a lot more of that – both because it helps kids develop the joy of cultural appreciation, but also because it helps to create good schools and a good atmosphere and a good learning environment, in a whole other kind of way.

So yes, I worry about it. And I worry particularly about what one might call the celebrity fascination and the sort of 'tabloidisation' of the range of cultural experiences which young people are exposed to, growing up. And I think it's the duty of schools and broadcasters, of artistic organisations and artists, to try as best they can to broaden the range of experience that they offer to kids. Because that's the way in which you'll overcome some of this problem. I don't think we're in a bad place. So I'm not sure I would agree with Richard Eyre entirely, but there is always a danger that we might head there.

PW: But is it not also a theoretical thing – that cultural relativism has effectively cut certain areas off from people? If people are told that Superman is just as good as Stravinsky, then why should they bother with Stravinsky?

CS: And of course Superman is not as good as Stravinsky. I got into terrible trouble about a year into being culture secretary, because I was asked the age-old question about, you know, is Bob Dylan as good as Keats? And

I said yes, because actually I think he is – he's a great poet, Bob Dylan. Keats was a great poet; that doesn't mean I believe in relativism. I do think we need to hold fast to the fact that some cultural experiences are going to be more fulfilling, more emotive, more intellectually stimulating and challenging than others. There are some pieces of poetry that are completely wonderful and spell-binding, and there are others that aren't.

We need to recognise that there are values and standards which we need to apply. But what we need to do is give kids, people growing up, the tools – the intellectual, the emotional, the artistic tools – to be able to make their own judgements about that. You are on relatively safe ground saying that Keats is a great poet. You are on probably less safe ground to say that Robert Southey is a great poet – there are some bits of Southey which are terrific, there are some which aren't quite so good. But giving kids, people growing up, the necessary intellectual tools to make those discriminating judgements for themselves is, I think, the important thing.

PW: The singer Ian Bostridge recently wrote that the need people once had to even *pretend* to understand high art – however easily mockable that social impulse might have been – is disappearing. He said that such an impulse at least showed that people felt that an aspiration towards understanding was important, if one wanted to be considered a well-rounded, educated person.

CS: It's a really interesting argument, and I find myself a bit divided about it. I think there is a role for saying to kids particularly: there are some things which are so good, which are so profound, which are so worth experiencing, that we're really going to make you do this. And OK, at the end of it you may still turn round and say: 'Look, I don't get this stuff.' And that's your right. But to reject it without at least giving it a chance is something that we're not going to allow you to do.

I would be horrified if we didn't make sure that every kid growing up in the UK experienced Shakespeare during the course of their education. Because, to allow them not to – that potentially deprives them of an enormous source of inspiration and intellectual wealth. Now, not every kid will get Shakespeare. Not every kid will like Shakespeare. But at least we have to make sure that we give them the chance, and give them the chance in a way that's likely to appeal to them – actually seeing it on the stage, and experiencing it. Not just sitting at a classroom desk and reading the text, but actually getting absorbed by the excitement of it.

PW: Do you think that's happening less?

> **I would be horrified if we didn't make sure that every kid growing up in the UK experienced Shakespeare during the course of their education.**

121

CS: I suspect it's happening a bit less. We need to try and make sure that some of this incredible richness that we have – and it's particularly in terms of drama and literature, because we have such a rich heritage of this in the UK – we have to make sure that it is part of the accepted norm of educational experience.

PW: The approach of some people working in the arts bureaucracies seems to be that, for example, to get more ethnic minorities involved in the arts there should simply be more hip-hop festivals alongside *La Bohème*.

CS: It doesn't just happen in relation to ethnicity. I think it happens more broadly in terms of – in inverted commas – 'youth culture'. I had a fascinating conversation quite recently with a wonderful guy called Vic Ecclestone, who started life as a teacher in Bristol. And he – on this really hard-bitten, deprived, huge council estate in south Bristol – he put together a dance programme for the kids on the estate, which was enormously successful. It ended up with the creation of a thing called the Hartcliffe Boys Dance Company – it completely transformed the lives of the kids who were engaged in it, but also transformed the life of the estate. And he said to me that the traditional view of the arts Establishment is that, if you're putting something on for kids in a deprived estate, what you're going to do is do courses on DJ-ing for them. And he said: if that's the level of aspiration that you put in front of the kids, that's what they're going to respond to.

But he said: what we decided to do was to sit these kids down and talk to them about the myth of Prometheus. And get them writing a dance opera about the Prometheus myth. And they completely got it. They were completely absorbed by it. They produced this fantastic piece of work, which they created themselves and they performed – it was a huge success. And he said: if you set their sights high, that's what they'll respond to as well. And what you shouldn't do is go into working in the field of arts with kids – you mustn't go in with low expectations, because then you'll get low outcomes. Go in with high expectations, high aspirations. Set their horizons really high, and they'll respond to it.

PW: When you were secretary of state, did you find that kind of low expectation level among people who ran arts organisations?

CS: In some bits of the arts Establishment and the arts funding system – yes. And, of course, you're not going to get every kid from a council estate responding well to a bit of ancient mythology and the chance to create an opera. But you're going to get quite a number who're really going to get turned on by it.

PW: You started off as minister during that 'Cool Britannia' era. How would you characterise the last decade in the arts?

122

CS: First a caveat, which is that I absolutely hated 'Cool Britannia'. In fact, I could show you four press releases issued by Virginia Bottomley when she was secretary of state, praising the notion of 'Cool Britannia'. But it became identified with Blair and the '97 election and so on. Totally unfairly.

How would I characterise things? Well, first of all, what I tried to do, as secretary of state, was to put in place four overarching themes for what government and culture – and the relationship between the two – were trying to achieve. The first of these was excellence, the second was access, the third was education, and the fourth was the creative economy. And they all sort of interlink: the making sure that we were stimulating and funding and nurturing real excellence in a whole range of different cultural fields; making sure that as many people as possible had the opportunity to experience it; making sure that we were binding in cultural experience to the education system, as best we possibly could; and seeing the importance of creative endeavour for economic success, as well as for aesthetic success. And I think, broadly speaking, that's not a bad encapsulation of what we were trying to do.

> **I absolutely hated 'Cool Britannia'.**

Now, what have the successes been, and what have the dangers been? The downside first: I think there has been, in some ways – with things like the onset of celebrity, the development of reality television, the obsession with lifestyle choices – I think there have been some elements of the indefinables of lifestyle and culture that have taken us away from seriousness and real fulfilment. But the other side of the coin is much more positive: if you look across virtually every single cultural sector, there is huge strength, there is enormous success, there's a lot of new work, new initiative, excitement, real success going on. That's certainly true in London, but it's true in a whole range of other cities, as well. It's not just confined to the capital. There are more people going to cultural events and institutions and experiences than for decades. And one of the things I'm really proud of is the way in which restoring free admission to the national museums and galleries has been an overwhelming success, in terms of the number of people that have taken advantage of it. And you can see the same thing happening with the £10 season at the National Theatre, and a whole range of other initiatives as well. So, in terms of the vibrancy of cultural life and activity – in terms of the number of people who are experiencing it – I think that there's been a lot of real success. If I weigh it all in the balance, I think the positives enormously outweigh the negatives.

PW: Looking at the broader picture, the book that you wrote, *Suicide of the West*, is a little pessimistic...

CS: Yes, although, actually, the ultimate conclusion is that we're in danger of going down the wrong road, but there's every opportunity for us to choose the right way.

PW: It was all about loss of confidence, wasn't it?

CS: Loss of confidence, loss of optimism, loss of a sense of the way in which the individual relates with society, and so on.

PW: Has your view changed since you wrote the book?

CS: I think, culturally, we're probably stronger than we were three or four years ago. Politically and ideologically, I'm not sure we are.

> I think, culturally, we're probably stronger than we were three or four years ago. Politically and ideologically, I'm not sure we are.

PW: If there were to be a Dome in 2010, how would it be different?

CS: Well, remember that I tried to stop us going ahead with the Dome. It was the first question I asked the prime minister when he appointed me as culture secretary: 'Do we have to go ahead with the Dome?' And I didn't get the answer I wanted. And I was always of the view that, if we were going to do something that was going to be, effectively, a large-scale exhibition experience, it needed to have a much more serious content to it than what we ended up with.

Would it be possible to create something that did? That was genuinely thought-provoking and intellectually stimulating, and looked at where we'd come from and where we're going to? It might be. But I don't think government is the right body to do it. And I don't think that trying to do it in the course of three or four years, with an absolute deadline, is the right way to go about it, either. One of the wonderful things that I do at the moment – that I'm able to do now I'm no longer secretary of state – is I chair the Wordsworth Trust, which is based up in Grasmere and holds something like 95 per cent of all Wordsworth's papers and manuscripts. It has a huge collection of Romantic material, books, papers, paintings, drawings, watercolours, and also has a very vibrant contemporary poetry programme – poetry readings through the whole of the summer, poets in residence, helping to stimulate and, in some cases, publish new poetry work. But it's done in the context of the setting of some of the greatest poetry of the past. And what I think that's able to do is to link the very best of the past with the best of the contemporary, in a very exciting way. And that's where I think we need to try and get to now. Whether it's possible to do on a huge scale, I don't

> I tried to stop us going ahead with the Dome. It was the first question I asked the prime minister when he appointed me as culture secretary: 'Do we have to go ahead with the Dome?' And I didn't get the answer I wanted.

know. But in thinking about the traditions, the provenance, where our cultural strengths come from as a country – we should not ignore those traditions, but we shouldn't just get absorbed by the traditions of the past. We need to relate it always to the new and the contemporary.

PW: There is a dialogue now about what Britishness is, and I wonder: could we be more confident about that now? The Dome was all about a corporate nothingness, really.

CS: The problem with the Dome was that it was a building in search of a content – and the content was flimsy. But just down the river, Tate Modern demonstrated that you can have a content, find the right building, and then match the two very successfully.

125

The Comedian – Reginald D Hunter

What's really edgy

Called by the *Sunday Times* 'one of the most brilliantly unpredictable comics in the country', Reginald D Hunter is originally from Georgia, USA. He studied at RADA, and performed his first stand-up as a 'dare'. Since then, he has achieved considerable success on the comedy circuit, being nominated three times in succession for the Perrier Award. After his successful debut show, 'I Said What I Said', at the 2001 Edinburgh Festival, he went on to further critical acclaim with his 2003 show, 'White Woman', and then, in 2004, 'A Mystery Wrapped in a Nigga'.

His approach to some of the most contentious issues of contemporary society has occasionally upset liberal commentators. His show, 'Reginald D Hunter: Pride & Prejudice & Niggas' attracted some criticism, and the poster was banned from the London Underground on account of the word 'Niggas'. The journalist Johann Hari has called him 'a black Bernard Manning'.

The success of his live shows has meant that he has become increasingly well-known on television, featuring in such programmes as Channel 5's *Comedy Store Stand-up* and the BBC's *Have I Got News for You*.

Peter Whittle (PW): Looking at comedy in this country, what do you think it tells us about the general culture at the moment?

Reginald D Hunter (RH): What comes to mind right away is the newer comics that are coming now – the comics that are proliferating, not just in stand-up but on television: silly, surreal, that sort of slacker, nerdish, do-nothing-but-good-hearted-guy kind of comedy. It implies that there's still a large degree of escapism. Comedy doesn't have that political edge that it enjoys every 10 years or so. We're kind of laughing at the same things still. And I think, particularly in this culture we live in, where we don't want to offend anybody – especially since the terrorist conflict – we're doubly keen not to offend anyone. Especially coming after George Bush's example of eight years! Everyone is going for the diplomatic badge these days. I think comedy is reflecting the fear of the culture. I think that comics are afraid to fail, afraid to innovate – which means you do what you've already seen.

Also, too, I think that women have more power in western culture than they've ever had in the history of the world – rightly. But when I think of the fear of offending, I think primarily of the fear of offending *women*. In my experience in comedy clubs, they tend to be the more easily offended, the more self-righteous about what is and is not funny. Even if they're in a room full of 299 other people who are laughing. And I think women as a whole – this is a generalisation, as it refers to the state of comedy – I think women are a little clumsy with their power right now. Won't always be so – in 15 or 20 years, they'll be chilled out a little bit. But now it's relatively new to them. So, I hope I answered that question.

PW: The received wisdom is that women have loosened up a bit since the more dogmatic days of feminism, but you say they're clumsy with their power. How do you mean?

RH: See, that's the thing, though: lots of women don't identify with feminism now. In fact, it has an unpleasant connotation for them. They don't want to be associated with that, although they still fervently believe in some of the tenets of feminism. There are lots of women who will accuse someone of being sexist or misogynist, and they don't really know the definition of the word; they simply know the *connotation* of the word. The same is true of a lot of black folks who accuse white folks of being racist, when actually the person they're talking about might just have been being prejudiced. A lot of people don't know the definitions of words, and so they use them loosely. And that's what I mean by, you know, women being clumsy with their power. I have this joke, where I say: 'Where I come from, our definition of racism is anything that white people do that you don't like.' For a lot of women, sexism is anything a man does that they don't like.

> I have this joke, where I say: 'Where I come from, our definition of racism is anything that white people do that you don't like.' For a lot of women, sexism is anything a man does that they don't like.

PW: You've been accused of that yourself, haven't you?

RH: True. Well, I've heard of some women's criticisms of me. After talking with these people, and reading some of their emails and posts and stuff, I'm convinced that many of them don't know. I don't believe anyone could listen to what I was saying – genuinely listen to what I was saying – and come away thinking that I was sexist or misogynist. Unless, as usually happens in the clubs, people are drinking. Sometimes women are in groups. They feel empowered. They're batteries for each other. And a guy like me – big, tall, black, masculine – says one or two buzz words that set them off thinking, and I may say these buzz words without what they perceive to be the proper reverence. To them, that is being sexist.

I slightly joke about it now, but I'm kind of half-and-half about it. I believe feminism, in its original concept, was very much about equality – I've got no problem with that. But like Islam, it broke off into splinter groups. And these splinter groups became less concerned about equality, and seemingly more concerned about control. I wonder if it's some splinter feminist plot to make men more feminine. I think this is happening. I think men have to care a lot more about things that they didn't have to care about before. They have to care about how their woman feels, and what she says. They care about their children – what they're saying, what they're feeling. They've got to care about sounding racist or homophobic, etc.

A lot of men – western men who've been educated – suffer from what I call 'man-guilt'. I suffer from it, too. I was raised, you know – my mum and five sisters and I grew up hearing the issues that they face, and how terrible my father was, and how terrible these men were. And I resolved not to be like that – I'm going to be better than that, I'm going to listen to my woman, I'm going to be more generous, I'm going to be more helpful around the house. Feeling this man-guilt, even though I've never punched a woman in the face, I've never raped one, I've never prevented one from getting a low-cost business loan...

It's not too dissimilar from white-guilt. And it's an unreasonable guilt, I think – the number of white people I know who feel guilty about the state of the world as it pertains to their race, and what their role is in it. And I'm not trying to discourage that concern, or their generosity of spirit, but I know lots of white people who seem to be embarrassed about white people and white European history – who have an embarrassment about it. They look at themselves as the descendants of imperialists, those who profited from imperialism. And while guilt can be used to propel people in, I guess, a positive direction, it looks ultimately destructive to me. Because there's always the next step: I know white people who used to feel guilty, and what they go back to after that is something harder, coarser, less forgiving.

PW: It seems that there are things comedy can talk about and things it can't – for example, the environment. Even people who see themselves as cutting edge say much the same things as they expect their audience to believe. Do you think that's a fair assessment?

RH: I do think that's fair. I think one of the killers for stand-up comedians, across the board, is a desire to be liked. If that becomes your primary focus – and it's hard for it not to be – then it pulls your teeth, in a way: it makes you unwilling to be disagreed with. And a lot of comics are unwilling to be disagreed with. I mean, who wants to be disliked? It is an unpleasant thing. Especially if you are saying something that is close to your heart, or you feel that in some way epitomises you. To have that attacked feels like having yourself attacked. So the desire to be liked pulls the teeth of stand-up. And you have to walk a really odd line: you have to walk the line between doing those things in a way that is likeable, while at the same time not being over-concerned about being liked. And that's a tough walk.

PW: When would you say was the last 'political' stage of comedy?

RH: Usually what happens is you get four or five comics doing the same type of thing, which is different than the thing that's most recently been done. That's more or less called a 'movement'. And I think every great stand-up really hurts stand-up as a whole, in a way, because he encourages a lot of copies, fakes – even very competent fakes. So I think Jerry Seinfeld, who I think is an exceptional comedian, probably ruined a couple of generations of stand-ups; Richard Pryor ruined about four or five generations of black stand-ups; Bill Hicks is still ruining stand-ups.

The whole comedy concept of 'not much happens', and over-analysing the mundane and the trivial, which is what Seinfeld sort of does... I mean, I see a lot of the young white kids who are coming out now, particularly the ones who went to university, expounding and getting really upset over, you know, that fourth wheel on a shopping cart – and being rewarded for that.

But it's also one of those things, too, where, if you can appear passionate about something, no matter how trivial your argument is, or how wrong your argument is, people enjoy the passion. Because we live in a culture that doesn't encourage passion. I think one of the reasons Tony Blair was able to pull off the whole Iraq thing was that he made all those impassioned speeches, both on TV and radio. And people who were in the know – people whose facts were different than Tony Blair's, who... they felt like they were sure of their facts – they looked at Tony and they were like: 'Oh, but he seems like he really knows what he's talking about. It sounds really important, sounds imperative to go. What my facts tell me about Iraq say no, but...'

PW: It seems that there's a cruelty now about some comedy. Do you think that's true?

RH: I think that's a basic element of stand-up that's fairly unchangeable. I think stand-up comedy is basically complaint: it is a complaint art form. It's Blues without the music. An achievement that stand-up is on the verge of having – and it's an odd achievement – but stand-up has nearly made subjects like rape and paedophilia hack [hackneyed – ed.]. We're on the verge of making that hack. And we've done that in about five years.

And I also think that when you look at stand-up, you are looking at where the next stand-up is at. Stand-ups who haven't changed their jokes in five or six years – they usually have some form of arrested development in their lives. You are an exaggerated version of yourself on stage. And I think our culture – I think western culture – is in a really weird bind, especially as it relates sexually, because a lot of stand-up comedy is sexual, maybe overly so. But on the one hand, you know, we have these social mores – we still have the influence of the Church, even if it's the Church from a century or two ago – that, you know, govern how we feel and think about sex. But at the same time, we have this pull, by the media and PR people, who try to sell us things through sex, and try to imply that our personal fulfilment will come through sexual encounters. And it's the implication that whatever you have, whatever you're doing, is imperfect. That's the problem with porn: no matter who you're married to, or who you're actually having sex with, you're not having sex with this. So there's a pull going on there. If you're getting pulled too much in two different directions, I think the result is inertia. And I think there's a slight bit of inertia that's set in. There's an unwillingness to be openly sexual, or completely not sexual on stage.

And so many people saying the same things about sex! The inability to get laid, or the dissatisfaction in their relationships. I mean, there used to be a time when women used to go on stage and talk about periods, and how crap men are. And now they just talk about not being able to get laid! And you're looking at usually physically attractive people, so what's the problem there? And many of those people have boyfriends or husbands, but they're still doing the shtick about not getting laid. So that implies that there's some dissatisfaction along the line somewhere. Most people – I've read a government study that said that some high number – like 70 per cent of people – believe that other people are having a better sex life than them. Most people seem to, in fact, believe that others are. I was talking about this with my lady the other day – the dissatisfaction that seems to be cultivated. Coco Chanel said in 1922 that the more we can make women dissatisfied with themselves…

PW: But what do you think all of this means? The subject of not being able to get laid: that seems like a traditional subject for comedy.

RH: But the thing is, though, you *can* get laid. That's the thing. Comedy is about dissatisfaction, and that's why comedians are unhappy. It's not that they're just naturally depressive, but stand-up comedy is about complaint and it's about dissatisfaction. And people want to stay good. They want to stay on top. So the best way to do that on stage is to stay in that area of your life where you are dissatisfied, even if the things in your life don't really reflect that: you've got a big house, nice kids, all that stuff there, all the things people are supposed to want. I believe, personally, that the second you see an established stand-up go on stage and say 'Let me tell you about this funny thing my kid said' – your heart sinks, because it doesn't have any edge anymore.

PW: A while ago – and it became a bit of a cliché – one would hear this idea that comedy was the new rock and roll...

RH: Somebody said that to me last night, as if it was being said for the first time.

PW: Do you think it's true? That for one generation comedy now has the political resonance that pop music lacks?

RH: Partly because of the generation doing it, but partly because of the generation that's going to see it. I mean, I'll be 40 next year, and I look at the audience, and they're a lot younger now. I see a lot of these girls – their skin all orange, Sixties bouffant kind of haircuts. And the guys trying to look like some guy out of *FHM*. And they look rudderless. They look like, you know: 'What do we do?' They look like they really want to know what to do.

> I look at the audience, and they're a lot younger now. I see a lot of these girls – their skin all orange, Sixties bouffant kind of haircuts. And the guys trying to look like some guy out of *FHM*. And they look rudderless. They look like, you know: 'What do we do?'

What they seem to be doing is mimicking each other. Or there seems to be a factory that produces this kind of people. And it is a factory mentality. Stand-ups – and the audience that goes to see them now, I think – have far fewer original ideas than they believe they do. What's that phrase? That term you use, for when you believe everything that everyone else believes, but you think it's just you...? Everyone has shared perceptions. And our shared perceptions are shaped by reading and watching the same things. It's become homogenised in a way. I'm not controversial, but I seem so, compared to who I'm around.

PW: Some commentators have attacked the things you've said on stage. Are you regarded in a certain way by the comedy community?

RH: The comedy community don't care as long as you get laughs and people come to see your shows. The thing I've learned is that you can say anything – you can, you really can! We're not in a third-world country. You're not likely to be shot. Comics who talk about what they 'can't' do on stage – they're talking about their own limitations. I used to have white comics tell me all the time: 'You get away with saying certain things because you're black, or you're American, or you have a deep voice.' And the reality is: I get away with saying what I'm saying because I'm willing to deal with the consequences of what I say.

PW: You mean they're just frightened?

RH: Yes, it's like the BBC, for instance. The BBC seems to not programme more aggressively for fear of getting letters from white people in the Home Counties. So what is perceived to be trouble is what's at issue. Yes, there will sometimes – there'll be two or three white women who've read a couple of books and are quite liberal in their point of view who want to tell me where the cold wind blows afterwards. But that's not trouble. Johann Hari wrote something not well thought-out about me in a newspaper – but that's not trouble.

PW: Real trouble would be some kind of violence?

RH: Yes, being censored. Or losing work. Or venues not booking you. That's trouble. It's a cultural thing. When British people tell me: 'Oh man, I got a real telling off for coming in late' – where I come from, a telling off means yelling into somebody's face, just being really dressed down verbally. But here, being told off simply means being chastised. What they call trouble is not trouble.

PW: What do you think of this view that, for a culture to be at one, it needs a set of shared references that everyone will get, and somehow that's been lost?

RH: I think society is fragmented. However, that argument presumes that society's fragmented to an extreme that I don't believe it is. I mean, we generally speak English here – generally, still. Generally still have money issues, marital relationships, sexual issues, we're honest with the politics of the country. I don't buy into that so much – I don't buy into the whole notion that there's not enough of a unifying force to have a great – or several great – stand-ups. It's simply not true. And you can look at the Barack Obama thing – how unifying he's been in a lot of ways, a lot of the things that he's been saying. And though it's not stand-up, he's managed to reach people that you traditionally would think he wouldn't be able to reach.

PW: Comedians now seem to be, as it were, working round the edges. We don't have big figures that can command a Saturday-night show anymore.

RH: It's also the times. The best stand-up – the best stand-up comedy – is about dissatisfaction. It is that thing of Groucho Marx not wanting to be a member of any club that would have him as a member. The best stand-ups occupy the place of outsiders. And as an outsider, you're more at liberty, at ease, to comment. I mean, I probably comment here in England in a way that I would not have been able to – to this point – in America, being somewhat complicit in America.

I think that television wants to appear innovative. But it wants to appear innovative while doing the same old things. And there's not an encouragement of a new style. I mean, you could say of Russell Brand that, apart from the comedy, just the physical aspect of what he does is a bit Eddie Izzard-esque. It's something that British culture, humour-wise, seems to dig about men that are a bit effeminate, or men dressed in drag. There's something British folks seem to find inherently really cool about that.

PW: Do you think that American comedy is less inhibited, less politically correct, than British comedy?

RH: I think it's more crass; I think it's slicker; I think in some ways it's less mature. We have to remember that America is Britain's younger brother. So America is still impressed with things like religion, in a way that Britain is pretty near over. I mean, you've had the religious wars over here. For centuries, you've had the Irish, the Protestants and the Catholics. It's still quite new to us. American stand-ups have the reputation of being quite slick – fairly deserved; and British stand-ups, in my reckoning, are usually a lot cleverer. But there are a lot of British stand-ups who feel like the jokes alone should be enough, so you should respect the cleverness of this joke. And there is a respect for it, but clever doesn't always make you laugh. Clever makes you go 'hmmm'.

I think that in American stand-up there is a greater sense of consequence of what you say, because we are a gun-toting culture. We are a more violent culture. We are a more reactionary culture. I've started to really come round to this notion of British repression: I think British repression is an extremity, but I think it exists for a reason. I think somewhere along the lines, probably around the Victorian era, those people worked out that emotions unchecked are quite messy. It's only when I watch American TV shows with my British fans, and see them just writhe in pain when they

> **I heard it said that left-wing politics are the convenience of those who haven't been punched in the mouth yet.**

look at Americans being over-sincere – I've got it now! I see somebody being over-sincere and I'm like: 'Steady on!' But remembering growing up, and the number of crass, just unkind, unpleasant things that were said in my community, even in my house – we could have done with a bit more British repression, when I look back at it.

So with that said, I think that America has garnered a reputation for being quite reactionary. In this country, you can say things like 'Fuck the flag', 'Damn the Queen', 'To hell with the prime minister'. But in America, no. There are people who get really worked up if you don't feel the way they do.

PW: Do you think that the comedy world is a particularly left-wing one?

RH: I think it's left wing in the way that young people are often left wing – before they get a job, and pay taxes and have kids. I think it's conveniently left wing. A lot of my friends who would make left-wing noises – since they've got a mortgage and all that, they're not left wing no more. I heard it said that left-wing politics are the convenience of those who haven't been punched in the mouth yet.

PW: Where do you think comedy is going to go? What would you call a right-wing comic?

RH: A working men's club comic?

PW: Exactly, a traditional working man's comic. It seems to me that that's one group of people who don't have much to laugh at.

RH: Well, see, the thing is: it seems like right-wing or conservative politics is not conducive to humour. There have been several films that the Right have tried to make in America. Jerry Zucker, who made the *Airplane* movies, has made one recently, and it's a piss-take on Michael Moore. And I saw some clips and just – it's barely forgivable. A conservative point of view typically, particularly from working-class people, often seems to be the passionate view of people who are under-informed. It seems to be people who are only aware of how the world affects people like them. That's how it appears, with working-class people who are conservative and right wing. Usually, a liberal point of view seems to have the connotation of having something more towards a world view, or at least a world beyond your immediate circumstances. There has yet to be, in the last 15–20 years, with the possible exception of maybe Jim Davidson, a conservative comic who does comedy that's just funny; that doesn't, somewhere along the way, make you wince by its depiction of some minority, or women. I can't imagine a comic like Jim Davidson making any of my friends from Hampstead Heath feel proud to be British.

PW: Do you think there are some things you can say that will be listened to and accepted, but if it was a white guy saying them would cause hostility in an audience?

RH: I think you get into a real world of hurt when you start trying to ask what should be, as it relates to people's feelings. I think that when Jimmy Carr does jokes about minorities or about women, it's sort of like if Americans did jokes about Canadians, or English people did jokes about the Welsh, or Australians did jokes about Kiwis. It has an element of a bigger person beating up a smaller person. And we don't like bullies. And so Jimmy Carr – physically, verbally – represents that class of people in Britain who will be OK. So, for him to – and this is how my friends explain it, or how I perceive it – for him to make jokes about minorities or women, it's like a bully knocking around a smaller person. Whereas, if somebody's black or a woman, you can say stuff about white people, you know, in moderation; and it's perceived as the little man getting a little of his own back.

PW: Where do you see it going? You said we might have another wave – what do you think it will be?

RH: Well, everything seems to really, really respond to the political times. The Bush years seemed to produce a lot of films – two types of films: paranoia films – paranoia about the government, paranoia about aliens and stuff like that; and they also produced – sooner than it normally would have taken – they produced another wave of superhero films, which is sort of a daddy wish-list: we wish there was this one guy in a cape who would just come fix this shit, instead of this quagmire that no one seems to quite know what to do about. So, this new wave – this new political wave – seems to be more about reasonableness. And that's a response to the Bush years, as well.

I think, comedically, for years it was pseudo-intellectual political outrage. Because there were lots of comics that would do stand-up, political stand-up, from just reading the headlines. I think the next wave – it depends on the slackers, it depends on the Josie Longs, and the Mark Watsons. It depends on what happens to them in their late twenties and early thirties. How the slackers (for lack of a better word), how they will deal with getting pregnant and having mortgages and that sort of thing. A major component of film, and even stand-up, seems to be about 'the hopeless man', the Simon Pegg, the guy who's a bit of a loser. But, you know, he's cute enough, and he's affable enough, harmless enough, that – you know, by golly he gets the girl in the end!

PW: How long will it be before there are jokes made about Obama?

RH: It depends. You remember a few months ago, when there was this big – well, minor – uproar in the States about this *New Yorker* cover, where Obama and his wife were depicted... The reason it's difficult to make jokes about Obama, and it will be difficult to make jokes about Obama, is because he's not generally perceived yet as being Establishment. Once he becomes perceived as Establishment, then it's bombs away. So, however long that takes.

Quite coincidentally it was during the week in which this interview took place that there occurred the now infamous incident that resulted in the three-month suspension from the BBC of the TV host Jonathan Ross. Ross and the comedian Russell Brand came under intense media fire for a series of phone calls made from Radio 2 to the home of the actor Andrew Sachs, the contents of which were broadcast.

The prank was universally branded as tasteless in the extreme, and resulted in tens of thousands of complaints to the BBC. Both Ross and Brand apologised, and Brand resigned. Following his suspension, Ross resumed his television chat show in January 2009.

I went back to Reginald after the controversy had died down to hear his thoughts.

PW: As a comedian yourself, do you think that what happened after the Ross–Brand affair was significant?

RH: I do think it was a warning shot across the bows for comedians. It's encouraged conservatism in comedy. As for the complaints, the whole 'X Factor' mentality has given people the idea that their opinions matter more than they do. I think it's a manufactured controversy.

It's meant that those who have a conservative approach to comedy – those people who talk about comedy being better in the days of Tommy Cooper, etc. – have become more entrenched in their view. I've heard Britain described as a post-Christian society, but there is still something there which requires retribution.

...a child can swear. A child can make jokes about faeces.

PW: Do you think what Ross and Brand did was indeed 'edgy'?

RH: No. Some comics think that 'edgy' means swearing, or something sexual. Real edginess is saying to an audience: 'However weird this is, it may well be true.' But a child can swear. A child can make jokes about faeces. 🖊

136

The Cultural Advisor –
Munira Mirza

Culture in the capital in the post-Livingstone era

Munira Mirza was appointed 'Director of Arts, Culture and Creative Industries Policy' in 2008 by the new mayor of London, Boris Johnson.

A journalist, lecturer and policy researcher, she has written and broadcast extensively about race, culture and identity, appearing on BBC 2's *Newsnight*, BBC Radio 4's *Today* programme, and in the *Guardian* and the *Daily Mail*. In 2005, she presented the BBC Radio 4 series, *The Business of Race.*

She was co-author of the Policy Exchange report *Living Apart Together: British Muslims and the Paradox of Multiculturalism*, and edited a collection of essays entitled *Culture Vultures: Is UK Arts Policy Damaging the Arts?* – also for Policy Exchange. She is a founding member of the Manifesto Club, whose tagline is 'History is Still Young'.

Peter Whittle (PW): There is a perception that there's been a difference in cultural tone under Boris Johnson than under Ken Livingstone. Has there been a desire to change the cultural tone?

Munira Mirza (MM): During the eight years of Ken's mayoralty, he and his officials talked about the importance of culture in the capital in the context of London's global profile and the contribution the arts can make to the economy and to broader society. I would certainly accept that an element of that is true. It is the case that large numbers of people visit London, live in London, study in London and set up businesses in London because of its status as a cultural city; possibly the most important cultural city in the world today.

However, there are very real points of difference between us and Ken as well. The previous mayor's office placed enormous emphasis on culture in the context of specific identities. Boris's administration, while recognising that cultures emerge from particular communities – ethnic, geographical, linguistic, socio-economic, whatever – also believes, both as an article of faith and as a matter of empirical observation, that culture can transcend such identities. That single point makes a huge difference to how you think about culture in society: what you value and, crucially, where you think public funding should go.

In my opinion, there are lots of areas, in both the artistic and geographical sense, that have been neglected in London. They have fallen through the cracks or not been seen as a political priority. One of the issues I've been working on since I began my current role is music education. It's been not so much *overlooked* – because significant work *has* been done on music education and it has received funding, particularly from central government – as suffered from a lack of clear, city-wide coordination and political championing, especially when it comes to instrument tuition. And certain types of music have – at least in the recent past – been regarded as more relevant to some pupils than to others. I'm particularly thinking of the way that people from certain socio-economic and ethnic backgrounds have been assumed to have no interest in, or aptitude for, classical music.

What I want – and what the mayor wants – is that in the next few years more children in London will have the opportunity to learn an instrument: so it's affordable and they have access to a range of music traditions. So it's not just a case of kids in inner cities getting hip-hop or urban music because that's seen as the only thing they'll be interested in. It needs to be broader than that. They should also have a chance to understand, hear and enjoy classical music.

PW: Do you think that was a deliberate approach – almost trying to maintain a kind of cultural segregation?

MM: I don't believe it was necessarily a deliberate act of policy, although I can't speak for what individuals may have thought or not thought. It certainly can't be attributed solely to a single political administration or agency. What I'm describing is a much broader and longer-term trend in the arts, culture and politics generally. It's that sentiment of the 'tyranny of relevance': it must be immediately relevant to kids; they must be able to see themselves reflected in the cultural product that they consume. This assumes that if they don't, they'll get bored, therefore how are we going to engage them?

I think it leads to a kind of paralysis about what kind of culture we want younger people to have. We are, as a society, generally quite nervous about using the word 'education' when it comes to culture, because we don't feel comfortable saying that some things are worth learning about and others, by implication, are less so. Add to that a pragmatic consideration – which I see as defeatist – about the difficulty of getting pupils to concentrate on things that take time and effort. That's the case particularly for young people from deprived backgrounds. We tend to have low expectations. It's not so much a deliberate strategy of segregation as a reflection of anxiety about whether certain kinds of art are appropriate for certain people.

PW: The 'tyranny of relevance' – where are we with that now? Is it crumbling, or does it still go on?

MM: It's interesting. Since I started this job, I've been heartened by the number of people who say things are improving: that there's more of a debate about previously sacred cows. So, for instance, when it comes to classical music, people tell me: yes, about maybe three or four years ago there was a real fear of talking about its importance, but that's starting to change, and we're regaining confidence in talking about the importance of musical tradition and skills. I think it's also probably true that the debate about whether the arts are of *intrinsic* or *extrinsic* benefit has also moved on. If that's really the case, then great: it means that we can start to reconstruct some of the important cultural blocks that we need.

> **I've been heartened by the number of people who say things are improving: that there's more of a debate about previously sacred cows.**

But my concern is that, while that conversation has moved on at the level of abstract discussion and high policy – people cite the Arts Council's McMaster report [on arts funding], for instance – change may not yet have worked its way down. On the ground we may still be mired in the old orthodoxies.

At the GLA [Greater London Authority] we're currently looking at the pattern of funding and provision to see if things have moved in a new direction. The GLA isn't a direct funder of culture: the mayor is charged with developing the cultural strategy for London, but we have to deliver that strategy through partnerships and advocacy. We do this by working with the key funding agencies and, of course, the boroughs, which are crucial, because they spend a huge amount on the arts and are at the forefront of delivering cultural services.

I suspect that the high-level debate about elitism and diversity, etc. has not fully worked itself through the funding system. My job, I believe, is to ensure that the debate is properly had. We need to enable people to speak up for good projects, but also be critical of poor projects. And there *are* sometimes poor projects – we have to be honest about that. Many people would agree that there has been a tendency to tick boxes in order to get funding. We want to change that and make sure people can talk about quality as if it matters.

> **Many people would agree that there has been a tendency to tick boxes in order to get funding. We want to change that and make sure people can talk about quality as if it matters.**

PW: You say that people are having a debate these days. Is that in the boroughs, or is it just the arts bureaucrats?

MM: London's boroughs are very diverse and have real pressures and challenges of their own. While some boroughs pride themselves on providing really strong cultural services, brilliant libraries and museums, others struggle to keep their cultural services going with very little funding. They may have arts and cultural provision as one strand within a wider directorate – which means these get lost or neglected in the hierarchy. There are many good people working extremely hard to make sure that culture is treated seriously by their management. Inevitably, those working at the coal face have to be pragmatic, and it's easier to obtain funding for culture if it's perceived as helping to deliver on other agendas, such as regeneration, education, community cohesion and so on. In that sense, local councils are the very places where these debates are hardest to have. It's not easy to talk about the importance of art for young people as a good thing in itself, when your management is picking apart budgets and asking about returns on investment.

PW: There is a sense, is there not, that the arts have become almost a sneaky way of implementing government policy, for example health policy? Do you think that approach is changing?

MM: I would characterise it slightly differently. It's not so much that the government is trying to drive forward other agendas through the arts; it's that the arts are trying to piggy-back onto other agendas, in order to get recognition and resources. As someone who is now in the position of trying to scrabble together bits of funding and justify the importance of culture, I can see why the temptation is there and why organisations do that. And obviously, the arts and culture do have certain spin-off benefits: these are very difficult to measure, and a lot of the research is inconclusive, but it makes it plausible to leap from one claim to another.

> Yes, culture can contribute to people's general well-being, but can it really reduce the number of suicides? Or deal with fundamental social or psychiatric problems that lead to schizophrenia or mental health problems?

I wrote a piece for a collection of essays I edited, *Culture Vultures*, in which I explored the claim that the arts can improve health outcomes. I'd seen numerous policy documents which pulled together bits and pieces of academic or clinical research to endorse this argument, and I wanted to interrogate it. The reality is a bit more nuanced. There are some aspects of the arts that do help in a clinical setting, but they're quite specific cases – you know, playing music to patients who are about to go into an operation tends to calm them. But the music is entirely the taste of the individual and could be heavy metal or classical. This kind of bedside care is not what I would see as being a primary focus for the arts. Ultimately, arts policy should not be confused with health policy.

Yes, culture can contribute to people's general well-being, but can it really reduce the number of suicides? Or deal with fundamental social or psychiatric problems that lead to schizophrenia or mental health problems? I just think those claims need to be scrutinised further. That's not to say that the case is closed – it's just to recognise that you can't base arts funding and support for the arts and culture on such weak ground. Rather, we need to be ambitious enough – and honest enough – to argue for the importance of culture in its own terms. I'm fortunate, in that the politician I work for endorses that position and believes in the intrinsic value of culture – partly because he's a writer, and personally loves the arts, but also because of his experience as shadow arts minister. He has seen the disparity – the staggering disparity – between the rich and poor growing up in London. The reality is that there's a massive gap in terms of music education, art history, poetry and so on. And this needs to be tackled head on, by reasserting the importance of arts funding and support.

PW: Richard Eyre has talked about the development of a 'cultural apartheid'...

MM: In terms of the development of arts policy in recent decades, obviously I wasn't around to see the process at first hand, but I can offer a worm's eye view, in that I certainly experienced an element of that in my early life. When I was young, I had very little contact with subjects like art history or classical music; and it was only later that I realised that not only did such things exist but that they weren't completely inaccessible.

So I think Richard Eyre has a point, in that the BBC has a public responsibility to use its resources to showcase culture. I've always been a bit concerned about the arrival of BBC 4, which has been fantastic for high-quality arts programming, but which takes the pressure off BBC 1 to show the same stuff to a wider audience that perhaps wouldn't go looking for it. Of course, it would be unfair to pick on the BBC; this is a broader cultural problem. Most of all, schools are where culture needs to be privileged. That's where young people are every day. It's universal. You have funding, structures, equipment. And it's not just about teaching kids the arts because it's a 'fun' thing to do, keeps them engaged or stops them from playing truant. I'm sure it does all those things. But we have to see that the arts are themselves serious subjects of study. It takes time and effort to learn! One of the biggest problems with music education in London, for example, is that we have lots of one-off initiatives that are great fun for a child to do for one day: you know what I mean, go and see an orchestra behind the scenes, or have a go at an instrument for a day and see if you like it. That's all great; but let's not pretend it's the same as five or six years of intensive tuition and getting up to Grade 8. That kind of serious, sustained interaction with the arts that *should* happen at school isn't currently happening for many. In London we can call for local authorities and arts organisations to work with young people and give them these opportunities, but it really has to start in schools.

PW: I talked to James Graham about how London is overwhelmingly the centre of the arts. Do you think that the way London looks at things is becoming like the way New York looks at America – as if the rest of the country should just be ignored?

MM: You mean that London is psychologically too distant from the rest of the UK? Yes, perhaps that's true. It's the age-old problem – which I think is probably accentuated today – of distance between the elite and the masses. Actually, it's probably not even just about London versus the rest of Britain: it's also about the distance within London between the Establishment at the centre and those who live in the suburbs, or in deprived areas. There is almost a sense of mystery, you know: 'Who are these people?' They live in *communities*. Poor people live in *communities*, whereas rich people don't!

I suppose we don't think enough about the exciting and genuinely interesting things going on around the country. There are pockets of cultural excellence outside London, such as the Manchester or Edinburgh festivals. It's not just the arts: there are remarkable, world-leading scientists working in different corners of the UK, and imaginative engineers and businesspeople. In a strange way, policy makers talk about Britishness, but you can't find it in Whitehall. You need to look at the rest of the country and see that Britishness has interesting textures, new dimensions, as well as a rich relationship to the past. It's a curious paradox that fashionable opinion in the metropolis will get very excited by a film from Vietnam or a dance troupe from Bolivia, while ignoring offerings of equal worth from Nottingham or Swansea.

One of the things that we're thinking about in 2011, as part of our London events programme, is how to celebrate the 60th anniversary of the 1951 Festival of Britain. It's a great chance, just before the Olympics, to think about what Britain looks like and to think about London's relationship to the regions. There are so many questions we could try to explore: what do we eat; who are our best musicians; our best artists; how do people work, live and socialise?

PW: The Olympics encouraged talk of putting money into sport. There was this unashamed talk about helping to create champions. But when it comes to art, it doesn't seem to be the same. Do you think that's because art forces us to think about people's natural talents, whereas sports can be learned – it's more external?

MM: I'm not sure if I do agree with you. I think we do fund excellence, and we certainly give a lot of money to high-quality institutions such as the Royal Opera House – just as we should. It's befitting of a capital city that we support world-class institutions. But I think probably what you mean – what I think is true – is that we don't really talk about champions or excellence in terms of the wider public engagement. We prefer to use the word 'participation', a word that conjures up an image of amateurishness and lack of discrimination. Sometimes it seems that just taking part – 'having a go' – is all we expect people to do. But I think that's only the start, and most people, with encouragement, can probably go further.

Sometimes it seems that just taking part – 'having a go' – is all we expect people to do.

The obvious example is when a young person is encouraged to try a musical instrument or learn to draw. What sometimes happens is that they have a good time, build their self-esteem and confidence, and then that's it – that's good enough. But it's *not* good enough, because even though it's fantastic to get people engaged, you could actually push them further.

PW: It's often been suggested that concepts such as 'self-esteem' and mental health can be helped by the arts, and they've often been laid at the door of the arts. But surely any collective activity, not just of the artistic sort, will make people feel better?

MM: I think it's healthy for people to do things collectively, whether it's art or sport, or just having a fun time. London has lots of carnivals and festivals, large sporting events like the London Marathon, and people love to get involved as participants or volunteers. I think these should be driven by people and by genuine communities of interest, rather than developed solely by politicians to make us feel good.

But you're right – there is also something else, something special about the arts which we can't do collectively or through those big, fun events. Sometimes, art demands a kind of seriousness: those quiet moments of thoughtfulness in a gallery, or reading a book. It's that side of the arts – because they're not sexy and don't involve mass participation – which is perhaps overlooked. We need to champion those things as well, because they are just as much a public good.

PW: Do you think it's true to say that there's a generally monolithic approach in terms of arts organisations and bureaucrats and so on? That they're cut from the same cloth politically? Or is that just a caricature?

MM: I think there is diversity within the arts as to what people think, although you might not always see it! I realise I have sounded quite pessimistic so far, complaining about how things are; but I should say that I have met many, many people in the last few months who, in their day-to-day work, strive for excellence and want to engage with the general public, and with young people in particular, at the highest level. I'm very keen to support and give succour to those artists and administrators who are trying extremely hard to defy the constraints of their jobs, push against low expectations and do the right thing. What they're doing is invaluable, and it should be recognised.

In terms of political orthodoxies, some of these things are breaking down and opening up for debate. So, for instance, when it comes to diversity policies and positive discrimination schemes in the arts (which have long gone unquestioned), there is more discussion about whether they actually work, or achieve the things people claim they do, or whether they can actually be counterproductive.

I've had many private conversations with people in the arts who see race-equality policies in the arts as flawed in one way or another, but wouldn't necessarily have the courage to come out and say that themselves at this stage. I would say we need more debate on such important issues. I doubt many people are fully signed up to the ideology of identity politics, diversity and so on. It's not so much a case of the 'long march through the institutions', with the cultural Left running everything. It's much more confused than that. Orthodoxies are not entrenched or deeply held, except by a few people. Rather, there is still sensitivity about debating them in the open, which means that bad ideas go unchallenged and become absorbed slowly, without resistance.

> **I've had many private conversations with people in the arts who see race-equality policies in the arts as flawed in one way or another, but wouldn't necessarily have the courage to come out and say that themselves at this stage.**

PW: You mentioned earlier the 'elite' and the 'masses'. Do you think that, as this is perceived as having grown, people feel powerless?

MM: I think that people don't trust cultural authority anymore, and that they are very cynical about why certain choices are made. Of course, in the past there was deference towards the Arts Council and the BBC, which in itself wasn't healthy. It was about class deference – these people have more class, therefore they are civilised. Authority was not explained or justified, just asserted and accepted.

The counter-culture of the Sixties argued against the Establishment and pushed for a new creative idea – it found its authority in the world around it, and the real experience of living through social change. That was certainly empowering on one level; but the gradual move towards criticising all authority, effectively undermining any idea of judgement as being 'elitist', means there is nothing left to believe in. Now you have the worst of both worlds. The majority of the public probably still feels alienated from the world of the arts, but many of them also think there's no point either. What you have now is the end of deference, but also cynicism about any new forms of cultural authority. I don't think that empowers us; it actually makes it harder for ordinary people to engage in culture and understand it.

When institutions like the BBC do make mistakes or come under fire, it reinforces the popular prejudice that all cultural authority is basically shallow. The same happens with art in galleries or the Turner Prize: 'They're only in there because they know the right people', or 'this is pretentious and not worth understanding'. I doubt there's a policy solution to that kind of cynicism, although I do think at some point the people who make judgements and give funding have to reassert their authority on the basis of expertise. Part of that process must involve explaining decisions.

> **What you have now is the end of deference, but also cynicism about any new forms of cultural authority.**

PW: Is there any chance of restoring confidence in those cultural authorities?

MM: Well, there is a strange contradiction when it comes to cultural authority today. On the one hand, we talk about 'value' in a very relativistic way, about how excellence has many different forms and it's very difficult to make judgements about one type of art over another, and so on. Yet we still *do* make judgements. We fund the Royal Opera House over other music institutions. Someone, somewhere has made a decision about what's worthy of public support.

Increasingly, funders feel compelled to pay for certain things not on artistic merit but as a gesture of inclusiveness. But at the end of the day, you can't get away from the fact that some things go in a gallery and other things don't. And the reason they go in a gallery is because the gallery has been endowed as a special space, curated by someone with expertise, sensitivity and understanding of their field. For me, this takes us straight to Matthew Arnold. His definition of culture as 'the best that has been thought and said' is something that's worth holding onto, because it is the only true basis upon which you can call for a democratic engagement in the arts. It is precisely because these judgements are more than just someone's personal taste that they have validity and can be shared by others.

In his book, *The Arts and the People*, Roy Shaw, who was chief executive of the Arts Council in the late Seventies, wrote something which I think is still pretty relevant. As a working-class man from Sheffield who came up through the Workers' Educational Association, Shaw was determined to make education a key plank of what the Arts Council did. He insisted on arts organisations appointing education officers for the first time, in order to make great art available to more people. But at the same time, he was committed to high standards and maintaining cultural authority. He argued with the community arts movement, accusing it of being patronising and of romanticising working-class life.

In his book, Shaw writes about how the community arts movement reminded him of this story: a Tory peeress, in the 1930s, went round telling housewives in depressed areas how to make soup out of cods' heads. He writes that this woman was generally very well received, until one of the women asked challengingly: *'Who gets the rest of the cod?'* And, he said: 'I wanted everyone to have some of the rest of the cod and was not happy about the provision of a cod's head culture for the poor.' It's a pretty inspiring story, and I think reminds us that excellence is not a bar to public engagement, but its purpose. *

The Historian – Michael Burleigh

Leaving academic fashion behind: the importance of going public

Michael Burleigh's books have been translated into 18 languages.

His best-selling *The Third Reich: A New History* won the 2001 Samuel Johnson Prize for Non-Fiction. Other works include his monumental study of religion and politics – *Earthly Powers: The Conflict Between Religion and Politics from the French Revolution to the Great War* – and its companion, *Sacred Causes: The Clash of Religion and Politics, from the Great War to the War on Terror.*

His most recent work is *Blood and Rage: A Cultural History of Terrorism*, published in 2008.

Burleigh has held posts at New College, Oxford, the London School of Economics, and the University of Cardiff, where he was Distinguished Research Professor in Modern History. He has also occupied the Raoul Wallenberg Chair of Human Rights at Rutgers University, and been William Rand Kenan Professor of History at Washington and Lee University in Virginia, and Kratter Visiting Professor at Stanford University.

In 2002, he gave the three Cardinal Basil Hume Memorial Lectures at Heythrop College, University of London. He is a member of the Academic Advisory Board of the Institut für Zeitgeschichte in Munich and a Fellow of the Royal Historical Society. He founded the journal *Totalitarian Movements and Political Religions* and is on the editorial boards of *Totalitarismus und Demokratie* and *Ethnic and Racial Studies.*

In 1991, he won the British Film Institute Award for Archival Achievement, for the Channel 4 documentary *Selling Murder: The Killing Films of the Third Reich.* He writes regularly for *The Times*, the *Daily Telegraph*, the *Daily Mail* and the *Guardian.*

Peter Whittle (PW): Could your *Blood and Rage* have been written 20 years ago?

Michael Burleigh (MB): No, because of the way that the Hobsbawms of this world have sort of stamped that type of general area. His most successful sort of serious book, as it were, is *Primitive Rebels* – I think it was called that – which was about bandits in places like Sicily in the eighteenth century, or in the Campagna, who plagued the general region. And, of course, it's a very romanticising book about them, which sees them as proto-revolutionaries; whereas they were just scumbags. So my book is a complete refutation of that type of romanticisation of crime studies, you might say.

PW: Eric Hobsbawm's reputation remains intact; he's still called one of our greatest historians.

MB: Yes, the BBC did [call him that]. Michael Gove wrote a very good piece in one of his columns a couple of weeks ago, saying this was just outrageous. I mean, it was on the BBC – maybe 15 or 20 years ago... When Michael Ignatieff asked him: 'Do you think that the great project, had it worked out in the end in Russia, would have been worth... Would the loss of 20 million lives have been justified?' And he paused for a minute, and said: 'Yes.' And that, for me, just disqualifies him as a sort of ghastly Stalinist. That's what he is. But he emits all the right, fashionable noises, and I find, looking at his big trilogy, and other books or articles by him, that it's rather like one of those con artists in Oxford Street with three shells and a pea under one. The way he operates is to switch from Venezuela to China to Indonesia, or something. But actually, if you know anything about Venezuela, China or Indonesia then it's invariably wrong. It's just done because people are actually so provincial in terms of their type of outlook. So that's how he gets away with it. But actually, then, superimposed on that is a very simplistic Marxist framework. He never asks any interesting questions; he's not interested in the motivations and psychology of real, breathing human beings, be they right at the top or be they at the bottom – it doesn't interest him. So it's a very abstract, schematic way of doing things.

PW: What influence do you think historians have now, on culture or policy makers?

MB: I certainly think my terror book has had an enormous influence on certain politicians, who will be nameless; and I've been quite genuinely surprised by the response of senior police officers or generals. General Lord Guthrie wrote a very nice letter to me about the book, after Spanish Prime Minister Aznar came to London to interview me about it, and said: 'I certainly hope all our politicians are reading this' – which some of them indeed are. So one would hope it would.

If you think about it, one of the prime concerns of people fighting terrorism of any sophistication is to destroy al-Qaeda as a global brand: one wants it to become a failed brand, as it were. A lot of this is because most terrorists are 15 to 35 years old; it's very fashion driven, and this is a fashionable brand. So what the people fighting terrorism think – and I think they're quite right – is: 'Well, we want it to become like an Amstrad computer rather than Coca Cola or Nike or Adidas.' The book is a very specific contribution to that process. It's actually saying: 'Look, these are self-romanticising, rather than romantic, figures using violence to satisfy some personal hang-up since the utopian goal is inherently unachievable; and the milieu they inhabit is fundamentally squalid, as Dostoevsky and Conrad pointed out decades ago.'

What always surprises me, as well, is that we don't use our full cultural resources to combat these people. When I wrote the book, I started looking at jihadist suicide videos, many from Afghanistan. And I watched a few of these things on the net, and after a while I began to think: 'Well, actually, I know what's going on here; these have all got the filmic structure of porn movies.' This country's universities are awash with film studies people: why aren't they pointing that out? I mean, just to say: 'Look, whoever made this knows about the "money shot" and all the rest of it in porn movies.' Because they do. And I just don't understand – we're curiously paralysed in the face of all this. And then, of course, political correctness has a stifling effect, so all our very bold, edgy stand-up comedians won't go there because they're frightened of being killed – that's an interesting comment on the limitations of that supposedly venturing-where-nobody-dares-to-go, supposedly 'edgy' type of approach to these things. But I somehow can't see the Institute of Contemporary Arts doing that amidst all its innovative conformist predictability.

PW: So why are we paralysed, then? Why are our institutions in a quandary over how to respond?

MB: Well, because they're still, in a way, operating with an ideology of multiculturalism, despite it being abandoned as a public doctrine. They're still trying to salvage some of that in their approach to the so-called 'communities', and their so-called 'leaders', rather than just scrapping the whole thing and starting from scratch, which is a much more difficult thing to do. And then, of course, the Americans – after 9/11 they took a solely military-based approach, thinking that they could just bring raw power to bear on it, with an army which had been very much trained in the warrior ethos; so they were not multi-tasking people who could be switched from one function to another, which is what this war actually requires.

> ...some parts of history are quite legitimately part of the light entertainment industry, and I don't mind that whatsoever.

But anyway, to come back to the point about history and all that: some parts of history are quite legitimately part of the light entertainment industry, and I don't mind that whatsoever. When it comes to actual policy making, it's very much a team activity, and I'm not sure historians are very good team players. In the way that you could obviously draw upon experts in pharmaceuticals to deal with some epidemic – you would have to talk to them, because they have very specific expertise, and with good reason the government has a chief scientific advisor. And likewise, although one is nowadays sceptical of it, the government's got top economists who advise on the credit crunch. But I'm not sure historians quite fit into the same bracket: the lessons, the instruction is not so straightforward, and politicians don't want the learned ambiguities of a seminar.

PW: If we take, for example, Paul Johnson's history of the modern world, that was one of the first revisionist histories...

MB: That was terribly influential, a great book. Of course, there are others – like Robert Conquest's *Great Terror*.

PW: Was it influential because politicians read it, or just simply influential on other historians, or what?

MB: It was influential on me because it's a marvellous book, and it's rather refreshing. But I think for politicians it just created a refreshingly centre-right view of the world, and covered a lot of subjects which had not been covered in that way before. So I suppose people on the Right would have read it and thought: 'Yes, this is roughly what we think.' And it's articulated – has put their world view – in time, as it were. So that's part of its achievement.

I mean, history, of course, can have potentially disastrous consequences on policy. Throughout my lifetime, you know, appeasement has been taken as something which we don't do: that justified the debacle of Suez, and then Thatcher with the junta in Argentina, then Blair with Saddam Hussein. Immediately, in the press, the people concerned become Hitlers, which is a farcical notion – Argentinian generals are not Hitlers, and nor was Saddam Hussein. That was a pretty middling little power; not a major industrial power in Europe. But by implication, diplomacy becomes synonymous with weakness. I've heard people talk about Dame Pauline Neville-Jones as Dame Pauline Neville-Chamberlain, because she's a career diplomat and is trying to do that.

I think that's very unfortunate: we go too quickly from half-hearted, ineffectual talks, say with the Iranians about their nuclear bomb project... The 'three stooges', including Jack Straw and his German and French equivalents, spent three years talking to them, and [the Iranians] gave them the run-around over the mint tea. Hopeless. We somehow go straight from that... This is our failure in Europe, since we claim we can deal with it through diplomacy... Therefore, the Americans or the Israelis think: 'Right, we've got no alternative other than the military strike!' So we are, in a way, responsible for them resorting to that option because we haven't effectively protected their existential security.

What we should be doing is revisiting Britain's very fine tradition of tough diplomacy. Start looking back at Castlereagh and Palmerston and the rest of the chaps I learnt about as a kid. I mean, they were not pushovers; and nor should the Foreign Office be regarded as synonymous with pushovers. I mean, these are people who know a lot about the world. They know a lot about the countries concerned. And they should be encouraged – given the resources and the back-up – to actually make diplomacy a very effective thing. Otherwise you will have other countries quickly resorting to force, which is not something any of us want to see – not that our economic resources these days really allow it. So that's an instance where history can have a rather inhibiting effect on policy.

PW: Some claim that the academic world is now far from a forum for free speech and instead is very hedged around with orthodoxies. Do you think that's a fair assessment?

MB: Well, I'd qualify it by saying that it's certainly not entirely so. One tends to get the humanities out of proportion – they undoubtedly are dominated by the political Left to a massive extent. But it wouldn't be true of lawyers or engineers or medics or scientists. One ought to acknowledge that fact, and maybe encourage them to have more say, since they're the money-men, apart from anything else, in universities, rather than English literature or history dons.

History in universities is incredibly fashion driven; so when I started as an undergraduate in the Seventies, French history was really the big thing still. I did a lot of medieval history as an undergraduate, and I would say 50 per cent of the books I read were in French – it was just assumed that you could do it. I wrote my first essay on the chronicle of the Albigensian Crusade, which was in medieval French. That was a shock to me – I'll never forget it. So these things are very fashionable. There was a large representation of French historians in all departments. Britain had some brilliant ones.

> **History in universities is incredibly fashion driven.**

And then suddenly German history – for reasons I can't quite figure – became enormous, so every department then had to equip itself with a German historian. German history is useful in terms of re-oxygenating the Left with a regular dose of anti-fascism. You can see this now, with the BBC and the Labour government talking up the march of the jackboot in Austria or Italy, whereas actually that doesn't convey any reality about the post-fascists in Italy. Mr Fini, who's the head of the Alleanza Nazionale, has been multi-recognised and honoured in Israel, whenever he goes there. He's a great friend of Israel, so let's get a sense of proportion.

Anyway, that's its function. German history, both here and in the United States, is totally dominated, with one or two exceptions, by leftists.

That's one reason why both Niall Ferguson and I decided to do different things, in both cases going global – although along rather different lines of enquiry. Niall is much more numerate than me. I think I failed Maths 'O' Level by the way. Russian history has always been, particularly in the Cold War, very strong. There was once a lot of money, obviously, to do it and East European studies. But all that collapsed – there's no money for that anymore. There's plenty of money to bankroll SOAS [School of Oriental and African Studies] or somewhere like that, because the Middle East is so rich – Africa not. But the whole field of Slavonic and East European studies is in a pretty parlous state, because it's completely irrelevant politically. I think Chinese studies will be – is – huge, for the obvious reasons about China. The one exception to that is that American studies has always been incredibly well bankrolled in this country, again for obvious reasons. A lot of money to do it, but somehow it never attracts very good people. I'll probably get my throat cut for saying this, but I think, because we share a common language, they're always going to be much better; whereas it is a fact that some British historians of Russia or Germany or Spain are, for all sorts of complex reasons, regarded as top historians in those fields by the countries concerned – chiefly, in the case of Spain, because everybody under Franco had to be a medievalist in Spain. It was too tricky to write anything after Ferdinand and Isabella. You'd probably get shot or put in prison.

PW: What exactly would it be that would be so frustrating, if you did not subscribe to the prevailing orthodoxy?

MB: Well, it depends where you work. I've worked in some places that weren't like that at all. It's just lack of imagination, or inability to think outside the box, and to try new things. It's all that, or a type of dreadful earnestness about everything, and a sort of trade unionist mentality, in which the least talented have the most to say. The Stalinist Left lives to manipulate meetings, which the rest of us flee from like the plague. Universities are still collectivist or oligarchic at departmental level – with an equally unsatisfactory overlayering of management and vice-chancellors seeking knighthoods. Anyway, I move in much more congenial circles nowadays – academics are so socially dreary. As it happens, Buckingham University has recently made me a research professor...

PW: That's the private one, isn't it?

MB: The one private one. In the States the best are all private, with enough money to educate any undergraduate they want to teach, regardless of their family income. Most postgrads also get paid a salary [to teach] at the

> **The Stalinist Left lives to manipulate meetings, which the rest of us flee from like the plague.**

big places like Stanford or Harvard. They are that rich.

PW: The books you've written, or, for example, Jung Chang's book on Mao – do they find their way back into history teaching, by academics?

MB: Yes, they can't avoid it. They can sort of make you a non-person. You'll disappear from their bibliographies, you know. They'll rip you off, but they won't cite you. But you just become a sort of non-person – that's the best way of describing it. The Germans call it being killed by silence. But I don't greatly care about that, because I've got a very big global audience now: my books are in 18 different languages, including Croatian and Estonian!

PW: But do you therefore think that your role, and the role of people who write history, is more relevant, more important, than what is taught?

MB: Yes, of course it is. But that has involved making the transition to being what the Americans grandly call a 'public intellectual'...

PW: But that's a change, isn't it?

MB: Yes. It's a big change. Just recently I was in Madrid for four days. I was in every single Spanish newspaper; I was on television three times; and I was in very big panel discussions with Socialist MPs. So I have a very big market there – and in Latin America through that. Much the same happens in the Netherlands and Belgium, as well as Italy to a lesser degree. It enables me to have a conversation with big audiences about things that matter to them. Likewise, I'm privileged to be able to comment on things in the *Daily Mail* and some other papers.

I think it's a pity, what the Republicans [in the USA] did. They just washed their hands of the universities, effectively. So they just set up think tanks – without students, obviously, but lots of interns... And then they're hugely bankrolled and employ hundreds of people: 400 people work at the Heritage Foundation, and the same amount at the AEI [American Enterprise Institute]. And Britain – even a think tank like Policy Exchange has got a very modest budget of about a million a year or something; it's trivial. And I think if it remains the case that diversity is not on the universities' agenda, then that might be one way for the Conservatives to go, by making it more feasible for people to fund things like that in order to establish intellectual diversity.

PW: Would you say that, in a way, American think tanks have almost become American universities, in the sense of the research they do?

MB: Yes, they are. They're not awarding degrees, and, because it's policy related, a lot of it is much more short-term relevance-focused, in a way that academic work often isn't. However, maybe you can actually extract more useful common sense from something which is of no apparent relevance than from something that seems terribly relevant. I mean, a lot of stuff coming out of think tanks just seems to me to restate the blindingly obvious, rather than saying anything of any great depth. I suppose that's just the nature of the conditions under which it's produced: people pay money and there's got to be a result, and the whole process is pretty quick. So I think I'd like to see them do a bit more long-term work than goes on at the moment – perhaps focusing more on cultural issues. The cultural atmosphere in think tanks seems happier – you encounter a lot of depressed people in universities, many of them suffering from 'donnish accidie'. They're trapped in a public-service ethos.

PW: It seems to me that your books are, in a way, charting a new era – where are we, if we're not at the 'end of history'?

MB: *The End of History,* Francis Fukuyama's book, sort of exemplifies what I was saying about think tanks. It's a very think-tanky book. It's a headline-grabbing title and thesis, and it's quite preposterous. It coincided with a time when there was a huge resurgence of nationalism in the West's decade of complacency after the Berlin Wall fell. Another example I can give is Philip Bobbitt – who, incidentally, nobody in America has heard of – with his market-state. I mean, for God's sake! That's a pretty discredited concept, since we're seeing the resurgence of nation states taking control of international capital flows and banks, as well as essaying protectionist measures. I also find pretty sinister the idea of stockpiling pre-emptive antiterrorist laws, like vaccines for a hypothetical epidemic. I'm very anti-lawyer: cut back on legislation as much as possible is a good Tory maxim.

My books are much more solutions to technical or formal problems I have identified, and far less ideologically driven than my critics think. I don't get up in the morning to write self-consciously 'conservative' history, even if it comes out as such – that's how I see it. And of course, there are innumerable varieties of conservatism, although that is often overlooked, too. Mine is sceptical of grandiose projects to engineer societies or human nature, including the projects of the neo-Jacobins in recent US administrations. Being preoccupied with formal questions does not mean I'm not interested in human beings – I wouldn't be doing this if I wasn't. History provides incredible raw insights into human nature. But I just wanted to create a body of work, which I've done. It's an ongoing thing, I hope.

> **History provides incredible raw insights into human nature.**

PW: Do you think that the Hobsbawm approach is ending? The Right previously ceded a lot of territory, and confined itself to just looking after the money. Do you think that is changing?

MB: Undoubtedly. The *Guardian* is doing a series of pamphlets about

World War One this week, connected to Remembrance Sunday, and I was pleasantly surprised that they asked me to do the one on the long-term consequences of World War One. So even though the *Guardian* is not a paper that shares my political outlook, nonetheless one has made an impact if the *Guardian* is asking me to do that. And I think some people on the Left are actually quite open-minded. I mean, there's a very nice chap called John Crace who interviewed me for the *Guardian*. There was a profile on me in the *Guardian* earlier this year, and he said – you know I write a lot in the *Daily Mail* – he said there wasn't a single article I'd written (with one or two exceptions) in the *Daily Mail* that couldn't have appeared in the *Guardian*. He was just surprised by this. So I think, with people who use their minds, there is some common ground. Apparently the *Mail* buys in more material from the *Guardian* than any other paper, by the way.

PW: What about the sort of popular history that people might see on TV and in films? I'm encouraged when films like *Elizabeth* come out: it keeps these things alive.

MB: Obviously human nature in some fundamental way doesn't change. But what such history could try to do better is to show how people's moral or mental outlook was very different – the things that informed them were very different.

So yes, alright: I can see why one makes programmes about Henry VIII – dramas where he's screwing everybody left, right and centre. But if it then doesn't explore the fact that he wrote tracts about theology and was a very cultivated man, then it's sort of failing. Or if it doesn't tell you that, you know, politics was 'high stakes', where you did get your head cut off if you got it wrong. And I think it could be more imaginative. Anyway, that's one for my old friend David Starkey to ponder. We used to interview new students at the LSE for a day each year – he was much kinder to them than me, as I wondered what on earth to ask about Henry VIII...

But actually, one thing I was thinking about before our conversation was to do with my hopelessly overloaded agenda for how history should be taught in schools. I mean, I could really make an argument for saying that it ought to be compulsory that – in addition to obviously studying your own history, which we've rather neglected – you should just pick somewhere almost at random. There ought to be a random element to it. So everybody has to study – I don't know – the history of modern Egypt, or Algeria... Just somewhere that has no practical use – although actually Algeria, since most of our liquid gas comes from there, is quite relevant. But just somewhere where you had to really put your mind around something, for no particular reason. You just had to figure it out. Give them Indonesia:

that would be a real test, because that's incredibly complicated. But I just think something that stretched people's imaginations, and which was non-European – wasn't, you know, Russia, Germany, all the predictable stuff, or the States... Just for once they had to try.

It is a hopelessly romantic suggestion, but it's what I would do. I think that just the discipline of thinking about something, with no possible gain in it, is actually something I would really like to see – especially since we live in an extremely complex world, and one really does have to know about these places. I mean, they still have the persecution of witches in parts of Indonesia, while the Muslims there bang on about 'Chinese Zionists'... ✿

The Broadcaster – Dennis Sewell

BBC bias, impartiality and the future of political broadcasting

Dennis Sewell is a writer and broadcaster.

Between 1986 and 2008, he worked in the current affairs department of BBC News, where he presented Radio 4's *Talking Politics*, as well as *Politics UK* on the BBC World Service. He was a reporter for *Newsnight* and the *World Tonight*, and worked as a producer on the *Week in Westminster* and the *Today* programme. He is an award-winning documentary maker.

Dennis Sewell is now a contributing editor on the *Spectator*. His book, *Catholics: Britain's Largest Minority*, was published in 2001. A new book, *The Political Gene – How Darwin's Ideas Changed Politics* is due to be published in November 2009.

Peter Whittle (PW): There is a view that now we have a kind of overall elite, a political class, and that the media is part of that. Do you think that's true?

Dennis Sewell (DS): I think it sometimes looks as if it is true, and Peter Oborne's made a good case for this in his *The Triumph of the Political Class*, in which he writes about a political class which is beyond ideology; which has similar ambitions; where people of left-wing and right-wing backgrounds, professional politicians, people working in the world of think tanks and so on have, in some way, captured the media, too. And that all are part of a class – which, I suppose, is something defined as having a common interest. But I think this is fairly superficial: a surface appearance more than a hard reality. I don't think the interests of the media and the interests of politicians of differing stripes are in any way identical. I think there's still quite a lot of guerrilla media, if you like – of which Peter Oborne himself is a prime example.

That said, there is – there has been – a pattern, and I think it's a pattern that repeats itself through history, which is that when a government comes in, particularly with a very strong prime minister – which was the case with Margaret Thatcher, as well as with Tony Blair – the media do tend to notice who is now in charge, and adapt themselves to the realities of the political power. That relationship lasts for a while, but then it begins to decay, typically; and so it has with this Labour government. I think that that relationship is one where the actors – the important actors – on the media side are the proprietors, not the jobbing journalists. Particularly Rupert Murdoch and the tabloid proprietors. The truth is that individual journalists don't count for much.

The truth is that individual journalists don't count for much.

There is, though, a class of, I suppose, the higher punditry: people who are very much at home around the dinner tables of politicians, and whose own dinner tables are frequented by politicians, and who do cut across party. They might be held in great esteem and respect by politicians in both parties. I don't think any of those people are in broadcasting – possibly Sky's Adam Bolton might qualify. But they are a small group, and they tend to be columnists on the major quality newspapers, who are not much read by people in the country as a whole. I wonder sometimes whether they have any real effect on events at all, but they certainly are close to people who do. I fancy that they are kept in the way that feudal monarchs may have kept fools, because of their witty conversation and their pleasant company. It would certainly be stretching things to see them as partners in power with elected politicians.

PW: The perception is that we're living in a time when these pundits are strong, because the politicians are weak. Do you think that perhaps there is too much punditry? That they, in fact, have a disproportionate effect on the people whose dinner tables they're at?

DS: I don't, actually. I think they're very useful in framing the issues, in conducting a rather narrow argument within public life. And, I suppose, in giving at least a sense that there is a national conversation going on. And in giving politics a character of pluralism, because there are many voices saying different things. They have different, sometimes very personal and idiosyncratic, approaches. That's all to the good. They don't change the way people vote. They don't change the big things in politics. But they may well change the way in which people think about certain issues, at a certain time. That's healthy.

PW: What effect has the blogosphere, civilian punditry, had on broadcasting?

DS: I think the internet is having an enormous effect. I think it is not so much the blogosphere or the citizen journalists themselves, but the way that technology has changed the terms of trade for the mainstream media. I think it's pretty universally recognised which way things are headed – and that the main way in which those people we still call 'broadcasters' will be delivering programmes in the future will be via the new media.

Now the BBC are sort of out in front there, changing the names of everything. People often think these labels are a bit silly and ridiculous, but they are significant. The fact that the heads of departments of the

BBC are now no longer head of radio, but head of audio, and the head of television has now become head of vision – they're signals that the digital future is mapped out. And the BBC has also responded very practically in creating this enormous news website, which is very popular right across the world. In a way, it is a launch pad for television and radio, as technology develops, to be delivered via the web.

PW: Do you think that, since you went into broadcasting, broadcasters feel less powerful now, as a result of the new media?

DS: There are people within the new media, say bloggers, who fancy that they own it; but actually they don't. It is not a different medium from the one in which broadcasters are operating, or the one in which national newspapers are operating. Indeed, the most frequented sites are the ones that belong to the broadcasters and the newspapers, and the distinction between new media and mainstream media is a false one. Because the real money and the power within the internet belong to the same people as with the mainstream media.

> **There are people within the new media, say bloggers, who fancy that they own it; but actually they don't.**

PW: How long were you at the BBC?

DS: Twenty-one years.

PW: The presenter Andrew Marr has said that culturally, the BBC has a liberal instinct. Do you agree?

DS: Often when Andrew says things, they sound so reasonable and plausible that one finds oneself nodding along as he's saying them; but then, when you actually unpack the box, how much of value is there in it? Let's look specifically at what he did say. He said the BBC was an organisation with an abnormally large number of people from ethnic minorities, young people, and gay people. Immediately upon hearing that, I should think most people think: 'Oh yes, that's probably right.' But is it?

Let's take the ethnic minorities – [an abnormal number] compared to what? Compared to a national health hospital in central London? I doubt it. I would have thought it likely that there are more people from ethnic minorities there: a higher proportion of hospital doctors are probably drawn from ethnic minorities than television producers. I think it's probably a higher proportion of nurses that are drawn from ethnic minorities than television technicians, and so on. So the BBC has indeed found it quite difficult to meet its own targets in terms of ethnic minority recruiting. It is, I think, somewhat higher than the national average of about 8 per cent: it is probably somewhere between 10 and 12, heading towards 12 per cent, which is low compared to London – where most of the BBC is – which is 25, heading towards 30 per cent. So it is somewhere practically in the middle, representing probably about the right number of people from ethnic minorities, given that it is more or less totally a graduate organisation.

Also, you then have to wonder about Marr's assumption that being from an ethnic minority necessarily lends you a liberal perspective. One's own experience is that quite a lot of people, particularly from Islamic backgrounds, are much more socially conservative than the mainstream. Moving on: I've no idea whether the BBC has more gay people, or about average, or fewer – I can't even see how anybody could ever know. Certainly, there doesn't seem to be any shortage of married people with young families at the BBC: you could never say that the voice of the family or the concerns of the person with young children are not heard within the BBC. They're there all the time.

Then you get onto young people. Well, once again, yes, of course it is true that the age profile, the employment profile, of the BBC is younger than it is in many other organisations; but no younger than it would be, say, in the armed forces. Again, there's not necessarily an equivalence between the left-liberal outlook and a young age profile, in terms of employment.

All that said, there are certain kinds of gaps, I suppose, that you get to notice after being in the organisation for a long time. There aren't that many, but one of them, I would say, is that the voice of the countryside is not very loud within the staff of the BBC. That is odd, because the staff of the BBC is middle class, and includes the middle class that does come from rural backgrounds and so on. But I noticed during the fox-hunting debate that there was really very little knowledge: it's not a question of sympathy, so much as of basic knowledge about the countryside.

But broadly speaking, the backgrounds of the people working in journalism, particularly in news, are pretty diverse. They do cover most of the country in terms of people coming from the north, the south, from Scotland, Northern Ireland and Wales, much more than they would do in any other organisation, I would have thought. And people have quite a variety of backgrounds – with that limitation that most of them are university graduates. But there are grammar-school people; there are comprehensive-school people; there are public-school people – right across the board. I think there is a great variety.

Where I'm leading to with this is that some critics of the BBC in this respect tend to imagine that it does have a common organisational culture, and I'm not sure that it does. I think it has lots of different organisational cultures. I think that BBC Drama and BBC News are so different from one another that you couldn't say there was a common culture between them. I think that people working in radio and people working in television have a completely different ethos and outlook, much of the time. And to say that there is a kind of single, uniform, corporate outlook is quite wrong.

PW: So you wouldn't agree with Robin Aitken, the ex-BBC reporter, who, in his book *Can We Trust the BBC?*, outlined a number of beliefs that, he said, were taken for granted as part of the BBC culture: that it was broadly pro-EU, anti-big business, generally anti-conservatism, pro-multiculturalism, etc.?

DS: Historically, at the time he was working at the BBC, there was, in BBC News, I think what is now admitted to have been a failure to recognise the importance of the Eurosceptic point of view. I think it was generally regarded as being not of the political mainstream; as being a faintly cranky perspective on politics. And the reason for that was that, in many ways, at Westminster that's how it looked. It seemed to be a problem within the Conservative party of a group of rebels, who did not have any prospect of ever winning, so they were a kind of guerrilla band, on the far-right fringe of the Conservative party, giving John Major a hard time over Maastricht.

I think that set the tone, and I think at that time BBC News automatically thought that the balances that it should have in politics are ones that should be drawn from the Westminster theatre of operations. They didn't, at that time, realise that there could be quite strong currents in the public – beyond Westminster – that were significant and that needed to be represented. And so a 'balanced' discussion of Europe might follow, reflecting the relative representation of the interest groups of Westminster, but ignoring something that was actually, by the end of it, something that 70 per cent of the people in the country believed.

It was a big mistake. And I think that certainly there was a recognition afterwards that people ought to take a different view of the way in which balance was achieved.

PW: Why did that change?

DS: Contrary to the view of the people who say the BBC is a kind of enormous monolith with a consistent world view, actually what goes on in the BBC every day is a constant criticism of its own output: so the programmes are constantly being reviewed, and individual items are discussed. There are editorial meetings all the time; there are editors delivering their pronouncements on yesterday's programme, on tomorrow's programme. And all of these are done in a kind of general discussion format, so lots of views are flying around the table. Nothing stays wrong for long in that situation.

> **...actually what goes on in the BBC every day is a constant criticism of its own output...**

PW: But, for example, recently David Cameron wrote in the *Sun* that he had been talking to a BBC producer at a social function, who had told him: 'We would have you on the airwaves, but we wouldn't want to socialise with you...'

DS: Sounds like a joke to me, don't you think? And if it wasn't a joke, I strongly suspect that the person wouldn't have actually voiced that thought. You see, again, it's part true, part not true. I think if you were to do a kind of serious count, make windows into the souls of everybody in BBC News, you would probably find that there was a left-of-centre majority. But until quite recently, you'd probably have found that in the country at large. Indeed, you still might – I mean, if you add up all the Labour supporters and the Liberal Democrat supporters, they outnumber the Conservatives, even now.

PW: But it's been observed again recently that the coverage of Barack Obama has been entirely positive – with an undisguised glee on the actual night of the election. Do you think that that showed the BBC in a good light?

DS: What troubled me was the relentless insistence on the significance of the racial element. Barack Obama had himself gone out of his way to say he doesn't want to be entirely defined by his race. And yet obviously, because of the part race plays in American political culture, it was going to be of some significance. It needed to be mentioned.

But it has just gone on and on. It is the only thing people report, and it is reported so often. I was watching the coverage the other day, and they were showing Obama visiting the White House to pay a call on Bush. And yet again, the reporter found it necessary to tell us that this was the first black president-elect, as if there were anyone left who did not know this! And it's certainly not the most interesting or important thing about what Barack Obama is doing. But for some reason this has been taken up by, I think, the media as a whole – I don't think it's just the BBC – as a matter of absolutely earth-shattering significance.

PW: Much of the coverage brings to mind the kind of thing that was written here about Blair when he was first elected in 1997.

DS: In a curious sort of way, the Obama treatment was more a kind of replay of the Diana thing – obviously except that, instead of tragedy, it was a celebration. I think one of the reasons for that is that the Diana thing changed the terms of trade, and so the media think that there's a big market now for curious and sometimes inappropriate public displays of emotion, and they cater to it. They assume it's there, and they may or may not be right.

But going back to the Obama story, and whether the campaign was even-handedly reported: if you think yourself into the position of a

162

journalist on the spot, there's a strong drive to 'call' it right. If you are a correspondent, you don't want to appear as if you're stupid, naïve, wrong. You want to make the right forecasts, and for your judgement calls to be ultimately vindicated by events.

Now, I think when Sarah Palin was chosen, quite soon afterwards it became apparent to journalists, perhaps quicker than to everybody else, that the Palin thing was going wrong. She was doing one of the jobs that she'd been selected for – she was energising the Republican base, the conservative base. But the second thing was that she was supposed to get white working-class voters from the key states to vote for McCain, and this wasn't happening.

But at the same time, she was having another effect that nobody had foreseen: almost the entire intelligentsia, even some people who had supported the Republicans, the war in Iraq and so on, were moving towards Obama as a result of finding Sarah Palin off-putting.

Now, I think that that realisation on the part of the people actually covering the campaign informed their reporting. But because they couldn't make that explicit, because you can only talk about that once you start looking at the numbers after the election... But if you see that happening, you want to 'call' it right. So I think there was a tendency to say 'Palin is not a good idea', without really quite explaining why, and this was interpreted by some consumers of news as being a bias against Palin.

PW: To me it seems that, in the media, the dislike of Palin came first.

DS: I think there are two obvious reasons why that might be true. And that is that there is a certain kind of graduate in England – and America probably – whose tendency is to be almost unquestioningly pro-abortion, and to look on the pro-life movement with great suspicion. There is an increasing tendency to be of the kind of Dawkins-ite atheist persuasion, and to regard religion negatively. I think that's just the time we live in, rather than the particular mindset of any particular organisation.

PW: There is the view that the campaign was more about elite versus the masses – almost a kind of court versus country contest...

DS: This is what worries me about much of, you might say, the kind of anti-BBC and anti-political-class and anti-elite rhetoric that we're beginning to hear in this country from the populist Right. If ever there was a demonstration of the folly of going down that route, of

> If ever there was a demonstration of the folly of going down that route, of that anti-elitist, anti-intellectual populism, it is this election in the United States. That it was so comprehensively defeated as a political strategy should give everybody pause.

that anti-elitist, anti-intellectual populism, it is this election in the United States. That it was so comprehensively defeated as a political strategy should give everybody pause. So when you start reading on blogs these constant rants against Oxbridge, the constant rants against the narrow political metropolitan bubble, the constant rants against the BBC, you think: 'Hang on – if what you guys want is a healthy market economy and centre-right political policies and a Conservative government, don't go that way: it doesn't work.' With this sort of anti-elitist populism, you can only throw up as your leader a Palin-type figure – who will bomb.

...as a result of the [Ross/Brand] fuss, people have woken up to the fact that they pay for this stuff, and that they therefore have some right to express a view as to what broadcasters do with their money.

Anyway, I don't think anybody who seriously considers themselves conservative, with a big or a small 'c', should be in the business of disparaging elitism. I don't think they should be in the business of dismissing the value of education, art and literature.

PW: Turning to the Jonathan Ross/Russell Brand controversy: was this just a moral panic that was whipped up, or does it show, as some commentators have said, that people have finally had enough of the arrogance of the BBC – that it was a sort of popular Middle England uprising? Or is that pitching it too high?

DS: No, I think it was a moment of enormous significance, in a number of ways. First, it brought into the national conversation the question of whether the BBC should be putting out this kind of thing; what conceivable public service function this provides; where it fits into the vision of public service broadcasting; and whether or not the criteria used for judging whether programmes are good should include terms like 'edgy'.

And, I think, as a result of the fuss, people have woken up to the fact that they pay for this stuff, and that they therefore have some right to express a view as to what broadcasters do with their money. I think it can do the BBC no harm whatsoever for people who pay for it to feel some sense of ownership of it. I think the BBC would be much happier belonging to the payers of the licence fee – those are, after all, the terms of the Trust that has been set up, to emphasise the fact that the BBC belongs to the licence-fee payer, not the State. The BBC has always disliked the idea of being seen as a state broadcaster. So therefore, it should be, in theory, more than happy that licence-fee payers are willing to express views, reservations, utter condemnation or whatever they feel like. Whether they will actually like what the licence-fee payers are going to tell them, I don't know.

PW: So you think that what's happened recently was quite important for the BBC?

DS: I think it will have a very long-term significance. I think that there will, in the future, be a much livelier debate about content. It won't be about channels or mechanisms of payment, so much as: 'You're using our money to make this kind of programme, and we don't approve.' Or: 'You're not using enough of our money to make the kind of programme that we want' – which is, I think, an equally important debate to have.

PW: Do you think that people trust broadcasting more or less than they did when you first started in it?

DS: Less. There was a time when I was growing up when there was a kind of common culture, a common set of references. The entire nation sat down and watched *Panorama* at the same time, and talked about it the following day. And that played a very large part in terms of establishing the brand and establishing the emotions attached to the brand, including trust. Inevitably, it was going to wear off a bit, whatever happened.

PW: What do you think of the view that the concept of impartiality in broadcasting was always flawed, was always impossible, and that therefore broadcasters should be allowed, editorially, to be more like newspapers?

DS: It's more complicated than it looks. The reasons why newspapers strike particular political attitudes and have their leader lines isn't something that is widely understood. There's been some very interesting recent research on it, actually, which showed that it is a mechanism. It's finely tuned to what works in the market, and the individual opinions of even megalomaniac press barons have less of an influence than actual pure market forces. Now, would the same be true of television? Newspapers can adjust and tilt if they have a new columnist who is taking a particular line and losing sales, or pulling up sales or something: they know what to do about it. Now, with something much bigger, something where productions take eight years and vast amounts of money, it would be like turning round an oil tanker. Would you just get networks which express the political will or biases of a megalomaniac television mogul, rather than a megalomaniac newspaper proprietor? I suspect you would. So I don't think it would necessarily be healthy.

That said, I would like to see more partisan television, but not necessarily in terms of rival networks, like in the USA. I wouldn't like to see a British Fox News. I think people live their lives in their own ideological bubble too much as it is. They should get out a bit, and people should expose themselves to more varied output. I think it's healthier: it produces a healthier polity if people read two newspapers rather than one, and watch different television news programmes, because I think the development comes out of the clash or contest of ideas and opinions; it doesn't come out of just reinforcing your own prejudices.

PW: How do you think political coverage in broadcasting will develop in the next 10 years?

DS: I think that when people have too much of one thing, they tend to create a demand for something else, to be different. And at the moment, we're in a phase where people have an awful lot of right-up-to-the-minute, instant news channels and so forth which don't tell them much – just enough to know roughly what's going on, but not enough to tell them why they should lean forward and take an interest; not enough to help them fully understand a story or an issue. But their curiosity about certain things will be, to some extent, sparked, and therefore I think the next phase, if you like, is that people start to notice that they know very little about quite a lot. And they'll want to know a lot more about some things, and they will want certain questions – which seem never to go away – to be answered at long last. There will be a demand for definitive programme making in current affairs. Go out, find out what is actually the truth about all this – yes, we've heard for years the same old arguments, x and y; but will somebody please go and do the research, do the leg-work, and come back and tell us whether x was right, or y was right, or neither of them was right after all?

I think there's an appetite for that. Whether actually television can deliver that, I don't know. It's certainly not geared up for it at the moment. Anybody that went to any of the big television companies and went to a producer and said 'I really want to settle one of the great perennial questions, and put lots of time and money and research into it' would be told: 'That's not how things work at the moment; there's not the money for that kind of stuff.' So it doesn't happen. But I think that one day it will have to happen. People will just stop watching unless somebody's going to give them value.

PW: Do you agree with the charge that broadcasters have become too timid, too worried about giving offence? Especially in relation to race and Islam?

DS: I think that what we've seen since 9/11 – in terms of the whole area of problems of social cohesion and the terrorism threat – is that broadcasters have shown themselves to be deeply pessimistic about the British national character, and unjustifiably so. I think there was an assumption that Muslims would be beaten up in the street and mosques would be burned down. But hardly anybody has been beaten up in the street, and, so far as I know, no mosques have been burned down. And then, when 52 people were killed on the London Underground and again nothing happened... There wasn't a huge backlash. But there seems to be an excessive caution that has been built into the system, both in the use of language and, to a certain degree, in what is reported, what is headlined and what is marginalised. I think the acute concern that the British public will once again disappoint in some way, and will all turn to the BNP if they are told too much about the level of the terrorist threat, or given any clue as to the kind of scale and the flavour of radical Islamist extremism in the universities or major cities, is wrong. A lot of it is – not exactly kept secret, but it's just not talked about much. And yet, it is actually one of the biggest stories of all our lifetimes, and one feels that it ought to have been examined much more closely. And it hasn't been. I think there is an anxiety that even reporting this – or reporting it well, reporting it fully – might be bad for community relations.

> [Islamist extremism] is actually one of the biggest stories of all our lifetimes, and one feels that it ought to have been examined much more closely. And it hasn't been. I think there is an anxiety that even reporting this – or reporting it well, reporting it fully – might be bad for community relations.

There's a parallel worry – apart from the worry about inciting our youth to go around beating people up and burning their mosques. There's also an excessive worry about offending Muslim sensibilities. There are radical Muslim groups who claim to take offence at the slightest thing, and there has also been a threat of violence which has been effective, to some extent, in limiting free expression. I think it would not be a good idea if the media showed themselves cowed by the threat of violence.

PW: So are they cowed?

DS: It sometimes looks that way. I am uncomfortable with hearing broadcasters talk about 'the prophet Mohammed', when I'm aware that there are very large numbers of people who don't think he's a prophet at all.

PW: Broadcasters wouldn't say, for example, 'Jesus Christ, the son of God'...

DS: No, they don't. It's noticeable. I don't know why there is this deference to Islamic sensibilities. I think it did antedate the threat of terrorism, so I think perhaps it's a function of the Islamist ability to project a kind of authority towards people who might comment on it.

PW: How does this sensitivity translate when actually doing the news coverage? What kind of conversation goes on to make a news event less provocative to the audience?

DS: I remember seeing live coverage of police operations in Birmingham, where there was an alleged plot to behead a British soldier. Despite the intrinsic drama of the unfolding story, much of the coverage was taken up with making clear to the viewer the fact that not all Muslims are terrorists, and that the local community is generally well disposed towards the rest of us, but that they might not be so for long, because all this police activity might make them feel victimised. It was almost like a propaganda exercise about how terrorism is only confined to a tiny minority, rather than a story about terrorists which was actually currently unfolding in front of us, with armed policemen going through the doors of houses. And what we want to know is the terrorist story – we don't need to be told that it's only a tiny minority of people. We know that. But this idea that there was a need to be fair to the Muslim community as a whole, to make clear that only a small number were involved, became a bigger part of the story even than the rumours about a soldier threatened with decapitation.

I am uncomfortable with hearing broadcasters talk about 'the prophet Mohammed', when I'm aware that there are very large numbers of people who don't think he's a prophet at all.

But the BBC did do a lot of original, highly researched journalism into Islamist extremism, which it doesn't get credit for – *Newsnight* were onto this in 2002, possibly earlier. *File on Four* have done all sorts of stuff. But given what I've said before about the excessive deference, the excessive anxiety, I wonder if that's been a factor in restraining journalists from doing the kind of investigation they might otherwise have done.

PW: Do you think that Islamic radicalism is one of the biggest problems facing broadcasters?

DS: Absolutely. There are a number of big stories at the moment, and all of them will test broadcasters in a way, because they suddenly throw into play highly charged, emotive events, which require quite a lot of deep reading, deep understanding, and the understanding of subtleties to be able to report them properly; and where it is of absolutely no use to anybody for reporters just to regurgitate platitudes. 🖉

The Newcomer (1) – James Graham

Political thinking among young writers and the cultural dominance of London

James Graham, 26, is playwright-in-residence at the Finborough Theatre in London.

His first play to be produced was *Coal Not Dole* at the 2002 Edinburgh Fringe Festival. *Albert's Boy* (2005) earned him a prestigious Pearson Award bursary. *Eden's Empire* (2006), produced at the Finborough, was described by Michael Billington of the *Guardian* newspaper as 'gripping... a dramatic piece of living history'. This was followed by *Little Madam* (2007), about Margaret Thatcher; *Tory Boyz* (2008), an exploration of gays in the Conservative party that was performed by the National Youth Theatre at London's Soho Theatre; and *Sons of York* (also 2008), a family drama set during the 'Winter of Discontent'.

Graham was the Finborough Theatre's nomination to the BBC and Royal Court's programme for young writers, 'The 50', celebrating the Royal Court's 50th anniversary.

His 90-minute television play, *Caught in a Trap*, aired on ITV at Christmas 2008.

James Graham's latest play is *A History of Falling Things*, which opened in May 2009 at Clwyd Theatr Cymru.

Peter Whittle (PW): You have written plays which have political subjects, but you don't look at them as being political drama in the accepted sense, do you?

James Graham (JG): I think, where they're explicitly dealing with the Westminster village, or political figures, such as the Thatcher play or the Eden play which I did, both, at the Finborough [Theatre] – then yes, I do think of them as just being political plays. Either political thrillers or whatever. The other things – more the *Tory Boyz*, which you saw, and *Sons of York*, which is more of a social drama about the Winter of Discontent – I think there's absolutely a political streak running through them, but I'd say they're more either socio-political or just drama with political elements in it.

I think all plays, all drama – whether it's on film or television or theatre – must have some measure of politics in them. Whether it's dealing with status or gender or the class system – even if they're not dealing directly with legislation or Westminster or political figures. But yes, I accept that

I'm more political than probably most of my peers.

PW: What would you say are the central issues dealt with by young writers that you know?

JG: For most young playwrights, I think there's a real fear or scepticism about taking ownership, I suppose, of politics. I don't know – maybe people don't feel justified in their knowledge, or maybe they don't feel it's their place or their responsibility to comment in the way that an older generation of playwrights can, Michael Frayn or David Hare... That feels like their 'bag', and we don't have a right yet to take ownership, either of our political history or of the culture politics. Which I disagree with. I think we absolutely have a right and responsibility to do that. For example, when I tackled Margaret Thatcher, I was nervous about it. Because I was very young, and it's more academic memory for me than living memory. I still just think that my generation is going to inherit everything that Thatcherism left, so it's our responsibility to ask questions of it, and form a perspective on it.

So there's a general fear among young writers that these themes are too big, or the world is too removed from what they know. And that they would be faking it. That it would be an inauthentic voice. Or they just don't have the right to comment on these big themes yet, which I do disagree with. We absolutely have the right and responsibility to do that. I think at the top of their agenda are social themes – so, relationships. Just general human relationships. Which is why you see a huge amount of plays from young writers either at the Royal Court or on the Fringe or regionally, which deal with young people under some kind of social stress, generally speaking. One location – the cliché would be a council flat, where the people are either dealing with their sexuality or some drug use or something like that. Those are the areas in the world and the voices, I think, that young writers, understandably, are probably comfortable with, because it's closer to what they know. Just general life experience, rather than the lofty world of Westminster.

PW: If you're talking about people who are writing in their early twenties now, who grew up in the 1990s, it would seem that they were not exposed to any great ideological battles...

JG: No, I think you're dead right. I think there's a natural apathy. Just working on *Tory Boyz* at the National Youth Theatre, it was a shock when I realised that most of the actors I was dealing with had only ever known Labour, really, in their adult life, when they were forming politically. And certainly, the opposition between left wing or right wing or Conservatism or Socialism was kind of alien to them, largely because, I think, it has become galvanised into this general 'centre politics'. And so the anger,

I think, has gone from our generation. I don't think people are angry anymore. I don't think it feels like there's much politically to fight for. I don't think young people and young writers necessarily stake a claim to one side or the other, because there aren't sides so much – in the way that our parents knew there were sides. Which maybe means they don't think there's a debate to be had.

PW: You've talked previously about a writers' group you were in. You said that they had a pretty homogeneous way of looking at the world. Is that right, or is that a caricature of what you said?

JG: No, I think that's absolutely right. I was part of something called the 'Royal Court 50', which was a really positive scheme. I think most young writers, certainly the ones that come to London to seek their fortune, generally go through these young writing programmes – either at the Royal Court or the Soho or places like that. Which I don't necessarily think naturally homogenises it. But I think that people who arrive there, by virtue of the fact that they want to write and that they're in the arts, generally speaking mostly lean towards the Left or some ideological liberalism or Socialism. I think anyone with more centre-right or right-wing opinions doesn't necessarily see the theatre as an outlet for them, so they don't arrive on the new writing scene so much.

PW: Are they right or wrong to think that?

JG: It's probably a little bit justified, because I think they would be a lone voice in that culture, in that world. So yeah, I mean, we were just talking, as a group of 50 young writers, about what people want to see. And I think Nick Hytner had recently – with you, I think – talked about a right-wing play and what that meant. I think there was just a general misunderstanding of what that meant, and the general feeling was: 'Why would he want to do that?'

The Right has lost the political war; they're now in opposition. The Right always lost the culture war. I don't think people gave it really much serious thought, and that's largely because people believed their audiences would be left wing and liberal as well, and they need to cater for them. And they just couldn't see themselves wandering over to that other side even for a minute, even just to see what was over there.

PW: Are there issues, like the environment, for example, that young creative people won't address? That they see as a simple open-and-shut case?

JG: Yes, I think so. Particularly with the environment and things like that – yes, even when you deal with some political ideology, it's just accepted that the left wing, or whatever it is, is the right course. I just don't think that, in our minds, as a generation there are many debates to be had. Hopefully, that will change. Hopefully, one of the benefits of the deteriorating economic condition will be to polarise people more, to get them to pick a side and start treating things less as read and more as open to discussion and debate and change.

> **I just don't think that, in our minds, as a generation there are many debates to be had. Hopefully, that will change.**

PW: One of the pushes with theatre is to get young people in. Do you think that young people, of university age, consider the theatre to be elitist, or irrelevant? If they're not going, maybe you can speculate as to why?

JG: I think both those things might exist for various different groups. A lot of students probably think of it as irrelevant, and I'm sure a lot of average young people might think of it as elitist, certainly, and irrelevant. There're different kinds of elitism as well. Some – most – of your average young people, inner-city kids, might think it elitist in terms of it being snobby, or too upper class. And there're also some people, maybe students, who might think of it as being too kind of pretentious and zany and bohemian. So I don't think elitism necessarily implies it's a class thing. I think a lot of people think it's a different group, outside of themselves. The great thing about *Tory Boyz* is that, because of the National Youth Theatre, it got a lot of young people in – which was great. But I do think it's a serious problem. Obviously cost is a problem, and it's going to be more of a problem in the next year or so than it used to be.

I think the subject matters that theatre tackles – and I don't know whether I'm helping it by tackling these political themes or these establishment characters or these figures... I don't think the way to attract these people is just by representing them on stage. I think they often feel patronised by that. They're looking for different kinds of truth than that. So no, it is a big problem. Things like the Travelex £10 theatre tickets do clearly work, from what I hear, in terms of the changing demographics of the audiences they get in. Until you get them in, there will always be weary scepticism about it. I was sceptical about it: I never went to the theatre as a young guy. There was no real theatre around me – we would go to see a panto in Nottingham or something like that. Or I would be dragged along to see some Shakespeare at school. But it would never make me fall in love with it, until I started going to see plays that *weren't* on the curriculum – that were plays by people like [John] Godber and Alan Ayckbourn and Willy Russell. They'd just make me laugh, and I just found them entertaining. And they had swear words in them, things like that. I found it a revelation. But unless you can get them in – and I don't know how you do that – the default position is always that it's not for them.

PW: What started you on that?

JG: It was mainly academic. It's probably not a very interesting answer, but I think I began just through school. And I got interested in drama by acting, which is probably the way for most young writers: you start acting and that's how your first relationship with the text happens – being in school plays, enjoying performing, and then just consequently studying drama more, and English literature, and being introduced to these texts. I remember Harold Pinter was a revelation; I remember Alan Bennett was a revelation. It just felt very accessible, in a world I felt I knew and voices I felt I knew. But yes, it was mainly on the page rather than on the stage that I was first introduced.

PW: Was it quite a lonely pursuit?

JG: Writing, when I began?

PW: Or even just getting interested in these new people, going to see things?

JG: Not necessarily. There was a group of school friends who similarly shared an interest in drama. So that introduced me. Then, when I went to university to study drama, obviously there was a whole network of people who could go on that journey with me. But certainly, then, when I went back home after university – I went to university in Hull, and then I returned home for a year, when you must get a gap job doing something like bar work or whatever, whilst you continue writing. I realised then that it could be a lonely pursuit. And I would just do it on my own, in my room quietly, and didn't really tell anybody what I was doing, because it wasn't a strong culture of theatre or the arts back home where I was from. Not that I wasn't supported, but I knew I had to go on that journey alone.

PW: Where are you from originally?

JG: From Mansfield, in Nottinghamshire. Which is part of the reason why I felt that I really had to go down to London. Not that I don't think Nottingham has a thriving cultural scene: I think the regions are often neglected, certainly in the press. But just being surrounded by people of a similar mind, as soon as I came to London, was brilliant. I still have it in me now – I still have a slight embarrassment talking about writing to non-writers. I still haven't even got the confidence really to use that term when someone – a cab driver or whatever – asks me what I do. I feel very presumptuous saying I'm a writer, because of all the implications of that. I just feel so self-important, and I don't mean to be.

So either by going to the theatre and meeting young people or getting on these courses like at the Royal Court – it felt less like I was on my own. And through people who were suffering the same problems, either creatively or financially, or all the other things that are wrapped up in trying to start out on a writing career... But no, I think that will always stay with me: the kind of – not *embarrassment*, but stuff like the sense of silliness at going to my desk, and beginning writing, not knowing necessarily where it's going to go, but making up stories and characters. I still have that feeling of being 14. And when all my other friends were out kicking a ball, I was pretending, playing around with make-believe. So I think it will always be there. But that's maybe quite healthy – I'm quite grateful that it is.

PW: Mansfield – I think you said – that's an ex-mining town...?

JG: Yes, the village I grew up in – in Mansfield – it's called Kirkby. And it was an ex-mining town, and obviously it began to be dismantled and changed during the late Eighties and early Nineties.

PW: There is a view that culture and the arts are a great way to rejuvenate areas of the country which have been laid waste. What do you think of that?

JG: I think it is a worthy idea. I do believe, certainly, that drama can play a therapeutic role and a cathartic role, and certainly has a social role. I very much believe in a *creative* health of the country as much as a *physical* one and a *mental* one and a *financial* one. I think, of course, that it can help people with issues – whether it's any kind of phobia or any kind of addiction or any kind of other social affliction.

Its prime and sole purpose must still be cultural. If it's purely to solve some social problems, then it won't succeed. I think culturally and creatively that has to be the main goal. And if it has a wider social implication, then fine. I'd be sceptical about how it's administered. I think if it's either sponsored by the state or some non-art organisation, then I'd be sceptical. The people it's applied to would be sceptical of that... It should be born out of the community rather than put on top of it.

> **I don't think you can just plug these centres in the middle of a council estate and expect them to flock. It has to be born out of the community.**

PW: You can't take art in a vacuum, can you, just by building an arts centre or whatever?

JG: No, I don't think you can just plug these centres in the middle of a council estate and expect them to flock. It has to be born out of the community. But yes, I can absolutely see how either poetry or music or film or art – having local members contribute to this and develop their own creative voice – would help them address some of the problems that they're facing, as will economic regeneration. And not to shove out the direct link between art and that – unless it does begin to solve crime, it does begin to solve youth apathy, it does begin to make people in the community more driven towards actually being involved in their communities, I suppose. But no, it's a tenuous link, and I think it has to be handled very sensitively. It does sound all very New Labour.

PW: How long have you been in London now?

JG: Moved down in 2004.

PW: Do you think it's true that in the UK culture is increasingly concentrated in the capital?

JG: Absolutely. It's one thing that utterly infuriates me, and I don't see it getting any better. I think there are very benevolent attempts to address that, certainly in the media, by the BBC moving its offices – some of its offices – to Manchester. But even then... Take the National Youth Theatre, which produced *Tory Boyz* – that now is taking huge steps to spread its wings, so they have productions in Manchester, and they cast from all over the country in some kind of *X Factor* rally-style thing.

But when I was growing up in the Eighties, I wasn't aware there was such a thing existing. And I think, why didn't I? Because I was interested in drama. But fundamentally, I wouldn't have been able to do anything about it anyway, because I would have had to come to London. I would have had to live here for two months, and that just wasn't feasible or possible. Luckily, as I said, the National Youth Theatre is one body that is now working hard to address that. But certainly most reviews that I would read in the newspaper would be from – would be about – shows in London. Or most of the shows that would pass through Nottingham would have opened in London a year ago, and we'd be getting the dregs: probably not the original cast – cast B.

...the review will say: 'It was worth the three-hour journey up.' Or: 'If you want to head up there to see it...' And you think: 'Well, if I'm reading this in Durham then it's "down". Or God forbid, I might actually live in the area you're talking about!'

I became even more aware of it when I went to university in Hull and, for the first time, got introduced to a whole raft of people who had grown up in London. And the theatres they had been to (which I had only ever read about in the front of play scripts), or the productions they had seen (which seemed monumental to me) – to them it was just normal. And so many of them had parents in the industry, or friends' dads who were famous actors, or their school had been used to film a movie, or they knew one of the actors in *Harry Potter* – and I'd just be like 'what?!' That would make you a minor celebrity in frigging Mansfield! But to them, it was normal.

It infuriates me, now still – even now I'm in London I read newspapers... Little slips that show you that not much has actually changed – the number of times that I'll read a review, in a national newspaper, that might say – it might be in Liverpool or Manchester, and the review will say: 'It was worth the three-hour journey up.' Or: 'If you want to head up there to see it...' And you think: 'Well, if I'm reading this in Durham then it's "down". Or God forbid, I might actually live in the area you're talking about!' And in most theatre listings, or in most theatre reviews, they will review the next play that's on at the Theatre Royal, and that will be the listing: Theatre Royal. And you think: 'Well, I assume that's the Theatre Royal London.' Because it could be Nottingham, it could be Durham, it could be... It's just the assumption that London is the default.

And I'm absolutely in favour of having a cultural capital. I think it's brilliant that it thrives here. But I think that the focus – certainly of the media, of the reviewers – is constantly on London, and then there's this rather patronising thing called 'the regions' or 'the provinces'. I think, as a writer, I felt that I had to be down here, because most of the new writing – a lot of the new writing venues – are down here, the [Royal] Court, the Hampstead. Even though there's some great regional places like the West Yorkshire Playhouse and even the Nottingham Playhouse, where I grew up.

I don't know how you address it, but I do think it's a massive problem still. I don't think it's a problem in funding – a lot of funding goes out to these regional venues. But as an actor, you have to be down here. I feel like, as a writer, it's useful at the moment in forging my career to be down here. Certainly in terms of television, all my meetings are here; radio, all my meetings are here. And I don't know how you solve it.

PW: So you think it's not about funding, it's about attitudes?

JG: Yes, absolutely. And it's projected through the media and the newspapers. There was an arts commentator on a national newspaper talking about Arts Council funding for regional theatres, and how best regional theatres could survive. And his opinion was that, obviously, they produce good work; it's popular and it gets a great audience response, critical response; and ultimately the objective then would be to move it to the West End. And I think: 'Well, no. I think the object would be to maybe tour it.' So that the 90 per cent of the country who don't live in London could see the show, rather than just the 10 per cent who do live in London, which is saturated by so many different shows, different playwrights, different work.

So yes, I certainly don't think it's funding. I just think it's outlook, it's perspective. Some newspapers are great – like the *Guardian* will send people everywhere, and you'll always get reviews from shows in Manchester. But even though I'm massively grateful for the attention I get at the Finborough Theatre, I'm also baffled why I do. Because it's a very small pub theatre, it's a 50-seater. And yet everything I ever do there will be reviewed by the national press. Obviously, I get all the casting agents coming, I get all the literary agents coming, I get directors coming and the producers coming. It's very easy. Whereas a big show by a new writer at the Liverpool Everyman – which is infinitely bigger and which has got an infinitely stronger budget and probably better production values – they all have to fight tooth and nail to get anyone to come and see it, critically. And then in terms of industry figures, agents and directors and producers and investors – even more so. It's much easier for me to get someone from the Ambassador [Theatre Group] to come to the Finborough than it would be if you were at the Derby Playhouse. There's something just inherently, structurally wrong about that, in its foundation. I think it's going to take years to unpick, and yet I don't really see any drive or impetus to unpick it.

PW: I see it almost as a contempt for anything that's not in London, even the people.

JG: I think you're probably right, yes.

PW: Where do you think this attitude might have come from? It seems like a disdain for the unknown, in the same way that New Yorkers pride themselves on not being part of America.

JG: I think that's probably right. People enjoy the sense of community and the identity you get when you're surrounded by your own kind. And I can't deny that I love the fact that I can go to see the opening of a new play at a theatre in London – I'd probably see seven people I know, it gives me a warm, fuzzy feeling, and I feel very nurtured and protected. So yes, I think it's absolutely scepticism of that otherness, and I don't know how it happened. But I do think we've sleepwalked into this, like a magnet and iron filings gathering around it.

I don't see any willingness to change that. And even in the media, there's talk of when the BBC, quite rightly, were going to break down the London-centric nature of its organisation and start properly spreading it about – that you heard stories of presenters, terrified and baulking at the idea because they might have to sell their Kensington house and go and get one in Leeds or something. Because we have formed a very isolated, insular community, and it's going to be very hard to break up.

But maybe the media's even worse. I know so many of the independent production companies are down here. And obviously, since ITV's no longer a national broadcaster, but has based itself entirely in London, that's fundamentally got more problematic. I don't know whether just shifting departments around the country's going to help. But I know – what's that ratio? It's like a given ratio that the BBC and other companies funded by the licence fee have to produce a certain amount of work outside of London... And it's horrendous how people get around that, just stepping outside of the M25 means you can tick the regional box status.

I shouldn't say this, but I know that my regional production, which was out at Christmas, was filmed outside of London so that somehow affects its status. And I know loads of independent companies who either have an office in Edinburgh which has got a phone and a desk in it, and maybe one person – and having that means they're not completely London, and so they can produce their programme outside, in the regions – or moving your office and going to Wales for three months to produce your programme. I've got friends who work in factual programming, and often they will just remove their office and go and produce it in Wales. And you use those facilities, but it's still just decamping from London to the regions, and then coming back again. Every creative decision still goes through the mind of someone who is living within the capital.

PW: How literate do you think that young people are, culturally? There aren't that many aspiring young playwrights: where is the dynamic of most of your peers? Where would that be going towards – would it be towards the internet, or technology?

JG: I think you're right. In fact, Simon Stephens, who was my mentor at the Royal Court when I was going through that system, instilled it in me – and in all of us, it was very useful – that most people don't write plays; 0.0001 per cent of people are playwrights, and that gives you a certain currency which you can spend, and you should be buoyed up and encouraged by that, which I was. I think that, again, one of the problems in the new writing culture – and one of the problems of the London-centric nature of this industry – is that you're so surrounded by like-minded people and your peers, and people within culture, that you do lose perspective of your audience, and you do think that the majority of young people – just because of the majority of young people that you know – are very literate, or very highly cultural, and do go to the theatre. And I think a lot of people might lose perspective on that, in terms of not writing something which is necessarily accessible or commercial, in the traditional sense. I do think that's potentially – in the future – a massive problem. I think a lot of writers write for other writers and write for directors and write for literary managers and write for cultural commentators. I don't necessarily think they write for people who don't go to the theatre. And you can understand why. But you're never going to get them there unless you start appealing to them.

> I think a lot of writers write for other writers and write for directors and write for literary managers and write for cultural commentators.

Theatre is not, generally speaking, embedded in most young people's culture. Probably certain communities are in it – I think that, for example, being educated in Hull, I was massively excited by the idea that theatre-going was something that everyday people did culturally, it was a working-class pursuit. John Godber – massively popular. Whatever you think of his work, it draws them in. And so, culturally, people of a certain class and a certain age – young people as well – it would be part of their choice: do you want to go to the pub, do you want to go to the cinema, do you want to go to the theatre? It was an option for them in a way that I don't generally think it is for young people; it certainly wasn't for me.

The internet has made it accessible to be in some way culturally involved, either through blogging or Myspace – creating your own page and promoting... What you promote, I don't know. Because the downside of that is that you're not promoting anything. Just by existing, you feel like you deserve to be heard and seen, even though you've got nothing to say or show. And so, yes, technology is certainly predominant, I think. Obviously, the whole concept of celebrity and fame, even though it's a well-worn... People have been speaking about this for ages. I do think that the emphasis for young people is on that kind of achievement. If you look at the magazines and the sites that they will view online, the general idea is that just because you want fame, you should get it – get it instantly. And so the pursuits of being famous for singing, or for being a footballer, I think, are becoming more central to young people's lives than perhaps was the case when I was growing up. *f*

The Newcomer (2) – Sarah Maple

Giving offence and the freedom of expression

Born in 1985, Sarah Maple grew up in Sussex, and did her BA in Fine Art at Kingston University. In October 2007, she won '4 New Sensations', a new art prize for graduates that is organised by Channel 4 and the Saatchi Gallery, and voted by the public online. She has been described by the *Independent on Sunday* as 'the heir to Tracey Emin's throne…the best of the new young British artists'.

She was brought up as a Muslim, with parents of mixed religious and cultural backgrounds, and this has informed and inspired much of her work.

In autumn 2008, her debut solo exhibition at the SaLon Gallery in London, entitled 'This Artist Blows', included self-portraits – one of them depicting her in a headscarf and holding a pig, and another showing her with a breast exposed. The show resulted in incidents of violence and intimidation, culminating in the gallery's glass frontage being smashed. Anonymous threats were made by telephone and email, and a woman wearing a burqa visited the gallery and threatened staff. The gallery was given 24-hour police protection.

Peter Whittle (PW): What was your response to the reaction to your show?

Sarah Maple (SM): It depends. When the brick first went through the window, I was quite upset. Because I felt that it had been misinterpreted and people had taken it the wrong way; but I think after a while of hearing the same thing, hearing what people are saying, you just try to ignore it.

PW: What have they been saying?

SM: Well, a lot of emails we've had through… A lot of stuff is positive, but a lot of people just completely miss the point and think I'm doing it just to piss everyone off, or make myself famous or something. A lot of stuff as well is just really 'Kill the bitch!' and stuff like that. It's horrible – on Facebook and stuff like that. But I've come to realise that I shouldn't really listen to what everyone's saying, because half these people haven't looked at the work.

PW: Do you know what kind of people are leaving messages? Whether they are young or old?

SM: I think probably quite young people – teenagers, people in their early twenties. And then I think there're also people who are older. It's probably from about teens to possibly people in their forties maybe. You can kind of guess from the way people write things what kind of person they'd be.

PW: You say they're missing the point. What are the points you're trying to make with this particular show?

SM: I started the work when I was at university, and it's basically exploring my cultural background, initially. Because my mother is Muslim. My father was brought up in a Christian family, but I was raised a Muslim. And my work was about growing up with the two, and kind of feeling torn between which one I was. I think mainly wanting to be Islamic and be a really good Muslim, but feeling like I was such a western girl. Thinking I couldn't be a good Muslim and be western as well. And I kind of always felt like I was a bad Muslim because I was western. And then when I went to university I met other Muslim people and then I realised that it's not necessarily people who go round wearing a hijab or praying five times a day... It doesn't necessarily mean that they're a better Muslim than me. And what people might perceive on the outside is not necessarily what they're like behind closed doors.

There's different elements to the work. That was kind of how it started – exploring what's a good or a bad Muslim, and kind of looking at what's in the religion and what's actually culture, and how the boundaries have blurred between the two.

PW: What kind of conclusions have you come to about how to be a good Muslim and a western girl? Or have you not reached any?

SM: I've thought about this, and I haven't come to a conclusion. Because I felt judged, I think, by other Muslims, and I've come to realise in the past couple of weeks that no one can judge me. Somebody might say to me I'm not a Muslim because of this; but, you know, he who is without sin...

PW: So essentially it's still a dilemma you haven't worked out?

SM: Yes, definitely. I think I'll still explore it, but it'll be different from how I explored it before, knowing the reaction it's had.

> **Somebody might say to me I'm not a Muslim because of this; but, you know, he who is without sin...**

PW: Were you aware before of any of the controversies there have been in the past to do with the arts and Islam – like Theo van Gogh or Salman Rushdie?

SM: Yes. I knew of them, and I read a lot about – is it [former Dutch MP and critic of Islam] Ayaan Hirsi Ali? I read her books, so I was quite interested in that side of it; but I didn't think that my work was offensive, and I didn't think I was doing anything wrong. I don't know how Theo van

Gogh felt – maybe he felt the same as me, I don't know. I was aware of it, but I don't think I really considered it too much when I made the work.

PW: So you weren't frightened of being attacked?

SM: No, I didn't really think of that. The only time I thought of it was when I was in the middle of the pig one [painting of a veiled Muslim woman cradling a pig], and my friend – who's Catholic – she came to look at the work, and she saw the pig, and she was like: 'Oh my God! What are you doing? You're going to get in so much trouble!' That's the only time I really thought, oh God!.. Because I hadn't had anyone else's reaction or interpretation – apart from my own, obviously.

PW: How do you feel about having to move some of your work downstairs in the gallery?

SM: Well, I think it would have been really nice to have them upstairs, because now when you look at the show it separates the two things. There's more attention drawn to this; it would have been nice to have the body of work woven in with each other. I suppose if it wasn't done this way then we don't know what could have happened: if it had been upstairs, the work could have been attacked. And that was one thing I was really worried about. I just didn't want the work to be destroyed. When the gallery was attacked, I was more worried about the work. So as long as it protects the work, I suppose...

PW: Your piece *Islam is the New Black* – what were you trying to say with that painting?

SM: A friend of mine said it to me: 'Islam's the new black.' And I thought: 'That sounds great!' And I thought that's true, because it's the hot topic: everyone's always talking about it – Islamic extremism – and it's always in the news. I thought it's great because it means that. And then it also means the negative connotations of black – you know, people associate Islam with terror and bombings and war and stuff. And I just thought it was a great word play.

> I don't agree with stuff that's just downright offensive for the sake of it.

PW: Do you think there are any limits to freedom of expression?

SM: I don't agree with stuff that's just downright offensive for the sake of it. I don't agree with that...

PW: What would that be?

SM: It's a tough one, because there are certain things that I would find offensive, like child abuse or something. If someone used pictures of that I would be horrified; I'd find that disgusting.

PW: Would you therefore think it shouldn't be made?

SM: It's difficult, because I probably have a different opinion now to what I would have had about three weeks ago. Because I'm in that position now: people think that my work is offensive – sorry, could you repeat the question?

PW: Do you think that there should be limits to freedom of speech, to what an artist is allowed to create?

SM: No, because if artists were restricted in some way and couldn't express themselves, then they wouldn't be artists. They would be controlled, and where is the art in that? But all cases of offence are individual, and what one person finds offensive another wouldn't. I know I have my own threshold... There are certain things that maybe I would think... But then we had these French people in today – a French camera crew – and they were saying about how they couldn't show some of my work because it would be offensive in France. I got really, like, outraged! I think it's ridiculous, they can't show paintings! Even on ITV they blurred out the pig and stuff, and I just thought: 'This is a bit ridiculous! It's not that bad!' But then again, who gauges it? I don't think it's that bad, but somebody else might think it is. I suppose all our levels of offence are different, aren't they?

> Even on ITV they blurred out the pig and stuff, and I just thought: 'This is a bit ridiculous! It's not that bad!' But then again, who gauges it?

PW: But do you think – with things you find offensive – that they should be banned?

SM: I do think it's a free country, and I don't think things should be banned. But I'm quite an easygoing person, so things like [the spoof television documentary series] *Brass Eye* – people thought that paedophile episode of *Brass Eye* should have been banned, but I want to watch it all the more, you know? I thought it was really funny – and good. And what people didn't get was that the show was satire on the media's handling of the subject, not the subject itself. The public reacted without even seeing it – a lot like in my case.

PW: A lot of people were offended by *The Life of Brian*; so what if people produced a 'Life of Mohammed' along the same lines? What would be your attitude to that? Would you say it should be banned?

SM: As a Muslim, I would be wary that someone was taking the piss out of my religion. But more than that, I would think about the repercussions for the people that had made it, because those people certainly would not get away with it in this current climate. As I said, I'm quite an easygoing person, so I'd probably be like: 'OK, let's have a look. Let's see what they've done.' But part of me would also think: 'No'. Because these people are probably going to get killed. With the Prophet, if you mention him in any

> With the Prophet, if you mention him in any sort of disrespectful light, then someone's going to... I haven't mentioned him in any of my work.

183

sort of disrespectful light, then someone's going to... I haven't mentioned him in any of my work.

PW: Was that a definite decision on your part? You would never depict the Prophet?

SM: No, I wouldn't do that. The closest I would go to that would be to imply in some way. There hasn't been a close issue for me to need to depict him at the moment. But I mean, people try to give me ideas and things, and say I should do a woman in a burqa pole-dancing or something, and really try and shock people. But my work isn't really about shock. I'm not trying to shock anyone or offend anyone. I just think I have my ideas, and I think they're intelligent ideas, and they're the best way to execute my concepts.

PW: So do you think that, with this exhibition, you have walked into something that you weren't quite aware of?

SM: People think that I'm doing all this work on Islam because it is the 'new black', and everyone's talking about it, and it's a great way for me to get famous or whatever. But I would have done this work even if no one was talking about Islam. Because this is all essentially about me and my thoughts about my upbringing, and my culture and stuff like that. So I suppose it happens to just be the timing.

PW: Are you aware of any peers – other young Muslim artists – of your age?

SM: I don't know of any others, no.

PW: Why do you think that is?

SM: I think it's a culture thing. I think a lot of Muslim kids are discouraged from the arts, unless it's graphic design or something. I think my mum wanted to do what I'm doing, but she was discouraged from it, because it wasn't a very prosperous career. So I don't think... You don't really get Muslim footballers either, do you? I think you're just discouraged away from sports or arts, really. My sister's a doctor, so she's the favourite.

PW: Graphic design – is that because of the traditional Islamic aesthetic of pattern?

SM: It's more to do with money, I think, and a good job. Good job, respectable, something to tell the relatives about, you know?

PW: What is your mother's attitude to what you've done?

SM: She is supportive, yes; but she worries about me because of all the controversy and all the problems. I know that she understands my concept, and agrees with it; but like any parent she's going to worry about the backlash. And my father's exactly the same – he's not Christian, but his family were Christians. He's not really anything, but he also felt that as well.

184

PW: Are you going to take this further – this phase of your work that concentrates on you being a Muslim woman?

SM: A lot of my work is edging towards feminism. But I think as long as I feel I've got things to explore, I will keep doing it. I wouldn't just do it as a gimmick, but I think being Muslim is part of who I am; and obviously art is a result of who I am. As long as I am living and breathing I will probably have something to say on the matter.

PW: Do you wear the veil yourself? What is your attitude to girls who wear the full burqa? Do you think there's almost a kind of grading?

SM: I think that's where my work comes from. Because when I used to see women in hijab, I would think: 'Oh, I bet they're such amazing Muslims, much better than me.' And that's like the one with the breast [self-portrait with headscarf and bare breast] – it's kind of about saying: 'Just because they're dressed traditionally, it doesn't necessarily mean they're a better Muslim than me.' If I wear the hijab, people just stare at me, because I'm white. So people are like: 'Why is that white girl wearing a hijab?' But when I see women in a burqa, I think... Well, you have to be careful of what you say, but I don't see the point of it. You don't need to wear it over here. I think the point of wearing a burqa when you're in Saudi Arabia or somewhere is to draw attention away from yourself. But if you wear it over here you're drawing attention to yourself, and I think: 'Are these people trying to make a point? Are they just really proud? Are they just saying: "We're not going to back down to western values, we're going to stay...".' So...

> I think the point of wearing a burqa when you're in Saudi Arabia or somewhere is to draw attention away from yourself. But if you wear it over here you're drawing attention to yourself...

PW: Are your Muslim girlfriends pretty westernised? Or are they seen and not heard?

SM: I don't have that many Muslim friends. But the people I do know – am friends with – all wear hijab, but are very bold women – very career-minded, very strong women. But are fully happy to accept their parents choosing their husband; they're very happy with that. It's just the way it is.

PW: You wouldn't be happy with your parents choosing your husband?

SM: Well, my mother is quite fickle, so I know she'd choose a hot guy, so I know it wouldn't be too bad! But if she was going to choose my husband, I wouldn't be that happy about it. And she wasn't very happy about it – that's why she married my father and went against all of the cultural values.

PW: So she was a bit of a forerunner to you?

SM: Yes. She's supportive of me, but she does kind of raise eyebrows at some of the things I do. And I say: 'I'm exactly what you are' – you know, a bit rebellious. And she probably sees herself in me, in her youth...

PW: How would you encourage more young Muslim men and women to get into the arts?

SM: I'm not sure, because a lot of kids are very influenced by their parents. And if their parents are going to disagree, they're not even going to have it in their mind; they're not even going to give it consideration, or even explore their artistic talent. But I think me getting in the public eye and people seeing what I'm doing is encouraging for Muslim artists. I've had quite a few write to me and feel really positive about my art and my work, and feeling that they could do a career in the arts. My brother is a stand-up comedian. He wasn't really going for it, and then when he saw me doing well he thought: 'Oh, why can't I do it?' So now he's doing that.

PW: Oh, is he on the circuit yet?

SM: Yes, he does a lot of gigs.

PW: You said you thought your attitudes might have changed in the last few weeks. I read something where you said that leaving a Koran on the floor should be banned. Is that right? Do you still feel that?

SM: I said that as an example of something I would find offensive to do with my religion. This is a very disrespectful thing to do in Islam, and I was saying my work was not as bad as something like this... But someone else may not agree! *⌒*

188

Published by the Social Affairs Unit

Look At Me: Celebrating the Self in Modern Britain

by Peter Whittle

This polemic explores the ways in which Britain's culture has succumbed to the all-pervasive need for individual self-glorification in all its forms, from the pursuit of fame for fame's sake to the need many have to impose themselves on the simplest public situation.

It looks for the reasons for the rise of unbridled self-belief, and asks whether our social and communal identity is in danger of being damaged.

'There is much intellectual meat in this short book... Look at Me *is the best kind of polemic: one that holds up a harsh mirror to the distinctive grotesqueries of our time.'*
Jenny McCartney, *Sunday Telegraph*

'Insightful... Peter Whittle pinpoints one of the most conspicuous but shallowly perceived phenomena of our times... What he has grasped, however, is that modern celebrity is not characterised, as it was in previous times, by the idea of "them and us", the sense of a curtain being lifted on a world ordinary people don't share and which draws its glamour precisely from its inaccessibility. On the contrary, the current obsession with fame actually represents a deeply narcissistic obsession with the self.'
Melanie Phillips, *Literary Review*

'...this phenomenon is brilliantly anatomised by writer Peter Whittle in his new book.'
James Delingpole, *Sunday Telegraph*

'...a timely, brief and very readable tract for our times by the formidable British cultural warrior Peter Whittle.'
Ruth Dudley Edwards, *Irish Independent*

*'*Look at Me *cheerfully mocks this cult with merciless accuracy and deadly disdain... Whittle's marvellously sneering rage fingers these vacuous drones perfectly, lethally.'*
Salisbury Review